Dramatic Satire in the Age of Walpole

1720-1750

DRAMATIC SATIRE IN THE AGE OF WALPOLE 1720-1750

JEAN B. KERN

A Replica Edition

The Iowa State University Press, AMES, Iowa

1 9 7 6

JEAN B. KERN is professor emerita and former chairman of
English, Speech, and Theatre, Coe College, Cedar Rapids,
Iowa. She holds the Ph.D. degree from the University of Wis-
consin. She has taught also in the Georgetown University
Program in Ankara, Turkey; the American University, Cairo,
U.A.R.; and has been guest lecturer at the University of
Tübingen, Tübingen, West Germany.

© 1976 The Iowa State University Press
Ames, Iowa, 50010. All rights reserved

Composed and printed by
The Iowa State University Press

First edition, 1976

International Standard Book Number: 0-8138-0450-7
Library of Congress Catalog Card Number: 75-32883

The Iowa State University Press REPLICA EDITIONS, reproduced
from typescript, are specialized studies selected for their
significance and scholarly appeal.

CONTENTS

INTRODUCTION

SATIRE in dramatic form seems to be at least as ancient as tragedy and comedy if we are to judge by what Aristotle says about invective, slight plots, and the "ludicrous style" of a satiric drama that preceded the tragedies of Aeschylus.[1] Unfortunately this earliest satiric drama is lost except for Aristotle's brief mention of it in his later criticism of Athenian drama of the fifth century B.C. We can only speculate, with the aid of twentieth-century anthropologists, about the almost universal urge in all cultures to release aggression by heaping abuse on a scapegoat. Okot p'Bitek, a contemporary Ugandan poet, for example, speaks of the oral tradition of "hitting" stories told by Africans around the family fire when a child who dislikes her treatment by a grandfather will tell an ironic allegory about an elephant who does all the unpleasant things her grandfather did. This preliterary form of ridicule is ably discussed by Robert C. Elliott in The Power of Satire,[2] but while it would be convenient to relate this primitive urge to castigate the socially undesirable to the alazon (scapegoat) of Greek satyr plays appended to trilogies of early tragedy, the evidence does not exist (only one such satyr play remains) to establish this as the form of the first dramatic satire. Satire on specific individuals and events is, however, clear in the comedies of Aristophanes; the fate of dramatic satire thereafter in western drama is almost inextricably associated with comedy. Stock characters—the imposter, the braggart, the soldier, the pretentious pedant, the parasite, the buffoon—pass from Aristophanes to the New Comedy and on to the Roman dramatists such as Plautus and Terrence. However, Roman satire also developed a poetic form, the satura of Horace and Juvenal, and this formal verse satire overshadowed dramatic satire in the literature of Renaissance England as Alvin Kernan's The Cankered Muse ably illustrates. What remains of satire in Elizabethan and Jacobean drama are satiric characters—Thersites, Bosola, Malevole—who are railers against society out of pride, loath-

ing or frustration. Unpleasant as they are, such satiric
characters no longer contribute to the form of dramatic satire. It is in the comedies of Ben Jonson, such as Everyman
Out of His Humor, Volpone, and The Alchemist, that satiric
comedy progressed. Kernan notes that Jonson not only disas-
sociates himself from the satirist (an obvious advantage in
the dramatic form of satire) but by crowding his plays with
details of unpleasantness and animal analogies (raven, crow,
fox, fly) fits his material together with little comic resolution. Humor is provided by the irony that his characters
do not see their goals as false, unable as they are to distinguish appearance from reality. Alchemy thus in The Alchemist becomes a central metaphor for Renaissance aspira-
tion.

With the closing of the theatres (1642-1660) English
dramatic development suffered a hiatus so that Jonson's con-
tribution to satiric drama almost disappeared from sight.
When Restoration drama re-emerged in the prose comedies of
manners and the verse couplets of heroic tragedy it reflected the French tastes of Charles II and his court returning from exile. It was drama for an elite theatre re-
sponding to the tastes and interests of the restored upper
class. As far as satiric form in drama was concerned, the
new comedy of manners offered the flexibility of prose and
little else. To be sure there were fools like Sir Fopling
Flutter and naive country wives among its characters, but
they were largely presented for what they were and realism
is not satire. When the intention of comedy is entertainment,
comedy of manners does not produce the grotesque wit, in-
version of values, deliberate allegory or other stylistic
qualities of an Aristophanes. A bon mot is a limited joke to
elicit laughter but the effect ends immediately. Thus the
witty rakes of Restoration comedies are not satirists but
entertainers. It was only in the minor plays of Shadwell
that Jonson's humor-ridden characters survived, or in Buckingham's The Rehearsal that parody was suggested as a satiric technique in drama; but both were outside the main-
stream of the Restoration stage.[3] Meanwhile formal verse
satire had revived with Butler, Rochester and Dryden whose
"Discourse on Satire" tended further to deflect the satirist
to imitate Horace and Juvenal rather than a dramatic satirist such as Aristophanes. By the early eighteenth century
Swift's Tale of a Tub added prose satire to literary satiric

form, and Augustan satire went on to flower in the parallel forms of verse satire like Pope's and Menippean (or Lucian) prose satire like <u>Gulliver's Travels</u>. How did this ebullience of satire affect eighteenth century satiric drama?

In general the eighteenth century has long been regarded as a period of transition and decline in drama. Restoration comedy, after Jeremy Collier's attack on its licentious morals, gave way to the sentimental comedies of Cibber and Steele. The excesses of bombastic rhetoric in the heroic tragedies of Dryden, Lee and Banks also gave place to domestic tragedies such as Lillo's <u>The London Merchant</u>. Early in the century Italian opera stole the favor of the upper class and became a serious competitor of drama. To retrieve their audiences, theatre managers added new attractions—pantomime and afterpieces—which further adulterated drama. Meanwhile the battle of the ancients versus moderns continued in dramatic critical theory.

While these facts of literary history are sufficient to explain the decline of eighteenth-century drama, they are tied to social and political changes which reinforced and extended the decline. Theatres no longer played to the elite as in the reign of Charles II but to an audience swelled by prosperous merchants, their footmen and apprentices. At the same time, with the accession of the Hanoverian monarchs, the country experienced a new phenomenon in Robert Walpole as prime minister from 1720 to 1742. The repressive effect of political power focused in one man profoundly affected the theatre as the Licensing Act of 1737 testifies. Yet recent work of the scholars who edit <u>The London Stage</u> indicates an unexpected vitality in the theatre, particularly unexpected in light of the critical neglect of drama in this part of the eighteenth century. For example, in the 1728-1729 season, London offered five plays on the same day for the first time in more than one hundred years.[4] Theatres had returned to their Elizabethan popularity as entertainment for the general public. As a result of this very active theatre, new dramatic forms—ballad opera, oratorios, sentimental comedy, domestic tragedy and dramatic satires—evolved. In other words the first half of the eighteenth century is a period of experimentation as well as change.

The purpose of this study, therefore, is to examine satire in English drama from 1720 to 1750. The focus is narrow and many of the dramatists are minor, even anonymous.

Yet their works, when examined in the context of experimentation and against the undisputed success of the great Augustan satirists, take on new interest for the student of satire. It is hoped such an examination of the details of political, social and literary satire in the drama will contribute to an understanding of satiric form as well as theory. This study which examines, then, anonymous plays as well as those by known authors, and plays which were only published as well as those which were acted, is an attempt to work from the particular to the general—what all satire has in common.[5] The assumption, of course, is that satire is recognizable even when it does not control form or lift the form into a separate genre.

I have made two arbitrary choices in this study of dramatic satire. One is the period 1720-1750 which corresponds roughly to the ministry of Sir Robert Walpole from 1720 to 1742. The second choice was a topical organization to discuss the extent of the satire rather than an organization by authors. The first choice was dictated by the unity of Walpole's long term in office and its immediate effect after his fall from power. The second choice results from the large number of dramatists who wrote only one play and the many anonymous plays. A topic organization has, thus, the advantage of avoiding short paragraphs and dreary, single-sentence discussions. My choice of topic organization does, however, mean that a single play may be discussed in more than one chapter.

A further problem is that despite my canvass of major collections in the libraries of this country and the British Museum, some plays have no known copy extant; for these I have had to rely on what standard histories of eighteenth-century drama say about the play's content (for example, Genest, Some Account of the English Stage from 1660 to 1830). Finally, I have had to distinguish between satiric and dramatic satire, a distinction I will save for discussion in Chapter 1.

Dramatic Satire in the Age of Walpole

1720-1750

CHAPTER 1

SATIRIC THEORY AND THE DRAMA

'Twas thus a while th'instructive Stage surveyed
From Breast to Breast its glowing Influence spread.
Till, from his nobler Task by Passions won,
The man unravel'd what the Bard had done;
And he, whose Warmth had fir'd a Nation's Heart,
Debas'd to private Picques the gen'rous Art.

—William Whitehead, on Aristophanes,
An Essay on Ridicule (1743)

I'll strip the ragged follies of the time
Naked as at their birth: . . .
. . . and with a whip of steel
Print wounding lashes in their iron ribs.

—Ben Jonson, Every Man Out of His Humour
(1599)

Satire has always shone among the best,
And is the boldest way, if not the best,
To tell men freely of their foulest faults;
To laugh at their vain deeds, and vainer thoughts.

—John Dryden's version of Buckingham,
An Essay on Satire (1680)

AS I HINTED in the Introduction, the dramatists of the Augustan Age of Satire had few models for the form of stage satire. It is not, therefore, surprising that in these three decades of the eighteenth century their efforts to translate satire to the public stage were both tentative and experimental. For this reason alone it is necessary to

construct a definition of dramatic satire in order to make
clear the direction of the experiments that will be discussed in the following chapters.

What is a dramatic satire? Obviously it is close to
comedy because of the accepted importance of wit and humor
in satire. This is why distinctions between comedy and satire are so often blurred and inconclusive. W. K. Wimsatt,
for example, in The Idea of Comedy: Essays in Prose and
Verse, Ben Jonson to George Meredith, states the problem of
separating the genres of comedy and satire as insoluble (p.
88). But such a conclusion is defeatist and fails to consider the difference in intention of the comic dramatist
and the satiric dramatist. It also assumes too much importance for wit and humor in satire and fails to recognize
what Northrop Frye in The Anatomy of Criticism calls the
"militant irony" which is characteristic of all satire
whether nondramatic or dramatic (p. 223). Comedy, as he
points out, works toward resolution—a happy outcome for disorder; satiric drama only displays the disorder without a
resolution. There is no happy ending to a dramatic satire,
or if there is, it is quixotic and accidental. The intention is to show the chaos to which irrational and foolish
acts lead. The world presented in satiric drama is not realistic or what it seems but ironically upside down, back-
wards, or inside out.

How does this difference of intention between comedy
which restores order or resolves problems and satire which
exposes disorder affect the form of dramatic satire? It al-
lows for multiplicity and fluidity, borrowing and juxtapos-
ing techniques to create new forms of drama. Parody of a
particular author's style for the purpose of ridicule, for
example, may control the form. Or the play may take the form
of a satiric allegory, or a mock-epic, or a rehearsal of a
play under attack by the satirist. In the last form, stage
characters watching the rehearsal may expand the satire to
critics as well as authors, to social and political satire
as well as literary satire. Because these three decades of
1720-1750 produced many experiments in drama (sentimental
comedy, domestic tragedy and ballad opera, most notably),
experiments in dramatic satire are also to be expected. Ballad opera, with short scenes interspersed with new words
written to popular tunes and songs, was particularly adapt-
able to dramatic satire.

Thus the form of dramatic satire is not singular but

inevitably multiple and is controlled by the intention of
the dramatist to expose folly, stupidity and ignorance which
are displayed but not removed or resolved as in comedy. Plots
of dramatic satire are chaotic; blocking characters are not
removed or reformed as in comedy. Disorder remains and irony
triumphs. The author's satisfaction is in showing and telling, displaying absurdities, allowing the characters to act
out the satiric intention. The stage of this period, before
the Licensing Act of 1737, becomes an adjunct of the political journalist. It can be used to show election abuses,
the unpopularity of new legislation such as the proposed
excise act or the gin act, or it can be used to attack the
Prime Minister himself. But it can also be used as a public
forum for social satire on auctions, masquerades and such
public orators as Henley. And it can be the satirist's outlet for literary satire on absurdities of style, or on
critical controversies, or on particular authors. In an absence of theory about dramatic satire, dramatists are free
to experiment with a variety of forms for the satiric mode.
In the final chapter, The Form of Dramatic Satire: 1720-
1750, I have summarized the stage experiments where the
author's ironic intention controlled the play sufficiently
to result in dramatic satire. Those plays which contain only
a satiric reference or a satiric character I have excluded
from the discussion of the form of dramatic satire. Satiric
reference to an event does not make a play a satire. In
fact, expecially after 1737, the satiric reference may be
buried in another form (such as a political tragedy) to escape the watchful eye of the Lord Chamberlain's Licenser
for the stage. The satiric is nonetheless interesting in re-
constructing who and what was satirized.

This study, then, is focused both on the extent of satire in the drama and on the form of dramatic satire. It
raises questions about the amount of political, social and
literary satire, the kinds of targets for the satirist's
arrows, and then moves through a consideration of the strategies of the satirist's style to the form, or forms, which
the dramatist developed. These experiments in dramatic satire are admittedly not equal to the best work of Dr. Swift,
Alexander Pope or the wits of the Scriblerus Club, but they
clearly reflect the influence of the Augustan satirists as
dramatists borrowed and adapted in their efforts to translate satire into a rorm for the stage.

Before turning to the evidence in the plays themselves,

I should attempt to make clear my own assumptions about what
satire is because the last decades of this century have produced a bewildering proliferation of critics writing about
satire. Why do I assume that all satire depends on grotesque
fantasy, wit, or irony to ridicule human folly or hypocrisy?
Or that satiric drama can be distinguished from comedy or
farce by the intention of the author? Or that a dramatic
satire has an unresolved plot? Much that has been written
since 1950 bogs down into questions: Is satire a genre or a
mode? Northrop Frye's Anatomy of Criticism assigns satire to
a broad category in a schemata of literature (romance, comedy, satire and tragedy) that obviously cuts across genres
like drama, novel, poetry and prose essays. For my purposes
in examining dramatic satire he is helpful in discussing
what he calls "low mimetic" or "low norm" satire closest to
comedy (p. 226), and less helpful at the other end of his
arc where satire disappears into "apocalyptic" irony closest to tragedy (pp. 237-39). Wayne C. Booth's 1974 study,
The Rhetoric of Irony, attempts a clearer separation of
irony and satire (p. 30): "In short, irony is used in some
satire, not in all; some irony is satiric, much is not."
While Booth's discussion of covert and overt irony, or of
stable and unstable irony is brilliant, there remains a
blurred definition of satire. Irony emerges as a broader
rhetorical strategy which is only "sometimes" satire. Thus
Frye's definition of satire as "militant irony" (p. 223)
survives as at least a parameter of satire. "Militant irony"
implies an object of attack which is close to the standard
definition in glossaries of literary terms: satire is an
attack upon prevailing vices or follies for the purpose of
ridicule. If there is agreement among critics and literary
historians, it therefore seems to be on the intention of
the satirist who attacks for the purpose of undercutting and
discrediting by ridicule whatever he dislikes.[1] Beyond this
agreement on the satirist's intention or objective there is
little agreement. Strict genre critics have trouble pigeon-
holing satire or distinguishing it from comedy, farce and
allegory. Is Gulliver's Travels a novel or Menippean satire?
Is Fielding's Tom Thumb comedy or burlesque? Is Dryden's Mac-
Flecknoe satiric verse or a verse satire? Such questions
lead to studies, some of them excellent,[2] of the technique
of the satirist—his method of achieving effects by indirec-
tion (irony), invective, understatement, hyperbole, extended

metaphor (allegory) or other tricks of rhetoric. Valuable as
some of these studies are, they seem to me to lose sight of
the forest while labeling the trees. Obviously satire bor-
rows techniques—wit from comedy, irony from rhetoric, allegory from morality, invective and physical abuse from farce.

The literary history of satire is equally confused. As
recently as the 1950's, listings under satire in the <u>Read-
er's Guide to Periodical Literature</u> were few and referred
to other headings—fantasy, burlesque, and farce. All three
references could be applied to drama, yet a student of drama
who begins with Aristotle finds only a bare reference to
satiric comedy, Homer's <u>Margites</u> which has not survived. As
G. C. Fiske pointed out in 1920,[3] Aristotle's brief reference to satiric comedy led to a confusion of the etymology
of <u>satire</u> with Greek <u>satyr</u> plays—comedies filled with slap-
stick abuse of a scapegoat (alazon). The only extant satyr
comedy (Euripides' <u>Cyclops</u>) gives us very limited evidence
of the technique of berating. Aristophanes' comedies clearly
did include satiric references to individuals of the Athenian city-state, but his attacks on "discernible, historically authentic particulars" (to use Rosenheim's definition
of satire), disappeared in New Comedy that developed non-
political stock characters (parasites, pedants, bearded
rustics) in plots of domestic comedy about marriages, mistaken identity and social situations. Again New Comedy is
known to literary historians only through the later Roman
imitations by Plautus and Terence. Thus little remains out
of the early history of comedy, except for the berating of
satyr plays and the satiric references in Old Comedy, which
could help define dramatic satire, although Aristophanes'
imaginative use of choruses of frogs, birds and wasps is a
hint of nonrealistic fantasy which a satirist might pick up
on.

By 35 B.C. Horace settled the etymology of satire in
the Fourth Satire of Book I as <u>satura</u>, or medley. While he
acknowledged his debt to Lucilius who, he said, copied Old
Comedy by attacking rogues, cutthroats and thieves, Horace
established verse as the form for satire, posing as the urbane critic who did not wish to give pain to his victims.
Whatever stock characters he may have taken over from drama—
the trickster, the grimacer or the <u>vir bonus</u> (usually the
bearded rustic or moral norm whose country simplicity is
uncorrupted by sophisticated urban hypocrisy), Horace, like

Juvenal, turned verse satire away from dramatic mimesis for
the stage. As Alvin Kernan in The Cankered Muse makes clear,
the Roman verse satirists influenced English satirists of
the sixteenth century and early seventeenth century to create, in verse, a crowded scene, landscapes like those of
Hieronymous Bosch (p. 8) presided over by a vir bonus capable of detecting human folly.

With this tradition of English verse satire then, it is
not surprising that Dryden's "Discourse concerning the Original and Progress of Satire," prefaced to his edition of
Juvenal (1693), should consider satire to be a verse form
whether the tone is of Horace's urbane variety or of Juvenal's harsh, abusive variety. Dryden's own verse satire when
he inveighs against Shadwell's humours comedies in MacFleck-
noe indicates he did not see in Shadwell's model, Ben Jonson, the possibility for stage satire with characters ridden
by a single humour such as avarice or lust and that, further,
he did not see in humours comedy a technique for developing
dramatic satire by satiric allegory. As Robert D. Hume
points out (Dryden's Criticism), Dryden stops his discussion
with the Romans—Horace, Juvenal, Persius (pp. 87-88).

As I have been suggesting, the dramatists writing from
1720 to 1750 had very little theory of satire to rely upon
and what little they had, such as Dryden's essay, was about
verse satire of the Roman satura variety. In groping toward
a dramatic form, they were hindered by a lack of definition.
Thus most of the playwrights of this period labeled their
efforts at dramatic satire as mixed (satura) plays—"Histerio-
Comical Satyr" or "A Serio-Tragi-Comi-Farcical Entertainment"—to indicate their confusion of distinctions between
comedy and satire or between satire and farce. Fielding, for
example, labeled only one of his dramatic satires, Pasquin:
a Satire on the Times. The emphasis on Entertainment probably stems from two sources: one, critical theory about the
effectiveness of laughter as a corrective (Shaftesbury's
idea of laughing men out of their folly), and two, a fact of
dramatic history, the popularity of afterpieces or entertainments attached to full-length plays, a fashion introduced by Charles II's court after his return from France.
Yet even after 1737 when the Licensing Act obviously made it
difficult to get political satire acted, writers still used
the label. The anonymous Fortune's Tricks in Forty-Six bore
the subtitle "an Allegorical Satire" and Aaron Hill called
his The Snake in the Grass "a dramatic satire," for example.

The critics who wrote about satire in these decades continued the pattern of Dryden's essay and, stimulated by Pope's Dunciad,[4] they hastened to warn against excessive abuse. Although John Brown's An Essay on Satire occasion'd by the death of Mr. Pope (1745) came to Pope's defense late in the period, he still limited his defense to tracing verse satire from Lucilius, Horace and Juvenal through Donne and Dryden's extremes of wit and meanness (Part III) to Pope's controlled wit where "Reason and Wit and Strength collected Shine" (1.490). Abuse or "billingsgate" seems the basis of eighteenth-century distrust of satire (see Spectator No. 209) and only Corbyn Morris in an Essay Toward Fixing the True Standards of Wit, Humour, Raillery, Satire and Ridicule . . . attempts to separate wit and humor in English comedies (pp. 23-25), thus moving the critical discussion away from verse satire and toward dramatic satire. But Morris failed to clarify that wit is only one ingredient of satire, and the examples he uses are not from drama (he omits any reference to Aristophanes or Molière) but from poetry. Morris dedicated his essay to Robert Walpole, by then Earl of Orford, commending him for "curbing the theatre" from "profligate attacks not fairly addressed to the Judgment, but immediately to the Sight and Passions." Thus while he indicates implicitly that there was dramatic satire which needed to be "curbed," his separation of wit and humor in English comedies moves satire back to the verse form where Dryden's essay left it.

From this brief literary history of satire and the criticism of satire in England, it is apparent that one, verse is considered the proper genre for satire, and two, satire by 1720 is viewed with alarm whenever it strays from raillery into abuse, invective or billingsgate. Thus neither literary history nor critics of satire are very helpful in distinguishing or defining dramatic satire. Is satire distinguishable from comedy and farce? I would argue that it is though admittedly it is difficult. The Restoration comedy of manners, for example, which carried over as an influence into the period of this study, used witty dialogue, and wit, whether in repartée or as the bon mot, is often called the identification mark of satire. But a witty remark, no matter how clever the turn of phrase, is not enough to distinguish a comedy from a dramatic satire. It may be only a decoration just as the Fopling Flutters are satiric characters in a comedy about Restoration society. Wit per se

was the language of Charles II's court and thus realistic,
according to the manners of the time. Satire is not realistic but exaggerated into more than surface meaning—what
Robert C. Elliott calls the "both-and" response to "either-
or" characters (The Power of Satire, p. 184). The Dorimants
and Harcourts of Restoration comedy are not exposed or unmasked but stand as portraits of a society where license as
well as wit is condoned. What about farce? The plotlessness
of farce might seem to be what Kernan in his later book, The
Plot of Satire, calls the circular plot which gets nowhere
(pp. 143 ff.). Yet farce seems to me to be actually a collection of jokes, often throw-away one-liners, jokes for the
sake of jokes. Thus the plotlessness of farce is not circular in terms of the intention of the satirist whose circular plot implies a criticism of a situation. Farce by contrast is entertainment; the jokes are for the sake of the
jokes with nothing more at stake, and no added meaning implied.

What then is a dramatic satire? Like any satire, verse
or prose narrative,[5] as well as play, it has a target. The
why of satire is its intention to ridicule, to expose by unmasking, and for this purpose the stage is an ideal locus.
By means of the actors' lines and their actions, the author
can make clear to his audience his satiric intention. A
character named Common Sense who is defeated by a character
named Ignorance is a patent alert to the audience. To such
overt illustration of the triumph of the irrational, the
dramatist may add techniques common to verse or prose satire
as well—grotesque fantasy, absurd wit, allegory or the complex rhetoric of irony. His invitation to his audience is
to look at and listen to the irrational, to share the satirist's own values. He may, for example, by the use of irony
invite his audience to reconstruct his meaning. A clue in
the title may alert the audience to irony (The South Sea
Bubble: or, the Biters Bit) or to the satiric allegory (The
Northern Election: or, the Nest of Beasts) or to parody for
the purpose of ridicule (The Tragedy of Tragedies: or, Tom
Thumb the Great) or to burlesque action, i.e., gross exaggeration for the purpose of attack (Harlequin Student: or,
the Fall of Pantomime). When the techniques of satire so
control the form of the play that no comic resolution soft-
ens the author's intention to attack, then the play is a
dramatic satire, distinct from either comedy or farce.

The adaptation of satire to the stage in this period did not always produce dramatic satire. Frequently the dramatist stopped short with only satiric bits or with the inclusion of a satiric character who is exploded or discredited before the end of the play. But the range of the experimentation to find a form for dramatic satire plus the extent of the satire in plays that are not controlled by the satirist's intention, encouraged me to study how the age of great English satirists was reflected in what was written for the theatres.

In suggesting some of the problems of etymology of the word satire and the literary history of satire before my period, I have wandered from the recent critical controversy over whether satire is a genre or a mode, and I have so far mentioned only a small segment of questions raised about satire in the recent wave of critical interest in this subject. Arguments also extend to the aesthetics of satire: When does satire become art? Is there a necessity for a masked persona? What is the rhetoric of satire? Is plot possible outside of satiric allegory? My earlier assumptions about the grotesque fantasy, wit or irony necessary to label a literary product as satire grow out of the discussion of the aesthetics of satire and need some further spelling out.

The most obvious common denominator of satire, whether it is of the satura medley type, or the satyricon, satyr-antics tradition, or the Menippean prose variety, is that it is rational criticism of human conduct. The satirist does not concern himself with the irrational in nature—sudden storms, stubborn animals or vast desert wastes—nor is he concerned with the cosmic ironies of history; he is concerned with the conduct of humans whom he perceives as rational but like Swift's man, only capable of reason (rationis capex) because man by no means always acts rationally either for his own good or for the good of society. Where he deviates, acts foolishly, interferes with the good of the state or the social or literary constructs of other men, he is ridiculed, insulted, castigated by the satirist. The folly of irrational behavior is constantly held up to the cold light of reason. This explains why the satirist attacks hypocrisy and affectation but not insanity. The insane man is incapable of distinguishing any discrepancy between what he says and what he does and is therefore outside the satirist's target. Beneath the satirist's attack on irrational behavior

from men who are capable of knowing better lies the serious
implication of human responsibility, although the satirist's
intention may be so masked by ridicule that his audience or
readers do not immediately grasp the implications of what
produced their laughter at the exposure of folly.

Perhaps it is the satirist's fate that in persuading
his audience of the follies of human behavior he often ali-
enates his readers. I am often asked by my students, What is
the use of satire? (The Roman Empire declined despite the
bitter castigation of Juvenal.) Was English poetry improved
by Pope's catalogue of dull writers in The Dunciad? Didn't
Swift immediately antagonize his contemporaries by Book IV
of Gulliver's Travels? To such questions I can only reply
that the satisfaction of writing satire is the satirist's
own because he has brought his private world into stable
focus by imaginatively displaying wherein and how far he
finds his fellow men irrational and ridiculous. I have argued elsewhere in a symposium on modern satire[6] that satiric catharsis is the satirist's own, developing from the
author's sense of relief as he ridicules, gently or bitterly,
human acts of which he disapproves. The idea is as old as
Freud's discussion of wit as a release of aggression, although it has been augmented by Robert C. Elliott's anthro-
pological analysis of a basic urge to rid oneself of hostility by expressing it, an idea that I referred to in the
Introduction (see Elliott, pp. 84-85, especially). It is
much easier for an audience to share in the catharsis of
tragedy where the hero suffers the consequences of his actions and we watch his self-knowledge come too late to re-
verse the consequences. An audience can also share in comic
catharsis when characters blocking a happy ending are exposed. (Witness the delight with which we watch the character hiding behind a screen, knowing full well that our
knowledge of his presence will soon be shared by all.) But
we cannot identify as easily with Lemuel Gulliver at the end
of Book IV as we can with Othello at the end of Act V. Gulliver has become less a man as he chooses his stable over
his family; Othello has become more a man as he painfully
learns of the innocence of his wife and the duplicity of
Iago. We reject the grotesque Gulliver who prefers the smell
of horses to the smell of his wife. Yet Swift forces us to
ask what does this exaggeration mean? Satiric characters are
thus controlled by the author's intention; they act and

speak to emphasize irrationality rather than reality. The
satirist's interest in characters who illustrate the particular thus leads him to create exaggerated, grotesque characters who are types or one-dimensional as opposed to characters of depth and individuality in realistic novels or
comedies of manners. The grotesque character's words and
acts are the satirist's method of picking out the ridiculous
and irrational—exaggeration for a purpose. Frequently the
purpose is oriented in the satirist's sense of irony, his
awareness of the difference between appearance and reality.
It is not tragic irony where the audience watches in horror
knowing more than the actors, but closer to comic irony
where the audience anticipates the exposure of the man hidden behind the screen. But satiric irony is stronger than
comic. It is the shock of the unmasking; the screen falls
with a crash. "Look," says the satirist, "the world is not
as you think!" It is the shock of Gulliver recoiling in
horror when he perceives his own resemblance to the Yahoo in
their reflected images in the water. Such irony enriches
satire as Wayne C. Booth, <u>The Rhetoric of Irony</u>, points out
because it engages the audience in an intellectual game of
reconstruction: what were the author's probable intentions
(p. 53)? Satire without irony quickly descends to name-
calling, and invective can be tiresomely unimaginative and
repetitive as anyone accustomed to locker-room chatter well
knows.

Satiric irony is developed not only by the shock of exposure but by the satirist's language. It appears often in
parody of another author's style. Parody depends on the audience knowing the style being lampooned well enough to recognize the ironic exaggeration in the satirist's copy. It is
an in-joke which the satirist shares with that portion of
the audience sophisticated enough to perceive the joke. Parody is difficult to establish and sustain and thus, like
burlesque action, is only one of the many devices used by
the satirist. While burlesque action suggests the antics of
a stand-up comedian, it can be an effective tool especially
in dramatic satire. Parody, however, is limited to attacks
on other authors (the modern author of <u>The Tale of a Tub</u>,
for example); it is the satirist's attack on a literary
target.

Allegory, the tool of the moralist, is often a convenient tool of the satirist. Instead of the reversal-reconstruc-

tion process that is necessary for an audience to appreciate irony, allegory, because it is a form of extended metaphor, is an additive process. In a beast fable like <u>Animal
Farm</u> we are invited to extend the relationship of the fictional character (pig) to satiric target (capitalist) in a
process of enrichment dependent on how well our own preju-
dice agrees with Orwell's. The audience watching Charles
Macklin's play <u>Covent Garden Theatre</u> (1752) would have no
trouble assigning added meaning in this "Dramatic Satire"
to characters with allegorical names: Sir Solomon Common
Sense is obviously a <u>vir</u> <u>bonus</u> to be trusted; Sir Positive
Conjecture is a self-important bore; Miss Brilliant is a
Blue-Stocking wit; Miss Diana Single-Life is an old maid.
Allegorical names cause no problem, but when a fable is extended allegorically (<u>The Deposing and Death of Queen Gin</u>),
the satirist may have difficulty sustaining the allegory,
keeping it consistent enough to make clear what he is attacking. The audience may also have difficulty in following
the fable; the enrichment of meaning may not be what the
satirist intended. However, allegory is a convenient defense
for the satirist during a period of political oppression.
When freedom of expression is curtailed, satire may be cam-
ouflaged in allegory. This is an advantage to the satirist
who can pretend innocence if he is called to political account; but it is also a disadvantage because the ambiguity
of the camouflage may weaken the satire.

Attention to the satirist's rhetoric has produced a
list of devices:

> <u>Invective</u>: easily exhausted and exhausting, frequently
> descending into scatology.
> <u>Hyperbole</u>: particularly the exaggeration of false,
> ironic praise.
> <u>Amplification</u>: as in Swift's long lists, frequently
> containing a disparate, jarring item.
> <u>Zeugma</u>: yoking by syntax of unequal items, as in Pope's
> <u>broken</u> <u>china</u> and <u>broken</u> <u>vow</u>.
> <u>Episeiopesis</u>: strategic omissions which cause the
> reader to supply what expectation has
> aroused when he is confronted by *****
> or -----.
> <u>Catechresis</u>: deliberately mixed metaphor.
> <u>Antonomasis</u>: negation by the use of contrasting words
> ("sweet little giant" or "foolish wisdom").

This list could be extended beyond this sample, but it is
sufficient to indicate how much irony there is in the rhetoric of satire. Even invective can be tinged with irony as
in the King of Brobdingnag's label, "little odious vermin."

Recent attention has also been called to the persona
in satire as a result of the social psychologist's interest
in role-playing. W. B. Ewald in The Masks of Jonathan Swift
points out that the reason Swift is so often misunderstood
is that he adopts the mask of a deceptively rational man in
A Modest Proposal, of a modern author in A Tale of a Tub and
of a naive Gulliver in Gulliver's Travels. The confusion of
Swift with Gulliver, for example, has led to the erroneous
assumption that Swift is Gulliver. But there is also an advantage to the satirist in adopting a persona and thus
standing outside his artistic construct. Aesthetic distance
from the object of attack is of course easy in drama. The
satirist author of the plays in this study is inevitably removed from the characters of his play. He may speak in his
own voice in a Dedication or Prologue of the printed version
and thus guide a reader to his satiric target, but even in
such addenda, he often adopts the persona of a stupid critic
whose pedantry is also under ironic attack. Writing for the
stage is such an obvious technique of creating "masked" personae that any study of dramatic satire must inevitably take
into account the appropriateness of drama for satire.

To recapitulate, dramatic satire is defined, in this
study, as ridicule of man's irrational behavior[7] by employ-
ing (1) grotesque exaggeration, (2) the fantasy of allegory, whether sustained or suggested by abstract characters,
and (3) irony plus a variety of rhetorical devices which
make the irony apparent. When the satirist's intention sufficiently controls his dramatic construct, the play is a
dramatic satire; otherwise it is a comedy or farce with
satiric elements. The boundary line between satire and comedy or farce is admittedly a thin one, as these eighteenth-
century satirists argue for a return to an established norm
such as England without Walpole, literature before it was
corrupted by hack writers and bad poets, a theatre which
does not cater to pantomime and opera. In the chapters which
follow, I hope to trace, one, the extent of satire written
for the theatre in these three decades, two, the variety of
its targets, and three, the forms which it develops.

CHAPTER 2

POLITICAL SATIRE

Negative criticism can be made in a meaningful way only
from an implicitly positive critical standpoint and thus in
itself points toward the discovery of what we should do.
　　　　　　　　　　—Fred H. Wilhoite, Beyond Nihilism (1968)

> As with a moral view design'd
> To cure the vices of mankind;
> His vein, ironically grave,
> Expos'd the fool, and lash'd the knave.
> 　　　　—Jonathan Swift, "Verses on the Death of Dr.
> 　　　　Swift, D.S.P.D."

SINCE THIS STUDY was begun, John Loftis's book, The Politics of Drama in Augustan England, has appeared with a discussion of the relations of the theatres to political
parties. Professor Loftis is interested not so much in the
form of dramatic satire as in the influence of Whig and
Tory doctrine on the dramatists. He concludes about the period of this study (1720-1750):

. . . Whig doctrine began to influence characterization,
satire, and even some comedies' pronouncements on norma-
tive characters. This is intermittent in the second and
third decades of the 18th century, reversions to the older
attitudes frequently occurring; but by the fourth decade
the new attitudes, which in origin were certainly Whig,
are so widespread in comedy that it would seem gratuitous
to associate them with the programme of any group. Just
as before 1710 the attitudes that were Royalist in origin

16

are so widespread in comedy as not to admit of association
with the Tory party, so after 1730 the new attitudes may
not properly be called Whig, even though they were Whig-
gish in origin (p. 156).

Sentimentalism, for example, he points out was not limited
to Whig dramatists. However, he found that politics hurt
the quality of the drama and propaganda "would seem to be a
major reason why the plays are remarkable chiefly as a
chronicle of the age" (p. 161).

The purpose of this study, on the other hand, is to examine the form which this political satire took in drama and
to study its relation to eighteenth-century satire in general. Political satire will not, therefore, be examined so
much as a "chronicle of the age" though that is certainly
evident, but will be considered as a part of the literary
expression of satire. What was the period like in which this
political satire was being written?

On the surface the period would seem to have little
cause for great antipathies. In contrast to the preceding
century of political strife, the eighteenth century was an
era of comparative peace. England had, in 1713, emerged victorious from a continental war which left her most formida-
ble enemy, Louis XIV, an old and powerless man. By 1720 the
country had settled into the quiet of a breathing spell—a
period of reconstruction between the wars of Marlborough
and the wars of the elder Pitt.

From 1720 to 1750 England was controlled by one political party. The Tories who lost power at the death of Anne
in 1714 were never to regain it until the days of Lord North,
and not all that the leadership of Bolingbroke could do
would unify their disrupted membership into an effective
political party. But if the Whig party dominated England in
this period, it is no less significant that except for eight
years (1742-1750) one man controlled the government. Sir
Robert Walpole came into power on the wave of the panic following the South Sea Bubble in 1720. Until 1730 he shared
his power with his brother-in-law, Lord Townshend, but for
the next twelve years his supremacy was unchallenged. Walpole believed in avoiding big issues at home, in keeping out
of wars on the continent, and in concentrating on the development of industry and commerce. However sound his policy
might have been, it was not inspiring. The old white heat of

enthusiasm which marked the struggles over the Clarendon
Code, the Bill of Rights, or the Stewart succession no
longer seized the minds and hearts of Englishmen. It might
seem that this pedestrian age, not distinguished by great
wars or great internal conflicts, would arouse little political satire from the pens of dramatists.

Appearances are, however, misleading. Already by 1720
Benjamin Griffin was attempting to capitalize on the popularity of politics in the title of his play Whig and Tory,
yet the prologue admits the title is a trick to attract a
large audience:

> As when the State has need of Volunteers,
> The Martial Drum beats loud to catch your Ears;
> So we, your full attention to engage,
> Beat up the Alarm on Warlike Title Page.
> We know your Expectations join to Night,
> To see two factions, Whig and Tory fight:
> But ev'n as when Recruit Projects are begun,
> And mighty Projects form'd, yet nothing done:
> So our sly Author, to avoid a Fray,
> Has made the Party Champions of his play,
> Tame as our Buff-coats on a Training Day.   (Prologue)

Griffin's trick is indicative of the undercurrent of excitement below the surface quiet of politics in this period. The
lack of big issues did not necessarily preclude an active
interest in government. What if the Hanoverian succession
was secure? What if the Whig party was firmly in the saddle?
People could still be expected to flock to a play just because its title was Whig and Tory. It was too recently that
the English had fought to define their constitutional rights
under their Stewart sovereigns and they were not yet pre-
pared to abandon politics to the hands of a few men.

Moreover, the man who occupied the throne in 1720 was a
German by birth and language. George I, forced to converse
with his chief minister in halting Latin, could play only a
slight role in government. Consequently it is not surprising
if the people were impressed with their own importance in
governing England. Furthermore, while Walpole's power was
to extend all but eight of these thirty years, there was always an articulate opposition collected; if Tory, around
Bolingbroke and The Craftsman; if Whig, around Pulteney and

Cartaret at first, and later around George II's son, Frederick, Prince of Wales.[1] Thus factions were constantly at odds although one party and one man dominated the political scene.

The close association of dramatists with party politics further explains why dramatic satire was so often concerned with political events and personalities. The association varied greatly. Some dramatists received pensions;[2] some (Cibber and Whitehead) were rewarded as Poet Laureate;[3] others were attached to Frederick, Prince of Wales, who for a time even kept a separate court.[4] A few held important posts, such as William Popple as Governor of Bermuda, and Richard West as Lord Chancellor of Ireland.[5] But others such as James Worsdale held posts as minor as painter to the master-painter in the Office of the Ordinance.[6] When James Sterling and Matthew Concanen came from their native Ireland to London, according to one story they flipped a coin to decide which would write for and which against the ministry. It fell to Sterling's lot to write against and thus two more playwrights joined the ranks of party journalists.[7] In all, roughly about 14 percent of the dramatists writing from 1720 to 1750 are known to have received pay from one or another political faction.[8] This is not a complete explanation of the prominence of politics in the drama, but it illustrates that the stage was close to the affairs of the day and might be expected to reflect those affairs in its productions.

Much of the political satire in the plays of this period is too general to be attached to any specific event, person or policy. It is often doubtful how much of this general satire was earnest and how much was added to bring a laugh from a contemporary audience. Comment on politicians was good copy for the dramatist in much the same manner that comment on the Establishment or the Military-Industrial Complex would be today. Thus, as I pointed out in the Introduction and in Chapter 1, it is necessary to distinguish between the adjective satiric and the noun satire in discussing the plays. Satiric bits and pieces do not make a play a satire though they do add a popular dimension to the drama which was easily the most popular literary form before the novel. Most of the plays of 1720-1750 are satiric and not satires. Only occasionally do they contain enough of the ingredients of satire—grotesque fantasy, constant irony

and witty distortion of accepted values—to have the consistency of satire. More often the political satire is inserted
into the traditional forms of drama.

General satire was often based on gossip of the court
and political world, as in three anonymous plays, Metamor-
phosis (1723), Callista (1731), and C---- and Country (1735).
The first was an attack on some political writers, and from
its subtitle, Harlequin Cato, was probably aimed at Addison's Whig successors of the Cato Letters. Callista was addressed to the Duchess of Queensbury, that outspoken lady
who befriended Gay, and, like C---- and Country, was based
entirely on gossip about court scandals. Such plays reflect
only personal pique and have practically no value as sincere criticism of politics, nor is it certain that the
anonymous author of Momus Turn'd Fabulist (1729) had politics in mind when he gave a warning to the unwary satirist.
(Momus is threatened with being banished from the skies if
he utters one satirical word against any of the gods.) However, there are plays where personal grudge and idle gossip
give way to more serious criticism of politics. Fainwell,
for example, who is the most realistic character in Mrs.
Centlivre's comedy, The Artiface (1722), attacks the politician in general terms: "I have known a statesman pawn his
Honour as often as Merchants enter the same Commodity for
Exportation; and like them, draw it back so cleverly, that
those who give him Credit upon't, never perceiv'd it 'till
the Great Man was out of Post" (Act I). Thomas Odell, in The
Patron, or Statesman's Opera (1729) is even more specific in
his criticism when he makes Lord Falcon, described as a minister of state, and his friend, Sir Jolly, both dupes of
Peggy Lure who attends Lord Falcon's levee disguised as the
wife of one of the Lord's dependents. In this play the politician whose levee is the breeding place for flattery and
whose business consists of evading the demands of others, is
himself cheated out of a patent for ₤400.

The satiric tone of Odell's play is typical of much of
the general satire on politics. Jobson in Charles Coffey's
The Merry Cobbler (1735) is quite willing, for example, that
his henchman should cobble ordinary shoes, but it is Jobson,
the master, who must make shoes for Sir John Loverule who is
a member of Parliament. "As for Sir John's," he says, "I'll
do them myself, he's a Parliament Man, and must be staunch
at the Bottom, or he'll never be able to bear up the weight

of the Nation. Besides, he may take off the Excise upon Leather" (sc. vi). The hint of expected recompense establishes the mock-seriousness of Jobson preparing a firm foundation for his representative in Parliament.

In Robert Dodsley's The King and the Miller of Mansfield (1737), it is Dick, the miller's son, who describes the means of gaining political preferment in London. Honesty, he reports, will get you no farther than a footman's position. To rise at court, "you must be master of the arts of flattery, insinuation, dissimulation, application and (pointing to his palm) right application, too, if you hope to succeed" (I, iv). The king who, in disguise, is a guest of the miller's, is startled by this frankness in a country bumpkin:

> The King: Why, Richard, you are a Satirist, I find.
> Dick: I love to speak the truth, sir; if that
>   happens to be Satire, I can't help it.
>   (I, iv)

In Dodsley's sequel, Sir John Cockle at Court (1737), the miller, now a knight, withstands all the temptations which his son Dick has previously described. Even the king, again in disguise, cannot bribe the honest miller who finds court vices as distasteful as the French cuisine and fashions.

Such general satiric reference to politics indicates that the stage was appreciated as a good medium for satire. Attendance at the theatres was popular and it assured the satirist a large audience. The stage also realized satire in a more effective visual way than one-dimensional printed satire or a one-shot satiric cartoon. The author of a dramatic satire could remain in the background while his actors took over his satiric theme. The audience watching his satire performed could also make its own application of attack to object-of-attack thus extending the intention of the author while shielding him from charges of libel. This amplification of technique gave the dramatic satirist a new range and, after the introduction of ballad opera in 1728 by John Gay, a multidimensional form of attack. Robert Dodsley is only one of many dramatists to see the possibilities for political satire on the stage.

John Kelly's The Levee (1741) is more specific than

Dodsley in satirizing the method of seeking preferment in
the political world. The eighteenth-century levee provided
the place to award whatever minor benefices a particular
politician might have at his disposal. Thus Kelly's Lord
Shuffle promises one post to three different men and finally
gives it to a fourth; disregards petitioners; will not help
authors who serve him; and tells young Brightly to go study
Spanish, only to reward him by saying he can now appreciate
Don Quixote. Cutwell, the tailor, discusses the levee with
Brightly who tells how he had been recommended to Lord
Shuffle by one to whom the latter is obligated. Cutwell replies, "Had you been recommended by one, to whom he was de-
sirous of being obliged; that is, by one who can serve his
interest, tho' he was his professed Enemy, I should have
greater hopes of your getting a post. Statesmen always
write the Obligations they receive and the Promises they
make on sand" (I, iii). Cutwell sarcastically assures young
Brightly that if he will not do hack writing, be a burough-
monger, a secret-service agent, a pimp, a husband for a
cast-off mistress, or if he cannot draw up a tax that will
not make people grumble, then he has nothing to recommend
him at the levee.

The heroine, Arabella, disguised as a beau, also attends Lord Shuffle's levee to observe the fate of young
Brightly's petition. When questioned about her reason for
attending, she replies that the "same Business of Consequence brought us here, which, I believe, brings other idle
young Fellows; to make a Bow to the great Man, shew our-
selves, look about us, put on an Air of public Business,
take Snuff out of some Nobleman's Box, talk of the weather,
look with Contempt on wanting Merit; and so brush off to a
Chair with an Air of Satisfaction" (I, iv). Kelly is clearly
contemptuous of the politician's levee when in this same
scene he introduces the three men petitioning to be chief of
the Panacoqua trade. Lord Shuffle tells the first to be patient, the second that he had spoken of him to the Directors,
and the third that he may look on the business as completed.
Yet before they leave the levee, the three hear that a
fourth man has already been awarded this post.[9] Although
labeled a "Farce," The Levee is dramatic satire.

By the early 1740's when Kelly wrote The Levee even
such general political satire might affect a play's success.
Dower in the preface to his unsuccessful The Salopian Es-

quire (1739) cites party and bigotry as well as the malevo-
lence of his manager for his play's failure. And as early as
1734 William Popple had made a similar complaint about the
relation of politics and the fate of his play, The Lady's
Revenge, or the Rover Reclaimed. Popple's preface blamed the
rumor that his play was "supported by the Court" for the
riot which occured when a crowd gathered at Bedford Coffee
House in the Piazza and declared they would damn such a
"party play." And Henry Brooke's Jack the Giant Queller
(1748) was prohibited after the first-night performance because of its satirical songs although these songs were aimed
only generally at lord mayors, aldermen and governors who
were incompetent in the administration of their offices.10
However, such general satire on politics would probably
never have crystallized the disfavor of the government in
power into the Licensing Act of 1737. To look for the explanation of such repression, we must turn from the satiric
general to more specific dramatic satire than that of Dodsley, Kelly, Dower and Brooke.

SPECIFIC EVENTS
    Direct or topical satire appeared in the drama of this
    period from the South Sea Bubble at the beginning to
    the peace of Aix la Chapelle at the end. It is more
significant than the satire couched in general terms because
it is more tangible and therefore easier to identify and
evaluate. It furnishes "the discernible, historically authentic particulars" which Edward W. Rosenheim finds essential to satire.11 Furthermore, the plays about these events
are closer to satires than the ones just discussed as satiric. They are evidence of the dramatist's increasing willingness to enter the political arena of propaganda and to
depart from formal English verse satire based on classical
models.12 Satire on Sir Robert Walpole is reserved for a
later section of this chapter.
    The period 1720-1750 opens with the collapse of perhaps
the greatest financial hoax the English have ever known. The
South Sea Bubble burst in September of 1720 after a summer
of wild speculation on Exchange Alley. What caused it? The
beginning was the formation of the South Sea Company in 1711
by the Oxford-Bolingbroke ministry. The next step was the
passage of a South Sea Act by Parliament early in 1720 "to

combine the advantages of the Sinking Fund with the machinery of a Joint-Stock Company." The Company in return for
agreeing to take up the national debt was to receive government aid and a monopoly of the South Sea trade. Inevitably
the Company's shares were inflated. In May a Ł100 stock had
risen to Ł890; by June 25th the same stock stood at Ł1060;
by September 21st it had fallen to Ł150. And there ended
the nightmare of speculation which had included companies
projected for Insurance against Losses by Servants, Making
Salt Water Fresh, Extracting Silver from Lead, Importing
Jackasses from Spain, Trading in Human Hair, and even one
company "For an undertaking which shall in due time be re-
vealed."[13]

This national scandal and financial disaster which
ruined merchants and ministers alike might well be expected
to attract both dramatists and artists as copy.[14] As late as
1729 there was still reference on the stage to "that fatal
year,"

> When <u>Stocks</u>, like <u>Syrens</u>, charm'd all ranks to <u>buy</u>,
> That their <u>directors</u> might, of course, destroy.
>   (1729 Prologue for revival of Aaron Hill's <u>Fatal</u>
>   <u>Extravagance</u>, 1720)

The fraudulent speculation that was responsible for the collapse of the grandiose scheme in 1720 immediately produced
a spate of plays with topical satire. Among the first were
two anonymous plays, <u>Exchange Alley</u> (1720) and <u>The Broken</u>
<u>Stock-Jobbers; or, Work for the Bailiffs</u> (1720), the latter
with a Prologue by <u>Gainer</u> and an Epilogue by <u>Looser</u>, to
italicize the effect of "that fatal year." William Chetwood
also contributed two topical plays about the Bubble: <u>The</u>
<u>Stock Jobbers; or, the Humours of Exchange Alley</u> (1720) and
<u>South Sea; or, the Biters Bit</u> (1720). The subtitle of <u>Ex-</u>
<u>change Alley</u> (the Stock-Jobber Turn'd Gentleman; <u>with the</u>
<u>Humours of our Modern Projectors)</u> along with the subtitle
of Chetwood's first play indicate how close these topical
satires were to Jonsonian humours comedy. While <u>the Biters</u>
<u>Bit</u> suggests a satiric metaphor, all the four reach a comic
resolution with the eccentric, humour-ridden projectors exposed and business back to normal as the final curtain falls.
Chetwood called <u>South Sea; or, the Biters Bit</u> a "tragi-comi-
pastoral." His rustic character, Plowshare, who speaks in

dialect, and his comic Irishman and alderman, Scrapeall, expect to make a fortune in South Sea stock. But the play drifts from its specific satire on Exchange Alley with its pickpockets and stolen stocks into the farcical complications of a love affair that is happily resolved just as Plowshare's money is restored to him by Scrapeall. Thus despite its exposure of abuses in 'Change Alley and its title, the play is not completely a satire.

Early in the following year Thomas Odell added his play on the mania of gambling, The Chimaera; or, an Hue and Cry to Change Alley (1721). A list of characters illustrates the satiric object of Odell's play: Selfroth, the Projector; Teartext, a sham Parson; Hide and Seek, a Banker; Sir Nicholas Ninnyhammer; Lord Gracebubble; Capt. Scout; Snap, a Stock Jobber; Scrawl, servant to Bubble; and Lady Meanwell. The plot shows Sir Nicholas coming to London to sell his country estate for speculation. He, of course, falls victim to the cheats, Selfroth and Hide, and loses his estate. In the end, however, the cheats are taken into custody when even the election of Lord Gracebubble as Governor of the Bubble cannot give it sanction enough to prevent a collapse. Lord Gracebubble may well be a reference to Sunderland who with Stanhope gave government sanction to the ill-fated South Sea scheme.[15] While the play is more specific in satiric references, it too resolves into comedy.

When Colley Cibber modelled his play The Refusal (1721) upon Molière's Les femmes savantes, he also inserted a satiric reference to the Bubble and made Sir Gilbert Wrangle a South Sea Director. The Prologue presents the director ironically:

But let none think we bring him here in spite,
For all their actions, sure, will bear the light;
Besides, he's painted here in Height of Power,
Long ere we laid such Ruin at his door:
When he was levee'd, like a Statesman, by the Town,
And thought his heap'd up Millions all his own.
No, no; Stock's always at a Thousand here.
He'll almost honest on the stage appear.

The most obvious satire on the Bubble incident is in the first act of Cibber's play. The men discuss Sir Gilbert before he arrives on stage, and Granger asks, "What! Is he

Lord Treasurer?" Frankly replies, "A much more considerable Person, I can assure you, he is a South Sea Director, Sir." Sir Gilbert, once he appears, occupies his time ostentatiously striking names off his list to reserve some stock for Granger. He gives false promises to Lords: he taunts Frankly about his Mississippi stock that is worthless now;[16] he reads letters from indigent relatives requesting that he use his influence to make their fortunes; and finally he alters his list of stocks in helter-skelter fashion whenever it pleases his fancy to include new names by striking out old ones. The scene, a convincing record of how unsound were the business principles behind the South Sea Company, does not make Cibber's adaptation a satire but it does indicate that he was willing to capitalize on the Bubble.

Because topical satire after an event quickly becomes stale material, the Bubble was soon forgotten. Under the wise financial management of Sir Robert Walpole, England settled down to a routine existence devoid of great issues. The old financial folly was not long remembered, except for occasional reference such as the 1729 prologue previously mentioned. A ridiculous footman in James Moore-Smythe's The Rival Modes (1727), for example, is called "the only Fool left of our last Ministery" (Act II, Clary to her mistress, Amoret). It was many years, on the stage at least, before another event could so tempt the pen of the political satirists. But in 1733 Walpole suffered what one biographer describes as one of his "rare lapses in the management of Parliament and public opinion."[17] The issue was his Excise Bill which gave his enemies plentiful ammunition for their attacks upon his administration. The Bill itself was harmless enough. It was intended only to remove customs and impose in their place excise duties at a slightly lower rate on tobacco and wine. By this new method of taxation, it was hoped smuggling could be abolished and a stable revenue established. However, in 1732 during debate on the salt tax, Walpole had said that he saw no reason why the country should be frightened by a general excise, whereupon the phrase was snatched up and made into an issue. Yet in the introductory speech for his Excise Bill on March 18, 1733, Walpole asserted that no plan for a general excise had ever entered his head. When he concluded the same speech by saying that his excise would "tend to make London a free port, and by consequence the market of the world," he thoroughly confused

the issue.[18] London was already the former; if she were to
be made the latter, he had apparently not given up the idea
of a general excise after all. The opposition dogged his
heels with cries of "No slavery, no excise, no wooden
shoes."[19] By willfully making it seem that the thoroughly
sound scheme was a deliberate attempt to impoverish the people, the opposition succeeded in arousing enough feeling so
that the plan had to be dropped. It was Walpole's first major defeat.

An affair that produced violent riots and fierce enthusiasm might be expected to produce satire, but this time
it was not satire after the event as it was in the plays reflecting the South Sea Bubble. Instead five anonymous ballad
operas appeared to help shape the event: The State Juggler
(1733), The Commodity Excis'd (1733), The Court Medley
(1733), The Honest Electors (1733) and The Sturdy Beggars
(1733). The State Juggler, or Sir Politick Ribband, a New
Excise Opera even printed on a frontispiece a quotation
from the Grubstreet Journal, No. 170: "O Merciful God, grant
that the Ministry may not be infatuated, nor the King lose
the hearts of his subjects." Sir Politick Ribband is quite
likely Walpole, who had revived the ribbon of the ancient
Order of Bath and accepted it though he refused a peerage as
long as he remained in the ministry. Sir Politick and Don
Gulimo in the play are bitter rivals who hire the same informer, and while much of the plot is taken up with crude
intrigues of the various wives, several scenes are obviously
aimed at the administration. Olympia, Sir Politick's wife,
asks her husband about the tax scheme:

Well, Sir Politick, have you perused the Scheme and ma-
turely weighed and considered every Particular? Remember,
that my namesake, Olympia, of the house of Barberini, the
greatest family in Italy, was the Projector of the tax
upon Wheat which was immediately approved by her uncle,
the Pope, who found it so beneficial, that though frequent
application has been made by all the Bakers, within the
Territories of his Holiness, to have it taken off, yet it
has been continued by his Successors to this very day.

(II, i)

Olympia's remark applied only too well in England where
the vintners and tobacconists, like the bakers in Italy,

were hounding Walpole continuously about the proposed
scheme. But Sir Politick is skeptical of a woman's advice.
He does, however, realize the necessity for revising his
scheme and tells Spywell, the informer, "I will make such
Alterations in my Scheme, as shall conceal the bitterness
of the Golden Pill, that they may swallow it without Keck-
ing" (II, i).

Don Gulimo (quite evidently William Pulteney, the
leader of the Opposition on this Bill) has other plans which
he confides to Spywell: "I have struck the People with such
a Terror, that their private Murmurs had proceeded to an
universal Out-Cry; and this Paper, which shall be printed
forthwith, and dispersed among them, will throw 'em into
Convulsions" (III, i). From the number of riots that actually did occur, Don Gulimo or his counterpart must be said
to have succeeded. But in the play Sir Politick only laughs
at Don Gulimo's threats when they are reported by Spywell.
He has the scheme now in so attractive a form that even Don
Gulimo must approve it in his own conscience when it is laid
before the "Great Council that very day" (III, iii). This
evidence that the play was written when the controversy was
at its height is also indicated by another incident when
Sir Politick rebukes Scribble who writes his newspaper:
"Truly, Mr. Scribble, you do not write with your usual Vi-
vacity and Spirit, your last Paper me thinks was very flat
and heavy—Besides you tell such bare-faced stories, that
you give our Enemies an Opportunity of falsifying you in
every Particular—Your arguments are too vapid and insipid"
(II, i). The anonymous author is clearly aware that Walpole,
who had made a half-confidence of his plans in 1732, was
without a defense in the paper war which followed.

None of these five ballad operas on the excise scheme
was acted in the public theatres although they all appeared
in print. One, the scurrilous The Commodity Excis'd: or the
Women in an Uproar, was privately acted in the secret apart-
ments of the vintners and tobacconists and its author was
humorously designated as Timothy Smoke. Its frontispiece
represents Sir Robert Walpole riding on a tun drawn by the
English lion and Hanoverian horse "together with circum-
stances too gross for description."[20] The Sturdy Beggars,
dedicated to the Lord Mayor and Citizens of London, for "The
bold, the brave, and the Seasonable Opposition you made to a
late Project," celebrates the end of the controversy by

burning in effigy a bulky man with a blue paper cross on his
shoulder, obviously Walpole (Act II). According to a pamphlet in the Newberry Library eighteenth-century pamphlet
collection entitled Dedication of the Select Orations of
Demosthenes to the late Sir Robert Walpole, Bart. by
Aeschines the Third (Dublin and London, 1748), Walpole's
derisive name for the citizens of London was "the sturdy
beggars" (p. 18). It is not surprising that these dramatic
satires are anonymous, for while Walpole was forced to
abandon his cherished plan, he nevertheless seized the opportunity to weed out the recalcitrant and make his position in the ministry firmer than ever.[21] Opposition Whigs
were, therefore, in a precarious position which made caution
necessary. What is surprising is the form of these satires
which reflect how quickly after John Gay's success, the ballad opera became an accepted format for political satire.

Again England settled into lethargy after the excitement of the Excise Bill. It was broken by occasional topical
satires such as the ballad opera, The Oxford Act (1733),
which ridiculed the University officials for refusing to allow the terrae filius to be read at the Anniversary exercises for that year. It had long been a custom to read such
a humorous speech from the Rostrum at certain seasons, but
the fact that Oxford was at this time predominantly Tory,
made refusal seem a base fear of the sarcasm and raillery
which the speech was known to contain. The University officials laid themselves open to criticism of another sort when
the whole of the exercises went very poorly and demonstrated
that there might be some fire behind the smoke of the terrae
filius charges. The play represents the Vice-Chancellor con-
gratulating the Proctors on escaping being all "bemir'd and
in the Suds."[22]

In 1736, an Act placing an additional duty on malt
spirits produced two satiric plays, the anonymous The Deposing and Death of Queen Gin and John Kelly's The Fall of Bob
or the Oracle of Gin. The Act which also forbade distillers
the retailing of spiritous liquors in quantities of less
than two gallons without paying a tax of ₺50 a year, was intended to reduce the number of Gin shops, but its unpopularity made it inoperative.[23] The Deposing and Death of Queen
Gin which called itself "an Heroic Comi-Tragical Farce" obviously was not sympathetic with the purpose of the Act.
Queen Gin, the Duke of Rum, the Marquis of Nantz and Lord

Sugarcane are the main characters in this combination of burlesque action and satiric allegory where the queen is killed by the harsh legislation. Kelly's burlesque tragedy in mock-heroic couplets adds a hint of the consequences to Walpole in the death of Gin when his play has a vintner hang himself because of the unpopular Act and adds a dead march of "Butchers with Marrow Bones and Cleavers, the Latter covered with Crepe follow'd by Men and Women, two and two, the Men with Mourning Hat-Bands and white Handkerchiefs at their Eyes, the Women with Crepe over their Faces, their Hair loose" to mourn the loss of Gin.[24] The boldness of these satires on the Gin Act undoubtedly contributed to the pressure on Walpole to curb his dramatic critics.

Walpole's Licensing Act of 1737, which will be discussed later with the specific satires on the Prime Minister, did not put an end to dramatic satire based on events but it necessarily changed the form of later satire. Ballad operas such as those on the Excise Act, and farce and burlesque tragedy on the Death of Queen Gin gave way before the Lord Chamberlain's power. Instead political satire took the form of veiled hints or plots revised to fit an event. The Jacobite invasion attempt of 1745 is a good example of how the format of satire was modified. After the peaceful Hanoverian succession in 1715, England had lost its fear of a Stewart claiming the English throne although an anonymous play, The Assembly (1722), attacked the abuses of the Whig party in Edinburgh and included ribald satirical sketches of Presbyterian divines.[25] Yet, on the whole, the issue was a dead one as Thomas Odell's The Smugglers (1729) made clear. When there is some talk in Odell's play of Irish smugglers going to Liverpool on a design to bring in a Stewart king, Bung replies:

> But we smugglers are his best friends, we don't ruin ourselves by running a'ter one that can hardly maintain himself; but stay at home and defraud the Publick of that Revenue which would otherwise be employ'd to his disadvantage; and as by such means we get Estates that in a lucky moment may be useful to him; so, however that may happen, they'll in time put us above the fear o' the Law, the trouble of keeping our Words, and paying our Debts, an' yet secure us a good Chance o' dying in our Beds too.
>
> (I, ii)

Before Charles Edward landed in Scotland in the summer of 1745, the old fears of Catholicism and the Stewarts had revived and already found expression on the stage. James II was too powerful a memory for such an event to be taken lightly. Dramatic references, however, to the danger of a Stewart invasion did not usually take the form of dramatic satire but appeared as political additions to other forms of drama. Colley Cibber's revision of Shakespeare's King John in 1745 is a good example. Cibber explained the timely occasion for the revision in the Dedication, February 25: "In all the History plays of Shakespeare there is scarce any fact that might better have employed his genius than the flaming contest between his insolent Holiness and King John." Cibber's changes in Shakespeare's play are, of course, numerous and not all political. Yet the fact that he sharpened King John's reply to Pandulph and changed the title to Papal Tyranny in the Reign of King John six months before the Catholic Stewart landed at Loch-na-Uamh shows the Catholic scare at its peak. King John tells Pandulph:

No, Sir, our English pastors shall be English subjects,
Not aliens, independent of our Crown; (Act II)

Cibber was pointing up one of the sorest points of English pride, a pride that had chafed openly at the advancement of foreign priests during the reign of James II. The revised play also makes Philip anxious to help Rome, a change that refers to England's fear that France would aid a Jacobite uprising. Cibber's emendations are not satire, but they are a reflection of the dominant Whig policy which was more effectively presented in the satiric pantomime Harlequin Incendiary: or Columbine Cameron (1746) where the subtitle refers to the willingness of the Highland clans to support Charles Edward. The pantomime also articulated the fear of Catholicism by making the Pope boast that he must once more subdue England. The exaggerations of the pantomime were a better vehicle for satire on Scots, Stewarts in particular, and Catholics than the few political additions Cibber made to his warmed over Shakespeare.[26]

Fear of the Catholic Stewarts extended to fear of the French which motivated a satirical afterpiece, King Pepin's Campaign (1745). England had become involved in 1744 in the complicated War of the Austrian Succession. Her chief enemy

was France whose influence she was growing to fear in the
colonial world as well as in the politics of Europe. Thus
the performance of this afterpiece on April 15, 1745, was a
response both to the Jacobite scare and to increasing anti-
French sentiment. The afterpiece is full of burlesque action.
The French king enters attended by a retinue of nobles,
cooks and dancers as well as his mistress, Margaret. Puff, a
disgraced Field Marshall, makes love to Margaret, and for
this he is imprisoned until by Margaret's request he is
pardoned. The King takes quarters in a nunnery, but when
Margaret becomes jealous, he allays her jealousy by award-
ing Puff to the first nun who desires a husband. In the last
scene with the prospect of Menin in the background, the King
falls flat when the first cannon is fired, thus burlesquing
the actual battle, for the French king had arrived at Lisle
May 12, 1744, to review the army. On the 18th the French
had invested Menin and on the 24th had surrendered the gar-
rison.[27]

Another anonymous piece appeared in 1748 satirizing the
treaty of Aix la Chapelle which ended this indecisive war.
The title reveals its content as well as its allegorical
form: The Congress of Beasts, under the Mediation of the
Goat, for negotiating a Peace between the Fox, the Ass wear-
ing the Lion's skin, the Horse, the Tigress, and other quad-
rupedes at War. The Goat, if it was an English character,
may have been intended for Lord Chesterfield who had long
advocated peace. The Fox is evidently France with whom England treated first when she was ready for peace. The Ass
with the Lion's skin is England under the Pelham ministry
that succeeded Walpole. The Horse is undoubtedly the Hanoverian horse, and the Tigress is certainly Maria Theresa of
Austria. The allegorical device for satire had already been
used in another anonymous play, Fortune's Tricks in Forty-
six—an Allegorical Satire (1747), whose Preface claims, self-
consciously, to have opened "a new Vein of Satyr." And the
beast fable as an allegorical device for satire was used
again in the anonymous The Northern Election or Nest of
Beasts (1748) that pretends to be a translation from "a Rus-
sian author by R.N. & B.W., Fellows of the Royal Society" as
a sequel to The Congress of Beasts. It seems obvious that in
allegorical beast fables, the stage satirists had hit upon a
safe device for avoiding the censorship of the Lord Chamberlain's office. Did these anonymous authors, casting about

for "a new Vein of Satyr," suddenly remember Swift's Houyhn-
hnms and Yahoos?

ELECTIONS
     Not all specific political satire is so topical that it
     can be pinned down to an act of Parliament or one event.
     This is especially true of the numerous dramatic sa-
tires on elections, and eighteenth-century elections were
certainly fit subject matter for satire. Voting was limited
and open; electoral divisions were unequal; certain groups
in new centers of population were without representation
entirely. Naturally under such a system of rotten boroughs,
pocket boroughs, and patronage, there was ample opportunity
for corruption. Nor was corruption limited to one party or
one man. Walpole's enemies elected their members under exactly the same system. Even the largest electorate did not
preclude bribery, and patronage was universally recognized
as the product of the franchise.[28]
     John Sturmy in The Compromise or Faults on Both Sides
(1722) gives one of the first criticisms of the electoral
system in this period. The scene of his play is a country
borough at the time of the election of the mayor. Sir Lewis
Despotick, a high Tory, and Sir Clement Harpye of the "godly
party" are the two candidates. In a scene in the third act
they are both shown soliciting votes from the butcher and
other tradespeople. But in the course of their campaign they
make up their quarrel over their cups, and when a mob attacks Sir Lewis, he is rescued by his new friends and former
opponents. The incident of the mob might well refer to the
unpopularity of the Tories who were rumored to have plotted
to take advantage of the South Sea Bubble in 1720 in order
to bring their Stewart pretender back to England.[29] The play,
however, has a comic resolution and is not a satire.
     Bribery at elections is also briefly satirized in
Thomas Odell's The Smugglers (1729). Crabb, one of the smugglers, has been in Liverpool standing for a seat in Parliament, and upon his return his confederates ask about his
success:

     Vulcan: Well, Brother Crabb, what news from Pool? Have you
             carried your Election?
     Crabb: No faith, I made the Swabbs so drunk they forgot

my Name, and so voted for the other Candidate! I'm
plaguely out o' Pocket by 't. (III, iv)

Crabb claims his bribes cost him £600; "an I'd carried the
Day, I hadn't matter'd it." Bribing with drinks was perhaps
the commonest of election bribes, since it cost less and
put the voter in a compliant mood. Lewis Namier records the
death of two voters at Gloucester as late as 1761 as a result of this particular electioneering method.[30]

Henry Fielding, perhaps the most prolific dramatic satirist of the period, found frequent occasion to ridicule
England's electoral system in his plays. In Don Quixote in
England (1734), for example, the visiting knight is suggested by the mayor as someone to stand for Parliament in
that borough. The corporation which the mayor heads is particularly anxious that Don Quixote shall offer some opposition to the old candidate, Sir Thomas Loveland, since they
suspect the latter of holding the corporation too cheap.
They prefer receiving bribes from both sides and then voting
as they please.

Mayor: Brother aldermen, I have reproved you already for
       that way of reasoning; it savours too much of brib-
       ery. I like an opposition, because otherwise a man
       may be obliged to vote against his own party; and
       when both parties have spent as much as they are
       able, every honest man will vote according to his
       conscience. (I, ix)

The mayor then pays a call on Don Quixote to tell him that
the corporation approves his opposing Sir Thomas. But the
poor knight is confused by this strange business of English
elections and assumes that he must fight the other knight.
He therefore replies politely, "Sir, you make me concerned
that it is not now in my power to give you whatever you desire; but rest secure of this, there is not one whom you
shall recommend that shall not within this twelve month be
governor of an island." The mayor is delighted by the mad
knight's extravagance and whispers in an aside, "This is a
courtier, I find, by his promises" (II, iii). Fielding's use
of the naive foreigner as the unwitting critic of election
practices, is an interesting innovation in dramatic satire,
but the election scenes are buried when the Don becomes involved in the comedy about the young lovers.

Fielding's Pasquin (1736) contains sharper satire on election bribes. Trapwit's comedy, The Election, is one of two plays being rehearsed as a play-within-the-play and the rehearsal permits the author and his companion to discuss The Election as it is being rehearsed. The result is a double satire of narrative plot and comment on the realism of the action. The mayor in Trapwit's play argues for the court candidates, Lord Place and Col. Promise, in the coming election, though he claims that he is impartial and would as willingly see Sir Henry Fox-Chase and Squire Tankard elected. Trapwit, as author, has to warn Lord Place to "bribe a little more openly, if you please, or the audience will lose that joke, and it is one of the strongest in my whole play." When it is discovered that no counters have been provided for the bribes, Fustian bursts into uncontrollable laughter; "upon my word, the courtiers have topped their part: the actor has outdone the author; this bribing with an empty hand is quite in the character of a courtier" (I, i). Thus Fielding, by making some of his satire seem unintentional and by putting the rest into the mouth of an author once removed from himself, is able to say as much as he pleases about English elections. Trapwit points out that Sir Henry Fox-Chase bribes in more subtle fashion, since he does not send money but venison to his constituents plus some wine to wash it down. This country squire furthermore orders a dozen great-coats from alderman Stitch and a hundred yards of silk from Mr. Damask to ensure their votes. Fielding's final bit of grotesque humor is that Miss Mayoress with the gift of a fan bribes Miss Stitch to bring her lover over to the side of Col. Promise. "And can I sell my country for a fan?" (II, i) asks Miss Stitch in a tone reminiscent of The Rape of the Lock.[31] Using the Rehearsal format of Buckingham, Fielding succeeds in writing a satire, whereas his election scenes in Don Quixote in England were only a satiric addition to a comedy.

Frequently plays were written as satire on particular elections as is evidenced by The Downfall of Bribery; or, the Honest Man of Taunton (1733). This ballad opera (which I have not seen) was supposedly written by Mark Freeman though the Biographia Dramatica believes the name is fictitious (I, 257). It appeared in a year when the general elections were particularly important because of the failure of Walpole's Excise Bill. The subject matter is apparently a hotly contested election for Somersetshire which reflects a small

portion of the general excitement in the 1733 contest for
party supremacy during the fight over the Excise Bill.

The 1742 election which finally defeated Sir Robert
Walpole was even referred to in a political tragedy, Robert
Morris's The Fatal Necessity or Liberty Regain'd (1742),
dedicated to Charles Edwin, Esq., who had been a victorious
candidate for Parliament.

> Sir, I shall make no more apology for the Freedom I take
> in addressing this Dramatick Essay to You, than I did
> when I went to join my voice to elect you one of our Rep-
> resentatives in Parliament. It was you, who so strenuously
> asserted the Cause of Freedom in Election, we thought
> worthy of defending it in that Place where our Liberties
> are most necessary to be preserved.

This dedicatory letter, which is signed "an Independent
Elector," also charges the newly elected member of Parliament with his duties:

> It is not enough to oppose Excise-Schemes, Standing Armies,
> Useless Fleets, Pensions, Etc. but also to endeavor as
> much as in You lies, to lessen the Weight of Taxes, which
> so heavily oppress us—And if any Great Men in Power have
> abused the confidence reposed in them, either by King or
> People, we hope you will bring them to accompt. Examine
> strictly how they strained their Authority or misapply'd,
> or squander'd away the Publick Treasure; or what they ne-
> glected to do, to the Shame and Dishonour of the Nation:
> and we expect the Corrupter and Corrupted will have impar-
> tial Justice done them, which the nature of their Crimes
> deserves.

The play which follows is the story of Appius and Vir-
ginia, depicting Appius as a tyrant who meets defeat before
the end of the last act. What is Morris saying? It would
seem that the instruction, "It is not enough to oppose Excise Schemes, Standing Armies, Useless Fleets, Pensions,
Etc." indicates that Charles Edwin was a member of the Walpole opposition which had a majority of sixteen following
this election. Further urging that "impartial Justice" be
done "any Great Men" who have "strained their Authority or
misapply'd or squander'd away the Publick Treasure" would

seem instruction to join in catching Walpole, for articles
of impeachment were drawn up soon after the victory of the
opposition in this election.[32] When such a dedication was
added to a play about a defeated tyrant, it is apparent that
Morris was not only celebrating a new administration but
also calling for revenge on the fallen minister; satire, in
other words, had strayed into open propaganda attached as a
Dedication to a tragedy representing a fallen tyrant who de-
served further punishment.

THE PRINCE OF WALES
     Another political circumstance that aroused the dra-
matic satirists of this period was the unhappy family
relationship between George II and Frederick, Prince of
Wales. George II had quarreled with his own father back in
the days when he was Prince,[33] but he seems to have forgotten the incident when trouble arose with his son. An open
breach came finally in 1738 when the Prince hurried the
Princess, on the point of confinement, out of Hampton Court
in the middle of the night. The king was furious and forbad
the court to pay any visits to the Prince in his exile.[34]
Consequently Carlton House, where the royal exiles took up
residence, became a center of the opposition to the Walpole
government.
     This quarrel and the whole unpleasant relationship were
soon reflected in the drama. Dramatists quickly took sides
for and against the Prince in his quarrel with George II.
The anonymous The Patriot (1736), which according to the Biographia Dramatica, II, 131, was not intended for the stage,
was a dramatic account of the life of William of Orange, but
its chief intent was to compliment the Prince and Princess
of Wales, in the characters of Frederic-Maurice and his wife
Augusta. (Prince Frederick's wife was Augusta of Saxe-Gotha.)
The obvious parallel names may well explain why the play
was "not aimed for the stage." It is not a satire but an
open compliment to the dissident Prince and thus an implied
criticism of the king.
     Another play appeared three years later which also re-
flected the friction between the Prince and George II. This
was James Thomson's tragedy Edward and Eleanora (1739) which
was banned by the Licenser after it had been rehearsed and
advertised. There seem to be excellent reasons why the Li-

censer should be harsh on this play. For one thing Thomson
was chiefly dependent on the Prince of Wales and he could
therefore be expected to side with his benefactor in a royal
quarrel. The text of the play bears out this expectation and
illustrates why, in the eyes of the Licenser who was but a
tool of the party in power, the play was dangerous. For
Thomson asks:

> Has not the royal heir a juster claim
> To share his father's inmost heart and counsels,
> Than aliens to his interest, those who make
> A property, a market of his honour?
>
> (I, i)

And he has Prince Edward exclaim, when he hears of Henry
III's death:

> Alas! my royal father is no more!
> The gentlest of mankind, the most abused!
> .   .   .   .
> O my deluded father! little joy
> Hadst thou in life, led from thy real good
> And genuine glory, from thy people's love,
> The noblest aim of Kings, by smiling traitors.
>
> (IV, vii)

Considering that this play was written in the year after the
serious quarrel, that the Prince of Wales was still in disgrace, and that the play is dedicated to the Princess of
Wales, it is understandable that the Licenser would easily
identify the "smiling traitors" as Walpole and the party
in power.[35]

Thomson, however, is no more a satirist than Colley
Cibber was when he adapted King John as Papal Tyranny (1745).
Thomson is writing a political tragedy like Brooke's Gustavus Vasa (1739) which also was banned by the Licenser for
its veiled reference to monarchs misled by evil counselors.
Both plays indicate one form which political criticism took
after the Licensing Act of 1737 and the subsequent extreme
sensitivity of the Lord Chamberlain's office. Like Cibber's
Papal Tyranny, these tragedies disguised their political
views not in satire but in vague narrative parallels in or-

der to escape the Licenser's disapproval. Yet even such
indirect political references did not escape the watchful eye
of the Licenser.

Perhaps the strangest example of a play which was mixed
up in this court quarrel between the king and his heir is
Captain Boaden's The Modish Couple (1732). The content of
the play had nothing to do with the quarrel; it is modelled
on the Cibber pattern of a Restoration-comedy plot with a
sentimental conclusion. But the fate of the play was decid-
edly involved in court politics. For Charles Boaden, while
he was Gentleman Usher and Quarterly Waiter in Ordinary to
both George I and II, was also the court pimp and general
scapegoat for court intrigue and scandal.[36] Thus it hap-
pened that the authorship of this play was shifted to him
although the Earl of Egmont's Diary says the play was written by the Prince of Wales and Lord Hervey who had quarreled
with Pulteney and the Whig opposition that same year. A
three-cornered political pull on this play from the Prince,
from the Court, and from Pulteney made it inevitable that
the play was damned by double opposition before its friends
among the Prince's followers could organize. Again the play
is not political satire; it is only another example of the
close interrelationship of politics and the stage.

The Prince's private life was more satirically exposed
on the stage. Two plays, the anonymous Humours of the Court
(1732) and James Miller's Vanelia, or the Amours of the
Great (1732), contained reference to the Prince's affair
with Mrs. Vane, the notorious Frances Anne Vane who was
prominent at court as well as in the society of Bath and
Tunbridge. In Humours of the Court she appears as Vanessa,
and the author claims in the preface that this is not a satire on any particular person. But the pursuit of Vanessa
by Prince Adonis is too pointed a reference to be innocent
of satire. Miller's play, printed "as it was acted by a Private Company near St. James," claims to have based the plot
on some private papers, but asserts that it is "a General
Satire upon Vice and Folly" (Introduction). To the Prince
Alexis-Vanelia plot, Miller adds a subplot concerning Skir-
rissa's affair with Lord Haughty—clearly a reference to Walpole's affair with Molly Skerritt. Thus Miller's satire has
a double political edge, cutting against the Prince of Wales
and also against his opponent, the Prime Minister.

WALPOLE AND THE STAGE

As the object of vicious personal satire, no political
figure was more vulnerable than Sir Robert Walpole,
the main character in politics for all but eight years
of this period. First of all he assumed more power than any
single minister had yet assumed under the limited monarchy.
By refusing a peerage and by insisting on the importance of
the House of Commons, he set the precedent for a Cabinet
responsible to Parliament and dependent on the support of
the lower house. By refusing grace to his enemies and by
dismissing his disloyal supporters, Walpole created the office of Prime Minister, and in his hands that Minister became the most important official in the administration of
the government. It was natural that the people should be
wary of his power, especially since they suspected that it
was maintained by an elaborate secret service and lavish
bribes. They both feared his power and hated his dishonest
practices.[37] Furthermore the man himself was not a pleasant
companion in polite society. "As matter-of-fact an Englishman as ever drank October Ale," he possessed as his only
virtues practical judgment and common sense. His tastes
were not cultivated. Except for painting,[38] he cared nothing for the arts. He was no orator like Pulteney; he was no
patron of letters like Lord Chesterfield. Men could find
little to admire in his opportunism. He inspired neither
high confidence nor fine sentiments. His faults were more
obvious than his virtues which is unfortunate in a man who
is in the public eye. And Walpole received more than his
share of criticism from the dramatists of his day. Scarcely
any plays are dedicated to him although the bootlicking
James Moore-Smythe did assign his play, The Rival Modes, to
Walpole's patronage, and even Fielding, perhaps with tongue
in cheek during the brief period when he was writing for
the Theatre Royal at Drury Lane, dedicated The Modern Husband (1732) to the Prime Minister along with a plea that he
patronize the drama. John Hewitt dedicated his tragedy, Fatal Falsehood (1734), to Walpole and his comedy, A Tutor for
the Beaus (1737), to "Miss Skerret," Walpole's mistress, but
such bows in Walpole's direction were rare among playwrights.

Immediately following the panic caused by the South Sea
Bubble, there were few attacks on Walpole, for the country
was still grateful for his sound management of finances.
However, when George II came to the throne and it was obvi-

ous that Walpole was more firmly than ever intrenched in
power, his literary enemies began to sharpen their pens.
Not all the attacks on the Prime Minister were bold enough
so that they can easily be recognized. There were undoubtedly countless veiled thrusts also hidden in these plays
which would have caused a ripple of laughter in an eighteenth-century audience but now pass unnoticed. For example,
it is difficult to know whether the praise given to Sohemus,
the first minister, in Elijah Fenton's Mariamne (1723) is
meant to identify Sohemus with Walpole, and, if Walpole is
meant, whether the praise of Sohemus is ironic.

> In that high sphere the Council, you, Sohemus, alone
> Must ever shine: and may your wisdom raise
> Your master's fortune to divide the Globe
> With this new Caesar.
>
> (I, ii)

Walpole too was best in Council. But Sohemus is the one who
foments the conspiracy against Mariamne, and the allusion,
if intentional, would therefore not be complimentary. Similarly in Philip Frowde's Philotas (1731) Craterus, discussing state affairs with Cassander, breaks out condemning

> Dissimulation, Avarice and Pride,
> Envy, Detraction of Superior Merit,
> With the long Train of Arts such Statesmen use,
> To crush the Brave, and cheat the deluded Monarch.

Walpole had been accused by his opposition's journalists of
these same faults himself, but whether this passage was
meant to have a contemporary ring to it can only be speculation. The fact is that many tragedies of this period followed the pattern of Thomson's Edward and Eleanora in which
monarchs are misled by evil ministers (see pp. 37-38). William Hatchett's The Chinese Orphan (1741), for example,
points out in the Dedication that "this Fable is political
. . . to represent Prime Ministers as so many Devils." How
many such "Fables" and veiled satiric thrusts there were in
such political tragedies is not easy to determine even before the Licensing Act of 1737. At any rate the tragedies
did nothing to affect the form of political satire. It was
the comedies, particularly farces and comic afterpieces, and

the new form—ballad opera—which John Gay made popular, that
most affected the form of political satire on the stage.

The satire on Walpole in Gay's The Beggar's Opera
(1728) was not veiled but pervasive and diverse. John Gay
had been disappointed in receiving court preferment, but
when he had finally given up hope and the opera was already
finished, he was appointed, late in 1727, to the unimpor-
tant position of Gentleman Usher to the youngest Princess.
He declined this questionable honor and wrote to Swift that
he now had no further hope of advancement.[39] It was from
the background of this relationship between Walpole and Gay
that The Beggar's Opera was written.

Gay's satire on Walpole in this ballad opera is exceptionally varied. He establishes the analogy between the
statesman's trade and a receiver of stolen goods in the
first scene of the first act when Peachum's song ends:

> And the Statesman, because he's so great
> Thinks his trade as honest as mine.

Then he changes the attack by naming one of the gang of robbers "Robin of Bagshot, alias Gorgon, alias Bluff Bob, alias
Carbuncle, alias Bob Booty" (I, iii). In this collection of
epithets all the habits and idiosyncrasies of Walpole are
described: Bagshot refers to his fondness for hunting, Gorgon to his coarse appearance, Bluff Bob to his heartiness
which did not stop short of a vulgar remark to Queen Caroline, Carbuncle to his intemperate habits, and Bob Booty to
his fortune supposedly acquired at the expense of England.
Then Mrs. Peachum tells her husband that Bob Booty gave her
a ring whereupon Mr. Peachum puts him on the "Black List"
for spending too much of his time among women (I, iv), which
could possibly refer to Sir Robert's frequent conferences
with Queen Caroline, but more likely to his weakness for
women, particularly Moll Skerritt with whom he was conducting an affair at the time.[40] Peachum also opposes Polly's
marriage because "My Daughter to me should be, like a Court
Lady to a Minister of State, a Key to the whole Gang" (I,
iv). However this remark was intended, it does not apply to
Walpole as aptly. Walpole never enjoyed the favor of either
George I's or George II's mistress so that he possessed no
such "Key to the whole Gang." He did possess a more powerful
weapon in the friendship of Queen Caroline, a highly intel-

ligent woman who held more power over George II than his
mistress, Mrs. Howard, could ever aspire to. He had won the
Queen's friendship by patching up a quarrel between her
husband and his father, George I, back in 1710-1720, and he
was rewarded by the Queen's support when George II mounted
the throne in 1727.[41] Thus it was not through a Court Lady
but through the Queen herself that Walpole possessed a "Key
to the whole Gang."

The most complex satire on Walpole in The Beggar's
Opera is the scene of the quarrel between Lockit and Peachum
(II, x). Peachum underscores the political satire when he
says, "like Great Statesmen, we encourage those who betray
their friends"—an intentionally nasty dig at Walpole's secret service agents. The song which Peachum sings in this
scene also shows that Gay realized the subject matter was
dangerous:

> When you censure the Age
> Be cautious and sage
> Lest the Courtiers offended should be:
> If you mention Vice or Bribe,
> 'Tis so pat to all the Tribe;
> Each cries—That was levell'd at me. (Air XXX)

The quarrel in this scene develops when Peachum claims
that Lockit, "for Value receiv'd," had promised Ned Clincher
"a Session or two longer without Molestation." Lockit is
also charged with neglecting to pay Mrs. Coaxer her Informa-
tion-Money. "Indeed, indeed, Brother," says Peachum, "we
must punctually pay our Spies, or we shall have no Information." Lockit replies that his honor has been insulted and
they end up collaring each other for a fight although
Peachum still protests "'tis for the Interest of the World
we should agree."

This scene has been thought to be an intentional burlesque of an actual quarrel between Walpole and his brother-
in-law, Lord Townshend, who was a Secretary of State until
1730.[42] There was such a quarrel between the brothers-in-law
when, according to contemporary accounts, they actually did
collar each other at Mrs. Selwyn's. But neither Hervey's
Memoirs nor Coxe's Memoirs of Sir Robert Walpole mention the
quarrel occurring before 1729.[43] Yet Gay's play which was
finished by October 22, 1727, and acted in January, 1728,

contains a scene almost exactly like the recorded quarrel at
Mrs. Selwyn's. It is almost as if Walpole and Townshend mod-
eled their quarrel on this scene from The Beggar's Opera.
What is the explanation? The scene is clearly political satire and Lockit and Peachum address each other as brother.
It quite evidently refers to friction between the two ministers. Such friction was undoubtedly developing before Gay
finished his play, for Lady Townshend, the most effective
mediator between the two, had died in 1726. Furthermore a
new sovereign had come to the throne in 1727 and Townshend
was not on good terms with George II.[44] There are two good
reasons then why Walpole and Townshend might be known to be
on bad terms before 1728 when The Beggar's Opera was first
performed. But this does not explain why the scene resembles accounts of the real quarrel at Mrs. Selwyn's. Hervey
and Coxe only knew that Walpole and Townshend became violently angry and had to be separated to keep from coming to
blows. The rest they may have filled in from the anticipatory scene in The Beggar's Opera. In other words the political satire in the play anticipated and became confused with
an actual event.[45]

      The significance of John Gay's development of a new
dramatic form—the ballad opera—will be more fully discussed
in the chapter on literary satire. The happy combination of
this new form, itself a satire on the popularity of Italian
opera, and Gay's many-faceted attack on Walpole as leader of
a gang of thieves, as quarreling brother, and as dishonest
fence for stolen goods, helps explain the extraordinary success of The Beggar's Opera which ran for 80 performances, a
unique record for the London stage in this period. His distortion of social values as when Peachum and his wife can
forgive Polly anything except marrying her lover, combined
with his metaphor of politicians as thieves, expressed in
numerous witty songs and comic short scenes, are evidence
that Gay had hit upon a form of dramatic satire so effective
that it would be often copied and survive in the twentieth-
century version of Brecht's Dreigroschenoper.[46]

      Walpole is reported to have attended the opening of The
Beggar's Opera and to have laughed at the pointed reference
to Robin of Bagshot and all his aliases. What else could he
do? But that Gay effectively got under his skin seems evident from the fate of the sequel, Polly, which was forbid-
den. Yet Gay loses control of his satire in this sequel when

he transfers his London characters to the West Indies. Macheath, who has turned pirate, is now disguised as a Negro slave. He has lost all his bravado and charm and it is difficult to imagine that he could be offensive even to the Prime Minister. The fate of Polly seems to indicate that while The Beggar's Opera may have taken Walpole by surprise, he was overcautious about the ineffectual sequel.

Henry Fielding soon joined the attack upon Walpole. His sharp satire on elections, already discussed, made it clear that he was part of the opposition. Lord Place in Pasquin, for example, represents the Whig party in power and calls his rival a "nasty stinking Tory" (II, i). And Lord Place makes the first voter who likes sack, poet laureate—a clear thrust at Walpole's bad literary taste as well as a jibe at his appointment of Colley Cibber. But Fielding could be much more specific and more personal.

As early as his Grub Street Opera (1731) Fielding had written with ridiculous extravagance of a love affair between Robin and Sweetissa by having the pair declare their love "as deep as the knowledge of physicians, the projects of statesmen, the honesty of lawyers" (I, vi). These ironic similes underscore the burlesque of Walpole's love affair with Molly Skerritt. Besides Robin, the butler, quarrels with William, the groom, with each giving the other the lie which, according to the Introduction between a Player and the author, Scriblerus Secondus, "is the whole wit of Grub street and long practiced by politicians." Apparently Fielding too could not resist a reference to the famous Walpole-Townshend fight, although William here could also be Walpole's opponent, William Pulteney. Other servants in the play are a coachman, John (Lord Hervey) and a gardener, Thomas (the Duke of Newcastle). They all serve, or trick, Squire and Mrs. Ap-Shinken who are Welsh and speak English as poorly as the German King and Queen. Fielding's opera, originally entitled the Welsh Opera, was to have been played as an afterpiece to William Hatchett's Fall of Mortimer so that the analogy of the tragedy on majesty misled and the satiric afterpiece on the roguish butler would constitute a double attack on Walpole.

By the time Fielding wrote his Historical Register (1737) he was clearly considered dangerous to the ministry; the proof is his own mock justification of the Register as a ministerial publication. In reply to an accusation in the

Gazeteer claiming that his plays aim at "the overthrow of
the m-----," he retorts ironically that, on the contrary,
he is writing _for_ the ministry:

> And here I must observe, that had not mankind been either
> very blind or very dishonest, I need not publicly have in-
> formed them that the Register is a ministerial pamphlet,
> calculated to infuse into the minds of the people a great
> opinion of their ministry, and thereby procure employment
> for the Author, who has often been promised one, whenever
> he would write on that side. (Dedication)

After this sly reminder that the ministry is not above bribing its opponents, Fielding adds, in mock-defense, that
since his characters are so low, he is shocked the _Gazeteer_
can discover any resemblance in them to the ministry. Indeed
it is so plain "who is meant by this Quidam that he who
maketh any wrong application thereof, might as well mistake
the name of Thomas for John, or old Nick for old Bob." Obviously Fielding was having fun linking Sir Robert's name
with the devil even while he was pretending to defend himself against the charge of political satire. He has the
audacity to add that he intends soon to write a paper defending the ministry "against the wicked, malicious, and
sly insinuations conveyed in the said paper." Fielding is
seldom cleverer than when he is making a left-handed apology
that still retains its satiric sting.

Despite his mock-protest in the Dedication, it is clear
that Quidam _is_ intended to represent Walpole. The scene in
which he appears portrays four patriots of different types—
the noisy, the cautious, the self-interested and the indo-
lent (Fielding's adaptation of the stock characters of classical satire). The patriots have one thing in common: they
all complain of poverty until Quidam enters and gives them
a purse. Again, as in _Pasquin_, Fielding uses the author of
the play-within-the-play to point up his satire. Here Medley,
the author, in response to criticism of the patriots scene,
observes, "Sir, everyone of those patriots have a hole in
their pockets, as Mr. Quidam the fiddler there knows; so
that he intends to make them dance 'till all the money is
fallen through, which he will pick up again, and so not lose
a half-penny by his generosity; so far from it, that he will
get his wine for nothing, and the poor people, alas! out of

their own pockets, pay the whole reckoning" (III, ii). Thus
Medley alerts the audience to the dumb-show dance which ends
his farce. Fielding is probably referring to a statement
Walpole is supposed to have made, "Every man has his price,
and I know that price." At any rate the scene is certainly
satire on Walpole's bribing so that it cost him little and
won him the votes of "patriots."

With Pasquin and the Historical Register Fielding developed an effective dramatic vehicle for satire on the
prime minister. Borrowing the rehearsal technique from
Buckingham, stock characters and the suggestion of satura
or hodgepodge in Medley whose very name suggests the Roman
satirists, he was able to give his plays an Aristophanic
topicality while ironically concealing his purpose by the
mock-defense of his Dedication. It is the author in Pasquin
who urges the politician to "bribe more openly" so the joke
will not be missed just as Medley points out Quidam's true
character, while Fielding, hiding behind the mask of Trapwit or Medley, can pretend innocence.

The effectiveness of these personal attacks on Walpole
combined with the many specific dramatic satires on his Excise scheme and Gin Act gave him a convenient excuse for the
Licensing Act of 1737 which limited the number of theatres
to those with royal patents and made illegal the performance
of any play, prologue or epilogue without the approval of
the Licenser from the Lord Chamberlain's office. Genest insists that while the Act was occasioned by political strokes
in Pasquin and other plays, it was being contemplated before,[47] and this is substantiated by arguments for further
regulation of the stage in the Gentleman's Magazine as
early as 1735 (V, 192). In fact Sir John Bernard had moved
in the House of Commons on March 5, 1735, for leave to introduce such a bill, but the bill did not then carry, despite Walpole's growing dissatisfaction with the antagonism
toward his person and policies in the plays of Fielding and
others. The immediate cause for the 1737 Licensing Act was
a lost play, The Golden Rump, which was apparently offered
to Giffard and then by him carried to Walpole. There is an
account of this lost play in the Gentleman's Magazine for
1737 (VII, 167-68) and one speech will serve to illustrate
the satire on Walpole's taxation: "Hearken to my Voice, all
ye People, I am the mightiest among the mighty, even he that
rideth on the back of the Great Bear. Offer up unto me your

Sons and your Sons sons, your Wives and your Daughters, your
Vessels of Silver and your Vessels of Gold. I say unto you,
Vessels of pure Gold, your own and your neighbor's Vessels,
so shall ye find Favour in my Sight, and the Man who chang-
eth his Rod into a Serpent shall fill you with Good Things."
This biblical language of a tyrant combined with the obscene
action[48] made the play intolerable to Walpole who now had
an excuse to push through Parliament an act regulating the
theatres.

There were objections to the Licensing Act even from
people not concerned with the theatre who saw it as an attempt to curb freedom of speech. Fielding as a dramatist
had already expressed such a fear in the dedicatory letter
to the Earl of Chesterfield published with his Don Quixote
in England (1734):

> The Freedom of the Stage is, perhaps, as well worth
> contending for as that of the press. It is the opinion of
> an author well known to your Lordship, that examples work
> quicker and stronger on the minds of men than precepts.
> This will, I believe, my Lord, be found truer with
> regard to politics than ethics: the most ridiculous ex-
> hibitions of luxury or avarice may likewise have little
> effect on the sensualist or miser; but I fancy a lively
> representation of the calamities brought on a country by
> general corruption might have a very sensible and useful
> effect on the spectators.

The gist of Fielding's argument was repeated and expanded by Chesterfield in opposing the Act in 1737.[49] Both
Chesterfield and an anonymous writer in the Gentleman's
Magazine for 1737 (VII, 409) saw the act as a limitation of
freedom of speech, a view shared by Thomas Cooke in his
preface to The Mournfull Nuptials or Love the Cure of all
Woes (1739). "What, alas! shall we say," Cooke asks, "when
we see in a nation whose greatest boast was its freedom and
its trade, large steps, or rather strides, taken to abridge
it of one of the most valuable branches of liberty, the liberty of the press? . . . What, but that they are afraid, if
a monstrous flagitious character of a person is represented
as moving in their own circle of life, that it should be
applied to themselves?" (p. vii).

Cooke's wry question indicates that the ministry had

missed its chance to make use of the stage for political
argument. In fact the writer for the Gentleman's Magazine
suggests that what the stage needs is not regulation but di-
version to a more profitable use: "And I see no Reason why
it is not well worth the Charge of a Ministry to send Companies of Strollers round to Corporations, to entertain them
gratis with Political Plays before an Election, as to cir-
culate Political News-Papers upon the like Occasion" (VII,
358). Walpole, it is indicated, had missed his chance to
annex the stage as an organ of political propaganda.

With the Licensing Act it was journalism and not the
stage which became the vehicle of the anti-Walpole crusade.
Fielding, for example, continued his attack in the Champion
and elsewhere.[50] However, the new restriction did enable
the Ministry to keep a stricter watch over the theatres,
and the number of satiric plays about Walpole decreased no-
ticeably. Francis Lynch slipped one small bit into his play,
The Independent Patriot (1737), but this was before the Act
went into effect.[51] The safest course was that adopted by
the anonymous author of The Projectors (1738) where the Minister on stage never says a word—a device which the author
points out in "Advice to the Reader" can give no offense to
the Ministry. The Lord Chamberlain's Office, which found
veiled references to monarchs misled by evil ministers in
Henry Brooke's Gustavus Vasa (1738) and James Thomson's Edward and Eleanora (1739) and refused them a license (see
pp. 37-38), was best satisfied by having a Minister say nothing at all.

Thus while the Licensing Act did not stop the satire on
Walpole, it did alter the form and usually it caused plays
to be read without being performed. John Kelly's The Levee
(1741), for example, was denied a license probably because
Lord Shuffle in this ballad opera was considered to be a
satire on Walpole, especially since the Lord tells one man
that he is indebted to him for saying fine things in his
poem The Patriot, and then gives the author no financial aid
except to wish him increased sales on his next piece (I,
iv). Walpole, like Lord Shuffle, failed to interest himself
in the affairs of men of letters. The rest of the scene,
with Lord Shuffle keeping three men thinking that they will
receive a post which he has already granted to a fourth,
would scarcely be complimentary to the Prime Minister.[52]

Walpole's fall from power in 1742 was celebrated by

dramatists both as the defeat of a tyrant (Robert Morris,
The Fatal Necessity, 1742) and as the end of a pantomime
(the anonymous Politicks in Miniature: or, the Humours of
Punch's Resignation, 1742). In the Morris play Numitorious
and Valerius, friends of liberty, bewail the loss of freedom under the rule of the tyrant, the "Prime Decemvir Appius":

> Rome cannot long subsist: The Bankrupt State,
> Oppress'd with heavy taxes, loss of Commerce,
> Of Friends, of Credit destitute, 's become
> The Scorn of ev'ry petty Tyrant Power
> That's leagu'd against us. (I, i)

Walpole had just led England unprepared into the war of
Jenkyn's Ear, which, besides making the charges of "heavy
taxes" and "loss of Commerce" applicable, severed finally
the last shred of friendship between England and France and
thus left England isolated from the continent of Europe.
Walpole's policy of avoiding foreign conflicts had eventually led him to neglect what F. S. Oliver calls "England's
prestige!" (II, 122).

But Numitorius continues his charge against the tyrant:

> And 'tis reported, he has abus'd his Trust,
> Has robb'd and misapply'd the Public Treasure,
> And squander'd it 'mongst fawning sychophants,
> His Dupes and Tools, the servile Senators,
> Who still oppress us with the Weight of Taxes,
> To feed these cringing Knaves, to bribe their Voice,
> And screen his Villanies. . . . (I, i)

Morris, in his dedicatory letter to the representative from
Westminster, had instructed the representative to prosecute
just such a man as Appius so that Numitorius's charges are
giving a blow to a man already down. It is interesting that
Morris even after Walpole's defeat puts his political criticism into tragedy not dramatic satire.

The anonymous author of Politicks in Miniature (1742)
returns criticism of Walpole to satire in what he calls "A
tragi-comi-Farcical-Operatical Puppet Show . . . to which
is added the Political Rehearsal, Harlequin the Grand: or,
the Tricks of Pierrot Le Primier." This political satire is

based on Walpole's retirement as Punch after 20 years and it
maintains the metaphor throughout that all politicians are
puppets. Apparently what prompted the play was the fear that
Punch will "speak from behind the Scenes" after he has left
the stage. "In short," the play warns, "we do nothing, if,
after we have turn'd him out from being an Actor, we make
him the Prompter." Thus Walpole-Punch is prevented in the
rehearsal which follows from prompting the Tory-Rorians or
the Merry Andrews of Farce (the Whigs). It seems a fitting
end to the satire on Walpole who after 1742 became the Earl
of Orford and shrank into impotence in the House of Lords.
The period when he made good copy for the stage satirist
was over.

After the fall of Walpole from power, political satire
of specific events such as the invasion attempt of 1745 and
the treaty of Aix la Chapelle, 1748, appeared occasionally
as did satiric references to changes in the Ministry as in
a revised version of Court and Country (1743),[53] but the
end of the period produced less satire on politics and more
social and literary satire, safer subjects for the dramatic
satirist after the 1737 Licensing Act.

What seems evident is that as politics became increasingly unsafe as subject matter, criticism of those in power
was suggested obliquely in political tragedies about evil
ministers of state or in allegories that might bemuse the
Licenser from the Lord Chamberlain's office. David Mallet's
Mustafa (1739) and the tragedies of Thomson, Brooke and Morris already mentioned are good examples of the former. One
anonymous tragedy, Majesty-Misled or the Overthrow of Evil
Ministers (1734) even stated such a political theme in its
title. Beast fables (The Congress of Beasts . . .) and allegorical names as in The Usurpers, or, The Coffee House
Politicians (1741) where Maskwell and Overreach as usurpers are matched against Col. Strut and Beau Puff-Paste,
were frequently used to obfuscate identification. Comic
treatment was clearly the most popular and most effective
vehicle for political satire and this took many forms. Even
pantomime was often adapted to satire although the afterpiece was more common since its shortness made it easier for
the satirist to sustain his intention. However, John Gay's
introduction of the ballad opera provided the most successful new form of political satire with its quick changes of
scene, variety of attack and sustaining wit and humor. In

the hands of Gay, Dodsley, Carey and Fielding and Kelly the
new form became the best dramatic tool of the political satirist and developed into an effective extension of party
journalism and pictorial caricature.

It was Fielding who extended farthest the possibilities of the ballad opera for political satire by the variety of his additional techniques. His use of the "rehearsal"
format provided fictional authors like Medley who could underscore the satiric hits. His use of a vir bonus like Don
Quixote and of stock characters of classical satire (boast-
er, sycophant, etc.) added contrast and depersonalization
to the contemporary political scene. His use of allegory
(The Grub Street Opera) further extended the possibility of
burlesque action. He also commanded a variety of stylistic
techniques—an ear for parody, an ability to burlesque political actions, and a pervasive irony which impregnated his
dedications and prologues as well as the plays themselves.
As long as the Haymarket Theatre remained open to him, he
continued to explore the variety possible in adapting comedy and ballad opera to political satire, but it would be a
mistake to suggest that it was only Walpole who was his
target as the following chapters will indicate. The multiplicity of his other targets (auctioneers, orators, poet
laureate and fellow playwrights and actors) diluted if it
did not diminish his effectiveness as a political satirist.
In such multiplicity no effective metaphor such as all ministers are thieves or all politicians are puppets could be
sustained. What seems evident is that for Fielding satire
remained a hodgepodge like the satura of Horace and Juvenal
of the classical verse satire tradition rather than a pervasive metaphor such as Aristophanes' Birds or Frogs into
which topical satire could be fitted. Only in his Grub
Street Opera, a revision of The Welsh Opera, did Fielding
expand the possibilities of ballad opera into a consistent
political allegory, with rascally servants who serve a non-
English speaking master and his wife. The Grub Street Opera
was a successful experiment in the form of dramatic satire,
but its political satire was too obvious; it was advertised
for the Haymarket Theatre for June 5, 1731, but never performed (Pt. 3, LS, I, 146). Thus while Fielding realized the
possibility of ballad opera for political satire more consistent than Gay's Beggar's Opera, he was forced to return
to a rehearsal-format in Pasquin (1736) and The Historical

Register (1737) to continue his ridicule of Walpole and the
Whig party in power. Only after his fall from power in 1742
did a dramatic satirist present Walpole again in a consistent political allegory as Punch, the Prompter for Puppets
(Politicks in Miniature: or the Humours of Punch's Resignation).

In summary, political satire at the beginning of this
period took the form of satiric plays after an event (the
collapse of the South Sea Bubble), and these plays were
comedies with satiric references to the event that brought
Walpole to power. As Walpole's policies and personal life
were increasingly attacked by dramatists, political satire
took on a variety of forms—ballad opera, rehearsal plays,
and pantomime—to prevent his Excise Bill, to attack his
Gin Act and election practices, and finally to call for his
impeachment in 1742. When the Licensing Act made political
satire more dangerous, dramatists were apt to turn away
from dramatic satire and to allude to the effect of evil
ministers in tragedies, although beast fables were revived
as satiric allegory on specific events such as the treaty
of Aix la Chapelle. One wonders why Walpole did not recognize satiric plays about his enemy, the Prince of Wales, as
proof that he could enlist the dramatist as a political
ally. Yet he seems never to have perceived the possibilities
of the stage as a public forum for attacking his opposition.
Thus the personality and policies of the Prime Minister became the chief targets of the political satirists writing
for the stage.

CHAPTER 3

SOCIAL SATIRE

The only source of the true Ridiculous (as it seems to me) is affectation.
—Henry Fielding, Author's Preface,
Joseph Andrews (1742)

Satire flourishes in a homogeneous society with a common conception of the moral law, for satirist and audience must agree as to how normal people can be expected to behave, and in times of relative stability and contentment, for satire cannot deal with serious evil and suffering.
—W. H. Auden, The Dyer's Hand and Other Essays (1962)

THE EVIDENCE in the previous chapter suggests that political satire was not a safe subject for drama. It was responsible for the failure of plays; it called down the Licensing Act on the heads of the dramatists; and it implicated the writer in personal quarrels of vicious animosity. Social satire in the drama of this period was a different matter. It was not, first of all, as dangerous because it seldom was concerned with personalities. There is a vast difference between laying a charge of corruption at the door of Sir Robert Walpole and laying a charge at the door of society, even of society with a capital S. A social class is less articulate and unable to organize its resentment. The dramatist therefore had little to fear as to specific forms of adverse legislation or retracted pensions and sinecures.

While social satire was less dangerous than political, it was also less topical. The South Sea Bubble undoubtedly stimulated the volume of attacks on wild speculation and the

Jacobite scare in 1745 increased the uncomplimentary portraits of Catholics in plays of that season. Yet never was
there the close cause-and-effect relationship between the
event and the satire about it that characterized the political satire in this same period. The social satirist was
more diffuse in his attacks. His targets were more often
generalities and types rather than specific incidents and
individuals. He also changed his weapons. Instead of shoot-
ing straight at the bull's eye, he spattered birdshot over
the social scene to fall where it would. With the loss of
his former accuracy of aim, he also lost the sharp sting of
his hit and thus limited his effectiveness.

It is, however, wrong to suppose that because the social satirist was in less danger and because he was more
diffuse, he was therefore less articulate. The social critic
was likewise the product of his century. He reflected, no
less than the political satirist, its crosscurrents, and behind his product is a basis of fact grounded in the social
history of these three decades.

THE MIDDLE CLASS

There is less satire on the middle class in the drama
from 1720 to 1750 than on any other social class. The
explanation lies in the cumulative importance of the
class. Stretching from tradespeople to the lesser gentry, it
embraced a section of England that was coming to recognize
itself as the backbone of the country. When the old seven-
teenth-century religious and political issues no longer divided the members of a single household, the strength and
solidarity of a community of interests drew this class into
self-confident unity. Sir Robert Walpole formulated his domestic policy in the interests of this class although he
considered the country squires rather than the merchants as
his chief support.[1] Because the majority of the dramatists
were from the middle class,[2] the dramatist was careful not
to satirize the class as a whole when its star was rising.
When he did criticize, his attack was chiefly on a profession (lawyers, doctors, clergymen) or peripheral tradesmen.
Thomas Odell, for example, based his play The Smugglers
(1729) on an actual instance of corruption in a customs
house of a Hampshire port. In 1727 officials in this port
were discovered receiving a fixed percentage on all goods

which they allowed to be smuggled freely into the country.
(See his Dedication to George Doddington.) Consequently the
chief of the smugglers in this play does not hold a customs
house oath very sacred. "A Custom-House oath, Child, is
like a Nutshell, no coming at the Kernel without breaking
it" (I, iii). Yet the play is written primarily to expose
smuggling rather than as a wholesale attack upon petty officials.

Occasionally a social satirist ran afoul of a group as
James Miller did of the Templars with his comedy The Coffee
House (1737). The play was supposedly aimed at Mrs. Yarrow
and her daughter who ran Dick's Coffee House between the
Temple gates. Because of its location this particular cof-
feehouse attracted many of the Templars as its patrons. To
them the play was more than an attack on the proprietess as
a member of the middle class; it was an infringement upon
their copyhold. Therefore they not only damned this play,
but they also dogged Miller's later Art and Nature (1738) to
make certain that he suffered for his satiric invasion of
their particular stronghold at Dick's.

Mrs. Weddell's The City Farce (1737) ridiculed the city
shopkeeper but not as severely as the city train-bands who
were militia or mustered men and the only police of eighteenth-century London. They were unpopular because they
lacked authority, and as the play indicates, they were often the cause of riots which in turn they were obliged to
quell.

Similarly Garrick's Lethe (1730) contains a foolish
tailor who comes along on the journey to Elysium because
his wife is a convert to Catholicism and he fears she has
made him a cuckold to punish his heresy, but the satire is
on Catholicism as much as on the tailor's trade. Besides the
tailor is joined by a Mr. Riot who enters drunk, and, as his
name suggests, his conduct is Garrick's comment on one cause
of the street riots in London whatever the social class.

John Kelly's The Levee (1741) indirectly attacks the
middle class by presenting the presumptuous butlers and
porters who imitate their masters. Gulph, the butler in this
play, entertains his father, an old Irishman fresh from the
country and unaccustomed to his son's splendor. The old man
is particularly worried about the large amount of money his
son handles, but is assured that "Father, here's nothing
done without Money." Besides showing off his city finery be-

fore his father, young Gulph boasts that butlers by their
elegant dress now have to keep the squires in their place.
He even asserts that the porter and butler govern the theatres, "and by a Disturbance baulks the Entertainment of
the Town whenever we see fit" (II, i).

A few plays were more explicit than Kelly's The Levee
in criticizing the middle class, particularly the merchants.
The anonymous Female Innocence (1732) gives an uncomplimentary portrait of a merchant so penurious that he uses the
food for his own wedding to celebrate his daughter's marriage also. And The Camp Visitants (1740), probably by
James Miller, suggests that citizens' wives are camp followers of the army. Yet such momentary pricks at individual
merchants and their wives were rare. Generally they were
treated well to offset what a writer in The Universal Journal for July 4, 1724, protested was a false portrait of
them as usurers and cuckolds in Restoration plays:

> I do believe that there have been, and may be still,
> some few Citts of that Character; . . . But throughout
> the whole Course of my Reading, I do not remember any one
> of our Comedies to have seen a polite Citizen; and yet I
> am sure it is not for want of a sufficient Number of real
> Examples from which they might draw their Characters. I
> have before now known a Merchant fit to preside at the
> Board of Trade, and a Banker every way qualified for a
> Lord Treasurer.
> View the Assemblies of our Citizens when met on Busi-
> ness; attend a General Court and you shall hear 'em debate
> with the same Ease, and the same Eloquence as at the Bar,
> or in the Senate: In Company with the Ladies we find 'em
> complaisant as Gallants, and enter on a Tea Table Topick
> with as much Humour as the best Lady's Men about Town.

The same writer suggests that authors opposed to "Citts" are
either themselves poor or envious of the new sophistication
and importance of the merchants.[3]

This plea for respect for the merchant sets the general
tone for his representation in the plays of this period. It
reflects the change in society which John Gay's posthumously
produced play, The Distrest Wife (1734), serves to illustrate, for here the butler complains that he is now forced
to wait on the wine merchant if he wants so much as six

dozen bottles of champagne. Furthermore, he must pay cash
for wine since his master's credit is no longer good indef-
initely. Barter, the merchant in the same play, makes an
impassioned defense of the rising middle class:

> Is the name of merchant then a term of reproach?—Where is
> the Profession that is so honourable?—What is it that sup-
> ports every individual of our country?—'tis Commerce. On
> what depends the glory, the credit, the power of the na-
> tion?—on Commerce. To what does the crown itself owe its
> splendour and dignity?—to Commerce. To what owe you the
> Lords the revenue of your own half-ruined estates?—to Com-
> merce: and are ye so ungreateful then to treat the profes-
> sion with contempt by which you are maintained? (IV)

This attitude of defiant self-assertion is more prevalent in
the drama of this period than satire on the middle class.
This was a period when rich Mr. Sealand could expect his
daughter to marry Sir John Bevil's son (Steele, The Conscious Lovers, 1722) or the noble Mr. Thorowgood could set
the moral tone for George Lillo's tragedy, The London Merchant (1731). Merchants suffered far more from sentimental
dramatists than they did from dramatic satirists in the
plays of 1720-1750.

THE PROFESSIONS
     When it came to the professional classes, dramatists
     were by no means so chary of their satire. Perhaps a
     type lawyer, a type doctor, or a type cleric was easier
to pick out than a type merchant, and types rather than realistic characters were more traditional in satire. Furthermore, the professional man did not as obviously contribute
to the country's welfare. He had little to do with the development of trade and industry, and he was, therefore, not
as essential to this newly awakened consciousness of the
English middle class, or to the growing optimism of the
eighteenth-century mercantile economy. He suggested rather
a kind of sickness and chaos in society. Corrupt judges and
lawyers were a threat to rule and order; the quack doctor
was a travesty of the order of science; the corrupt or hypocritical cleric exposed a lack of moral order.[4] Such professional men also fitted easily the stereotypes of both

stage comedy and classical verse satire, particularly the
pretentious pedant, the mock doctor and the hypocritical
moralist.

The lawyer suffered perhaps most severely from the
dramatic satirists of this period. He was too closely related to the notoriously loose and inefficient administration of justice in eighteenth-century England not to furnish
a pertinent target. In fact the satirist often hit at the
law as well as at the lawyer so that the two tended to be
indistinguishable once under the fire of ridicule. Was justice or the agent of justice most at fault? The satirist
found the man, not the abstraction, a more effective target
to answer this question.

By 1720 rascally lawyers appeared often in comedies
though sometimes they were only impersonated to draw up
false wills or marriage contracts. Yet occasionally their
appearance is direct and unmistakably intentional satire.
The lawyer in Odell's The Smugglers (1729), for example, is
certainly no credit to his profession. As an agent of the
band of smugglers, he draws up false conveyances to make
their new estates seem legal, and he bribes the jury (with
liquor) to decide all lawsuits in the smugglers' favor. Yet
in the end when the king's officers begin to close in on
the band of outlaws, he switches his allegiance when it will
now be to his advantage to defend the law. His ironic name,
Mr. Conscience, only emphasizes his lack of scruples. Odell's
play, however, despite its satiric portraits of smugglers
and this rascally lawyer, is a comedy and not a satire.

In Gay's The Beggar's Opera (1728) both law and the
lawyer fare poorly. For one thing the satiric parallel of
honor among thieves is constantly stressed. Filch refuses to
tell on Polly because of his honor (I, vi); Macheath's gang
despises avarice and all mean vice (II, i); Peachum regrets
getting rid of Macheath because he cannot help admiring his
fine strategem (I, xi). Yet the gang of robbers has only
contempt for the honor of the law and its administrators.
Mrs. Trapes does admit that the act for destroying the mint
and against imprisonment for small fines went hard on her
business (III, vi), but on the whole the entire gang knows
how to cheat the law. Peachum scorns murder only because the
jury can always be bribed to bring in a verdict of man-
slaughter (I, iv). Not one of them trusts a lawyer (I, ix,
Air XI). Lockit, the jailor, is a confederate of the thieves

and serves as an excellent commentary on the corrupt prison system. He takes money for every smallest convenience to his prisoners, even a lighter set of fetters for Macheath (II, vii). Because of its consistency, this social satire seems a much more integral part of Gay's play than the political or literary satire.[5]

In aiming the brunt of his social satire at the loose administration of the law, Gay was not exaggerating the London of his day. He wrote to Swift that he actually visited Newgate so that his information was firsthand, and a copy of the "Proceedings of the London Sessions from December, 1732 to October, 1733 bound up with the Accounts of the Ordinary of Newgate, etc." shows the same strange literary names and the same artlessness among criminals that distinguish Macheath's gang.[6] In a London without police and without street lights, countless thieves could operate; it was not until 1774 that fees paid to jailors were made illegal. Clearly not all the blame lay on the shoulders of the lawyer whose business was the law already codified more than the law which ought to be drafted. The lawyer who knew the system and yet was as corrupt as the system is not represented in Gay's cast of characters, but his profession is named in the first song. Like the cleric and statesman, the lawyer shirks his responsibility by shifting the blame to others: "All professions be-rogue one another" (I, i, Air I).

Fielding was the most savage of the satiric dramatists in his attack upon lawyers as incapable and corrupt. What begins as a joking reference in his first comedy, continues throughout his dramatic career. In his first play, Love in Several Masques (1728), the ladies in naming for each other a list of disagreeable suitors, include "the lawyer who attacks me as he would a jury, with a cringe and a lie at the tip of his tongue" (II, i). Besides, they point out, a lawyer's clients always win when he is well paid (IV, ii). These satiric references are extended in The Temple Beau (1730), where young Wilding illustrates how a law student could while away his time in London. Dallying at coffeehouses, flattering the ladies, and indulging in clandestine affairs with them, this Temple rake is a sorry figure for a person about to be admitted to the bar. He even sends his father to Pedant's rooms in order to preserve the old man's illusion that his son is a student. But in the end his intrigues pile up and expose him to all for what he is, the

Temple beau. In The Author's Farce (1730), Fielding claims
that lawyers hang thieves while they themselves are the
greatest robbers (III, i, Air XIV). But the constable in
this play is equally corrupt. When he is sent to stop the
show, he promises the author, "Come down a good guinea, and
you shall be clear" (III, Air XXII). Evidently not only the
lawyer irritated Fielding but the officers of the law as
well. Of the latter, the greatest rogue is Justice Squeezum
in the comedy Rape upon Rape, or, The Justice Caught in his
own Trap (1730).

Justice Squeezum insists that "he is the greatest of
fools who holds the sword of justice and hurts himself with
it" (V, vi). The best that can be said of this official of
the law is that he practices his own theory. He protects
bawdy houses in return for bribes, dismisses criminals for
a substantial recompense, and provides himself with a retinue of bribed deputies who will swear to anything he does.
He arrests the young people in the play for rapes that were
never committed and then tries to have intrigues with his
women prisoners. When he is caught attempting to violate
one of them, he claims she swore it on purpose to incrimi-
nate him. It is only when his wife finds his notes to this
prisoner that the judge has evidence enough to convict him.
Fielding makes Squeezum a thoroughly disreputable character
yet convincing enough to prove there was some truth behind
the satiric portrait.

Don Quixote and Sancho, as foreigners, are also both-
ered by the sad state of the law in England in Don Quixote
in England (1734). Sancho thinks that twelve lawyers would
not make one honest man (I, iii), while his master laments
whenever he sees "A low, mean, tricking lord" that here is
another lawyer lost to England (I, ii). In Pasquin (1736),
Law even disclaims, in Fustian's tragedy, being descended
from Reason, "We hardly deign to own from whence we came"
(III, i). Thus Fielding's satire on law moved from a joking
reference in his first comedy to the portrait of Law in his
dramatic satire, Pasquin, as an abstract character denying
any descent from Reason.

Even after the Licensing Act diverted his attacks on
lawyers and the law to novel form, Fielding persisted in his
stage satire on corruption in the profession. By 1737 he was
himself a law student at the Middle Temple. Mr. Mutable in
The Wedding Day (1743) tells about a raucous party he at-

tended with a justice of the peace and four whores. "His
worship did not sit late; he was obliged to go home at three
and take a nap to be sober at the sessions." "And," another
character adds ironically, "punish wickedness and debauchery" there (II, iii). Fielding was plainly aware wherein
the responsibility lay for loosely administered laws of
England as he indicated in his plays, novels and his pamphlet, An Enquiry into the Causes of the Late Increase of
Robbers (1751): lawyers were corrupt and officials were lewd
and unreliable. Out of such a combination the harsh criminal
laws could be neither justly administered nor relaxed. His
satire on the law and lawyers is a kind of moral preparation for his appointment as a Bow Street magistrate.

Other dramatists continued Fielding's satire on the
profession of law. Sometimes the attack was not specific as,
for example, in Robert Dodsley's The Toy Shop (1735) where
the master of the shop sells the smallest box of his collection, a box still large enough to contain the honesty of
lawyers (sc. ii). Sometimes the attack was very specific as
in Samuel Foote's Diversions of a Morning (1747) for which
he could not procure a license so that he finally invited
the public to a dish of chocolate in order to present his
collections of satiric imitations of individuals about London.[7] Foote's collection included Sir Thomas de Veil, a
justice of the peace for Westminster. Although this gentleman was already dead when the Cup of Chocolate, or Auction
of Pictures first took place (1748), Foote did not hesitate
to include his unflattering portrait of the Westminister official. Whether the satire on lawyers and officials was general or specific, it continued throughout this period. Naturally the profession resented stage satire on their profession and grew touchy on the point of their honor, as has
already been mentioned in the example of James Miller's The
Coffee House which was damned by the Templars.[8]

However, lawyers and officials of the law were not the
only professional men satirized on the stage. The doctor received his share of ridicule as well. Fielding again led the
attack with The Author's Farce (1730) when he has Charon
grow suspicious as his passengers suddenly arrive in great
numbers. Charon is certain that this influx of deaths is
either the result of the plague or a fresh shipment of physicians who have come to town from the universities (III,
i). Two years later Fielding's The Mock Doctor (1732),

adapted from Molière's <u>Le Medecin Malgré Lui</u>, continued the
presentation of quacks. While the main outline of the plot
follows that of Molière, Fielding adds his own touches. His
ironic dedication to Dr. John Misaubin called attention to
an individual quack or "pill Doctor" who lived near Drury
Lane. In the play itself, Gregory, the mock doctor, blames
his mistakes and confusion either on the "New Science" and
new methods being taught at the college (II, i) or on make-
believe drugs, "some, sir, lately discovered by the Royal-
Society" (II, iii).

Thus Fielding uses <u>The Mock Doctor</u> to show his distrust
of the orthodox training with its narrow-minded devotion to
classic courses which characterized the preparation of the
eighteenth-century physician. He also shows his dislike of
the pompous self-assurance which led the doctor to discourse at length in a lingo as meaningless as Gregory's
while the patient was left to suffer. He furthermore ridicules the common practice of making all cases, whatever
their nature, seem serious, and the equally common, though
absurd, policy of trying all cures in the repertoire in the
hope that one would prove successful. Thus Dr. Drunk in <u>Don
Quixote in England</u> (1734) assures the Don that he will be
incurably mad unless he is blooded, cupped, sweated, blis-
tered, vomited and purged on the instant (III, xv). Fielding
suggests that by such an omnibus method the doctor concealed
his own ignorance and, while trying all his arts, hoped to
stumble on a cure. The incompetence and pretentious learning most offended Fielding.[9] In his late play, <u>The Wedding
Day</u> (1742), when Millamour pretends he is a doctor, Sted-
fast commends him because he never took a University degree.
Millamour replies, "You are a man of understanding, sir. The
University is the very worst place to educate a physician
in. A man, sir, contracts the narrow habit of observing the
rules of a set of ancients. Not one in fifty of them ever
ventures to strike a bold stroke. A quack, sir, is the only
man who can put you out of your pain at once" (IV, v). As
Fustian says, when Sneerwell objects to the satire on physicians in <u>Pasquin</u>, "What is here said can't hurt an honest
lawyer or a good physician" (III, i).

Fielding's attack on pseudo-science and quack doctors
is also the satiric theme of several other plays. <u>The Jew
Decoyed, or, the Harlot's Progress</u> (1735), an anonymous ballad opera which, according to the Prologue, draws its satire

from Hogarth's Harlot's Progress, includes two quacks,
Meagre and Nostrum, who allow the Harlot, Moll, to die while
they continue to quarrel over her treatment (III, ii).
Charles Johnson's The Female Fortune Teller (1736), which
takes its motto from the fifth satire of Persius, opens with
a vicious attack on Mrs. Joiner who refuses to divide the
earnings from her fake cures with her confederates. Spring
warns her, "Yes, Faith, I will spoil your whole Machinery;
I will deface your Lamens, Sigills, Spells, Amulets, Phil-
ters, and your whole Cart of Charms; I will demolish your
Pantacles, your Magic Glasses and Geomantick Figures; I will
chace away your Familiars, Pugs, Ghosts, and all your rascally crew of dependent Beggars" (Act I). In Act II further
tricks of "Varsal Lixor, Pouder of Projection and Oyl of
Bones" are listed for exposure, but only in Act V does Mrs.
Joiner confess her quackery when she is frightened by the
feigned madness and threatened violence of one of her victims. Richard Baker's burlesque rehearsal of a ballad opera
The Madhouse (1737) "after the Manner of Pasquin," also was
aimed at quack doctors. Dr. Hyppo, who conducts the Madhouse, confines people whether they are mad or not so long
as their relatives are willing to pay a substantial sum to
have them put out of the way. Sir Solomon Testy, for example, has his daughter confined to keep her from marrying
against his will. The hospital is well named, for with no
segregation of the sane from the insane, it rivals Bedlam.
Another ballad opera, The Woman of Taste, or, The Yorkshire
Lady (1738), attributed to Joseph Dorman (Nicoll dates it
1736) contained a Dr. Pill and Drops who, according to one
young lady, had killed more people than the plague (II,
iii).

While most dramatic satirists used metaphorical names
(Meagre, Nostrum, Dr. Hyppo, Dr. Pill and Drops) instead of
calling attention to specific quack doctors as Fielding did
to Dr. John Misaubin (Dedication to The Mock Doctor), John
Kelly, in his ballad opera The Plot (1735), named a Dr.
Ward, commonly known as Dr. Pill and Drops, as the object of
a plot by eight doctors eager to discredit a charlatan who
is stealing their fees and patients.

> Ward is an Otter, which I fear
>   Will much our Pool annoy,
> Him we should hunt with Hound and Spear
>   Lest he our Store destroy.

"Otter" Ward later in the opera becomes "this Pole-Cat Ward"
and "an eating Cancer" who ruins not only doctors but cof-
fin makers, nurses, grave diggers and parish clerks because
his pill causes patients to recover. Thus Kelly implies
that the self-interested doctors are no better than the
quack Dr. Ward. The Epilogue says the poet was cautioned
but refused to change the Plot:

> The Pictures I have drawn, are Foils to Merit;
> The Bully kick'd, can touch no Man of Spirit.

Such a disclaimer, like Fielding's in Pasquin—"what is here
said can't hurt an honest lawyer or a good physician"—is
the satirist's usual excuse that only those who need correc-
tion will be hurt by ridicule.

The anonymous The Projectors (1737) attacked pseudo-
science as well as quack doctors. The play is full of fake
scientific schemes: to drain the Thames in 24 hours; to ex-
tract silver from lead; to flow diamonds; and there are
also quacks who project to cure the bite of a mad dog. Each
of the fantastic projects or projectors is matched against
actual projects and people: "your York-Buildings work," "the
Drop-doctor," or "the new author of Fog." The Prologue makes
no secret of the author's purpose:

> This night our author means to view
> A group of figures to the Stage are new,
> Yet to keen Satyr's Lash who've long been due.

Perhaps not surprisingly, Charles Fleetwood, to whom the
play is dedicated, refused to apply for a license from the
Lord Chamberlain's office to perform such pointed satire.
The Projectors comes close, except for a clumsily contrived
ending, to being a consistent dramatic satire on science. It
exploits the absurdities of projects and projectors and
shows a clear knowledge of where the power over the theatres
lay by the neat device of including a Prime Minister who
never utters a word during the play. Whoever the "W.H." was
who signed the Dedication,[10] he might well have been encouraged to continue writing satire for the stage. This play,
at least, is more a dramatic satire than a comedy.

What is evident in the social satire on the professions
of lawyer and doctor is that it took the form of satirical
portraits in comedies, generally without altering the comic

resolution of plot. The dishonest lawyers or quack doctors
who pervaded the popular literature of pamphlets, ballads
and broadsides (Thomas Wright, Caricature History of the
Georges . . ., pp. 66-142, lists numerous examples) were
stock characters also in the drama and such stock characters
are only additions to comedies. Fielding's lawyers and doctors, for example, appear oftener in such social comedies
as The Mock Doctor or The Wedding Day, and are only inci-
dentally referred to in such dramatic satires as The Author's Farce. While Kelly's The Plot is entirely devoted to
self-interested doctors and their plots against the quack
Dr. Ward, it too lacks the concentration of dramatic satire
by including irrelevant interludes of French comedians who
have nothing to do with The Plot. Samuel Foote's Auction of
Pictures (1748) that includes a ridiculous portrait of a
quack oculist, Chevalier Taylor (Hogarth placed this man
prominently in the foreground of his Consultation of Physicians), is closest to dramatic satire when he mimicks the
quack mercilessly in his plotless pot-pourri. Foote's satiric skits suggest a satiric form for the stage that is a
departure from comedy of manners or social comedy. Except
for the anonymous The Projectors which satirized all science, Foote's collection of satiric portraits was the one
dramatic technique that enlarged and extended the presentation of satiric characters in comedy. The technique allowed
easily identifiable satiric targets to emerge from the
vague stock characters of social satire. But the technique
led only to a series of skits, a kind of vaudeville entertainment, rather than to unified dramatic satire.

The clergy were spared no more than lawyers and doctors
by the dramatists of this period though the Established
Church escaped fairly well. Puzzletext in Fielding's The
Grub Street Opera, revised from The Welsh Opera (1731), is
a typical portrait of the rural Church of England cleric.
According to Sheridan W. Baker's Introduction to an edition
of Shamela (Berkeley: University of California, 1953) Puzzletext like the Tickletext of Fielding's later parody novel,
was based on the Rev. Conyers Middleton. Whoever was his
model, Puzzletext has degenerated until he writes but half a
sermon in half a year. Tobacco, backgammon and wine are much
more familiar to him, and he assures Lady Apshinken that he
can preach with perspicuity even after the fourth bottle.
His speech is the only mark of his profession which remains.

He still talks in theretos and thereuntos but such formalism
is the only serious trademark of his profession.

The individual clergyman who was the target for much of
the dramatic satire was John Henley who came to London in
1721 as a reader at the Church of George the Martyr. This
eccentric man, noted for his oratory, was forced to retire
from his London church in 1724, but two years later he was
back in the city giving his own sermons at rented rooms in
Newport Market. In his theological lectures every Sunday
evening he proved a great showman. Besides his flamboyant
oratory, his "pulpit" blazed with gold and velvet. He was
also good at publicity, for he had medals struck to be used
as admission to his lectures, and he had a habit of giving
out his text a week in advance to pique the curiosity of his
audience. On one occasion he had all the shoemakers in London at his evening lecture because his text seemed to promise a secret new way of making soles.[11]

Such an eccentric could scarcely avoid attracting satire. Fielding paid him mock tribute at the end of The Author's Farce when the Epilogue, spoken by a cat disguised
as a lady, concluded that Henley might prove all men are
cats. Anthony Aston, the strolling actor, added a burlesque
imitation of Henley in The Fool's Opera, or, The Taste of
the Town (1731), and Samuel Foote also included him among
his satiric portraits in The Auction of Pictures (1748).
According to the DNB there was good reason why Foote should
satirize Henley since the two had engaged in a public controversy on the stage of the Haymarket Theatre in 1747. On
that occasion Henley proved himself so great an artist at
buffoonery that Foote might well have become anxious for
revenge (DNB, IX, 415).

While the Church of England did not entirely escape
satire on the stage, most of the attacks on clerics were on
Catholics or Dissenters (Presbyterians, Quakers and, later,
Methodists). The established church, in fact, exerted enough
influence so that Genest even suggests that Mahomet (1744),
translated from Voltaire by Miller and Hoadly, was with-
drawn after three performances because it contained sentiments offensive to high churchmen (Genest, IV, 66-67).
Whether or not this charge is justified (and there seems
little in the translation to support the claim except for
the ostentatious self-worship of Mahomet), it indicates why
the Church of England clergy were less likely to suffer from

dramatic satirists than clerics of minority religious
groups. Again, most attacks were short jabs rather than sustained satire. For example, when Commons in Fielding's The
Letter Writers (1731) is asked for a light, he retorts
sharply, "Want a light, sir, ay sir? Do you take me for a
Dissenter, you rascal? Do you think I carry my light within,
sirrah?" (II, ii). And when Lord Bawble in Fielding's one-
act Miss Lucy in Town (1742) asks whether Miss Jenny, a former resident of the bawdy house, is dead, Mrs. Midnight replies, "Worse if possible—she is—she is turned Methodist
and married to one of the Brethern." Such isolated jokes at
the expense of Dissenters were, however, sometimes extended
into more sustained satire.

Early in this period it was the Quakers who were attacked most often. Their eccentricities of dress, language
and religious practice were ridiculed in a series of ballad
operas beginning with Thomas Walker's The Quaker's Opera
(1728). One year later William Chetwood added The Lover's
Opera where the maid Lucy is wooed by a Quaker named Prim.
To add to the satire on this sect, Robert Dodsley's The
Blind Beggar of Bethnal Green (1741) also contained a Quaker
character, Friend Sly, who has evil designs on the heroine
and is willing to help the villain carry her off.[12] Another
ballad opera, The Whim, or, The Merry Cheat, published anon-
ymously the same year, has a character, Fairlove, disguised
as a Quaker, who mimicks Quaker speech when he is accused
by Cutely of being of the tribe of "Satan! Satan! the Devil!
One of his spiritual relations!" Fairlove's mock reply is,
"Yea, thou are of the Seed of the Serpent; who is continu-
ally condemning the Inward Light of the Spirit. And I say
unto thee, the Vengeance of the Incarnal Powers shall thunder upon thee with great fury. Hum!" Since Cutely is posing
as the mock Judge Mittimus, the play strikes both at Quakers and the law as the Epilogue, spoken by Cutely, makes
clear:

> Not he whose cause is Best shall gain the Day
> But he whose Pocket best can pay the way.
> A Mock 'tis here, but not just here alone,
> For ev'ry Court ne'er fails to make it one.
> And though it here may seem a Ridicule
> The World itself is but a mocking school.

Although the tone of this Epilogue indicates the consistency

aimed at, the anonymous author of The Whim unfortunately
does not fully exploit the trick of disguise as license for
satire.

About 1738, when John Wesley had returned from his
first trip to Georgia, the Methodists also came in for their
share of stage satire. The anonymous The Mock Preacher, a
Satyrical-Comical-Allegorical Farce (1739) appeared first.
Its elaborate Prologue struck out in all directions. When
told that the custom is to have a political friend usher in
a new play, the author says he does not know Pope "who is
grown dull and declining." He likewise discards as patrons
Stephen Duck, the Four Seasons (Thomson), and the Laureate
(Cibber) who "was possessed but of one Talent, which he hid
in the Earth, and labour'd hard to dig it out once a Year to
show his Master he had not improv'd it." Then in a catalogue
of satiric dramatists, he continues that some advised him to
try The Honest Yorkshire Man (Carey) "but his Brains were
swallow'd up alive by The Dragon of Wantley"; some advised
The Toy Shop (Dodsley) but "there were nothing but Trifles
left," for the owner had pawned "his last valuable at Mansfield when he sent the Miller to Court." Told that nothing
will succeed on the stage "but severe Satire, Bawdy, or
some very smart political Piece," the author launches into
a mock pedigree and concludes:

> I have ventur'd to introduce my First-born Satire into the
> World in spite of Pope, or the Devil himself, assisted by
> a whole train of Conjurors, Wits, etc. against whom, and
> all others who shall dare oppose me as a Satirist, I make
> publick Declaration of War, without the Assistance of
> Friend or Ally; Therefore let 'em all take care of Them-
> selves.

Having established his satiric intention, the author
produces a series of scenes about Methodists. Scene one is
laid in Moorfields where the preacher likens himself to
Christ and gives a rhetorical parody of a sermon asking for
alms for the orphans of Georgia. Scene two is laid in a
bookseller's shop where the Preacher reads his fan mail and
instructs his followers to solicit funds in The Daily Advertiser, exclaiming, "What a fine Scheme is Religion . . . Who
would be a poor curate under a lazy Vicar when by taking a
little pains to gull the Publick, I have two Tides of Money
flow in a Day." In scene three on Kennington Common the

Preacher in another sample sermon mentions his <u>Journal</u> and trip to Spain. By scene four his enemies begin to collect and call for a Protestant Inquisition. The Preacher is then arrested in a tavern and subsequently tried (sc. vi) for "preaching in Fields and Commons." Lest anyone misinterpret this "Universo-comico-hieroglyphical Farce," the Epilogue spells out the "universal satire" on Methodists: "For it is agreed Methodists are Enthusiasts; and I intend to satirize the whole tribe of 'em." Not even the acquittal of the Preacher to the wild huzzas of the crowd in the final scene could soften the harsh satire on Methodists.

This play appeared in the same year John Wesley was confronted by Beau Nash at Bath, and according to Wesley's <u>Journal</u> (I, 198), for June 5, 1739, Nash came off second best. It is interesting that this same journal entry contains a report of a street full of people asking for Wesley: "Which is he? and I replied, 'I am he,' they were immediately silent." The incident seems a serious parallel of the satiric Christ-Wesley analogy in the first scene of <u>The Mock Preacher</u>.

Methodists were again satirized in a one-act farce by Thomas Este, <u>Methodism Display'd</u> (1743), intended for a performance at Moot Hall in Newcastle.[13] Este claims in the introduction that he had been assaulted by a Methodist mob when he went out of curiosity to hear their preaching and that he was threatened, if he continued his plans for the production of his farce. But his play, altered from <u>Trick upon Trick</u>, was never performed because the building collapsed.[14]

Catholics, of course, aroused dramatic satire because of their political connections with the Stewart pretender to the throne. The previous chapter has already illustrated how the Jacobite scare was reflected in the drama by attacks on Catholics, who, like Jews, were still outlawed in England during this period. Thus there was at best a foreign flavor about the Catholic clergy. However, occasionally satire on Catholics was stimulated by an incident that had neither political nor national connotations. A ballad opera, <u>The Wanton Jesuit</u> (1731), for example, was based on an actual incident that shocked all England. For it seems that a Catholic priest, Father Girard, had seduced his ward, Miss Cadiere, "an affair," says Genest, "which at this time made a great noise, as well it might" (III, 322). The incident undoubt-

edly took on enormity in English minds because the celibacy
of the Catholic clergy was to them one of the most obvious
differences between the Catholic clergy and their own. Thus
the discordant action of an individual priest aroused the
satiric pen of an English Protestant playwright, whose play
was revived again in 1745 at the time of the Jacobite invasion.

The same incident probably stimulated Fielding's The
Old Debauchees; or The Jesuit Caught (1732) which had almost
the same theme. In this play old Jordain is intimidated by
Father Martin, a Jesuit priest, into thinking that he will
remain in purgatory if his daughter is allowed to marry
young Laroon. In reality the Jesuit himself has designs on
the girl, but he is exposed when young Laroon, dressed in
woman's clothing, poses as a girl and substitutes for his
fiancée. The exceptionally black picture of the Catholic
clergy that Fielding paints in Father Martin undoubtedly
stemmed from the incident of Father Girard in the previous
year, yet despite the satiric portrait of Father Martin,
the play is more comedy than dramatic satire.

Firebrand in Fustian's tragedy within Pasquin (1736) is
possibly Fielding's condemnation of the fundamentals of
Catholicism. Firebrand, who is a priest of the Sun, quarrels
with Commonsense because she refuses to accept on faith his
claim that his authority is derived from the Sun. He finally
stabs her as his greatest enemy, and then embraces the cause
of the Queen of Ignorance to give his priests "a just degree
of power and more than half the profits of the land." If
Firebrand typifies Fielding's idea of the greed, twisting of
authority, and impatience of the Catholic priesthood, then
he wisely shifts the responsibility for this wholesale condemnation to his invented author, Fustian. Firebrand is a
bitter contrast to the country parson, Puzzletext, in his
earlier Grub Street Opera.

Satire on the clergy, like that of the other professions, had little effect on the form of dramatic satire.
Usually it was confined to satiric characters in comedies,
mildly satiric if they were Church of England parsons like
Puzzletext, sometimes bitterly satiric if they were Quakers,
Methodists or Catholics. Methodism Display'd was, however,
displayed to show a comic resolution of order restored.
Particular Catholic priests were discredited in social comedy where the dissolute priest was foiled (Fielding's The Old

Debauchees; or The Jesuit Caught). Quakers were imitated by
non-Quakers (The Whim) or were comically exploited in ballad
operas (Walker's The Quaker's Opera, Chetwood's The Lover's
Opera, Dodsley's Blind Beggar of Bethnal Green). Henley's
oratory did produce the burlesque imitation of Aston's The
Fool's Opera and the satiric portrait in Foote's Auction of
Pictures. Otherwise, except for Fielding's hint that Firebrand in Fustian's tragedy (Pasquin) is a Catholic priest,
the clergy as a profession, while they were often treated
satirically, did not succeed in transforming comedy into
satire. The Mock Preacher, for example, with its satiric intentions announced in both Prologue and Epilogue is one of
the few where the ridicule of Methodists is consistent
throughout and even here the trial at the end is a comic
restitution of order.

FASHIONABLE SOCIETY
        If the middle class suffered little and the profes-
        sional class but slightly more at the hands of the dra-
        matic satirist, fashionable society did not escape so
easily. This is to be expected because of the increasing
importance of the middle class and the dramatist's identification of himself with that class. Obviously, in defending
his own class, he would direct his satire at the portion of
society that seemed most to hinder the rapid progress of
the merchant economy. On such progress fashionable society
was a dead weight. It squandered its fortune at court; it
dawdled over chocolate and cards; it was not actively pro-
ductive in a century that was laying the commercial foundation for the industrial revolution. Of course other contrib-
utory factors are present in the abundance of satire on
fashionable society. At the beginning of this period a res-
idue of reaction to the Restoration comedies so roundly condemned by Jeremy Collier still existed. And new dramatic
forms, sentimental comedy and domestic tragedy, help to explain the war on loose morals that was an important part of
the criticism of the upper class. Yet it is not erroneous to
say that one fact, the importance of the middle class, gave
the initial impetus to the bulk of the satire on fashionable
society.
        Now fashionable society is a large category which does
not exactly exclude some of the types already discussed. A

professional man or even a very wealthy merchant might claim
to be a member. In fact with new fortunes appearing frequently, some wealthy merchants made so ostentatious an ef-
fort to be accepted by the beau monde that they courted,
even before they were well established in society, the derision of those both above and below them. Such derision
crystallized into the satire on the nouveau riche. Defoe's
Tour through Britain (1724) called attention early in the
period to these wealthy merchants who, bent on acquiring
culture by means of their wealth, were building country estates on the outskirts of London. In one place he found an
iron merchant and a greengrocer who had purchased large estates (Letter I, p. 17). This contemporary evidence that
the wealthy middle class was forcing its way into polite
society explains the amount of satire on this borderline
portion of fashionable society. There was inevitably some
crudity, some discrepancy between these new recruits and the
standard behavior of the class with which they were anxious
to be identified.

Satire on the nouveau riche usually took one of two
forms. Either it was ridicule of their passion for money, or
it attacked their weakness for adding the weight of a title
to their fortunes. Gabriel Odingsells in The Bath Unmasked
(1725) chose the former of the two. In this play the lady
whose passion for money amounts to cheating or close bar-
gaining bordering on cheating, sells her daughter in marriage to Count Nipor for ₺5000. But the Count proves a cheat
also, and the lady's folly returns to her with good measure.
Genest insists that the intent of the play is to describe
"the humours of Bath" (III, 168), which identifies Odingsells' play as a humours comedy set in the most fashionable
gathering place outside of London.

Ducat in Gay's Polly (1729) is another character who
frankly admits his attempt to make his wealth serve the
fashion:

> Besides, madam, in most of my expences I run into the po-
> lite taste. I have a fine library of books that I never
> read; I have a fine stable of horses that I never ride; I
> build, I buy plate, jewels, pictures, or anything that is
> valuable and curious, as your great men do, merely out of
> ostentation.
>
> (I, i)

Ducat's gross materialism is exactly what Allen Ramsay complained of when he dedicated his pastoral The Gentle Shepherd (1725) to the Countess of Eglintoun. Complaining of the corrosive effect of money on honor, Ramsay chose to celebrate the rural joys that once pervaded the countryside which are lost now since "The rust of lucre stained the gold of love." Violence and dissimulation, he says, have replaced happiness in the country as well as in town. Ramsay's idyllic pastoral is no more successful than Gay's satiric character removed to a West Indian setting. Neither hit upon an effective dramatic form for their criticism of materialism. Ramsay's idealization of pastoral life is only implied criticism, while Gay's removal of Ducat to the land of noble savages results in dull didacticism.

Fielding's comedies attack the greed for a good name as well as the greed for money. Lady Matchless in Love in Several Masques (1729) finds that every ambitious squire "would put my life into half his estate, provided I would put his whole family's into mine" (II, i). In the one act An Old Man Taught Wisdom (1735), a footman, Mr. Thomas, has lived in the houses of great families where "I have seen that no one is respected for what he is, but for what he has." But he also has observed that times have changed so that a lord's name is easily purchased with an adequate sum. Thus when old Goldwill is enraged to find that he has a footman for a son-in-law, Mr. Thomas tells him, "if my own industry should add to your fortune, so as to entitle any of my posterity to grandeur, it will be no reason against making my son, or grandson, a lord, that his father, or grandfather, was a footman."

Whether Fielding is criticizing the nouveau riche or the fashionable society to which they aspired is not always easy to detect. Lord Puff, for example, in The Intriguing Chambermaid (1734) is shocked when Goodall senior interrupts his son's dinner party: "I see if a man hath not good blood in his veins, riches won't teach him to behave like a gentleman" (II, ii). But Lord Puff who lives by his friends' generosity is no model as a gentleman either, so that putting the sharp retort into his mouth takes some of the sting out of his remark. Fielding seems to stand on middle ground, hating ostentation but respecting, since he is obviously sympathetic with the senior Goodall, recently acquired wealth that was honestly come by and modestly employed. Only

when this new wealth is won by fraud and when greed for
money extends into pretentiousness and ambition to marry a
title, is he clearly satiric.

David Garrick satirized the female counterpart of the
obnoxious, pushing type of ambition in Lethe (1740). In this
"Dramatic Satire" Mrs. Riot, a merchant's wife, asks to be
rowed across the Styx. Fussy and impatient, she has plainly
come because she thought she would be in fine company. She
mispronounces all the big words she attempts to use and she
mistakes Elysium for Elysian, an opera house. Consequently
she is noisily disappointed when she discovers how she has
been cheated. "What, no operas!" And as a final thrust Garrick ironically has her add, "Your taste here, I suppose, is
no higher than your Shakespeare and your Johnson. . . ."

However, the new recruits into fashionable society did
not always receive the brunt of the dramatist's satire. The
foolish tastes of established London society were constantly
the objects of complaint. Charles Coffey, in the final song,
justifies his play The Boarding School (1733) by claiming
that all England is like a boarding school:

> For the Lord Apes the Footman, the Footman his Grace,
>   In this Pantomime Age:
> Fawning and Sneaking, Promises Breaking,
>   O rare work for the Stage!

This theme of servants who ape their masters appeared the
year before in an anonymous ballad opera, The Footmen (1732),
where the servants have formed a Society that will refuse
castoff clothing if the lace and ruffles have been ripped,
and will charge set fees for delivering their masters' bil-
lets doux to abet their love affairs. The Epilogue makes
clear the author's purpose in attacking the masters through
their servants:

> His Satyr's sting, he offers like a Friend
> To spur the Vicious that are slow to Mend.

Such a Footmen's Society had been mentioned as early in this
period as 1720 in John Leigh's Kensington Gardens where the
footmen were called "Knights of the Rainbow." These "Knights"
"never admit any who have not been at least 7 years in London, wear their Silver Watches and their Master's Linen,

game in the Lobby, play at Shuttlecock with the young ladies, and never appear abroad without a Black Bag, Red-Topped Shoes, an amber-headed Cane, and a Silver Snuff-box, Cram'd with Orangerie or Bergamot" (II, i). This belittling of the Lords through the servants who imitated them was indicative of a new attitude toward fashionable society unlike the Restoration comedy of manners where the Mirabells and Dorimants were celebrated for their cleverness. Now the taste of the town was defined and satirized. The masquerades, auctions, lotteries and fashionable gathering places were exposed to attack and even the clichés of polite conversation were parodied. Gambling at cards, rioting in the streets and at playhouses were condemned. Effete beaux were shown as cowards when challenged to fight, and the corruption of the city by newcomers from the country was repeatedly decried.

Fielding satirized women succumbing to the dictatorship of fashion in Miss Lucy in Town (1742). In this one act farce, a countrywoman, just arrived in London, is being instructed in the peculiarities of city life, but she cannot understand why she should prefer the beaux she has seen to her own husband until Tawdry explains:

> Because it's the fashion, madam. Fine ladies do everything because it's the fashion. They spoil their shapes to appear big with child because it's the fashion. They lose their money at whist, without understanding the game; they go to auctions, without intending to buy; they go to operas, without any ear; and slight their husbands without disliking them; and all because it is the fashion.

Miss Lucy, then, determines to be a fashionable lady even to running off with Lord Bawble, but she is rescued by her husband and carried back to the country. She excuses her actions at the end because "what I did was only to be a fine lady, and what they told me other fine ladies do, and I should never have thought of in the country; but if you will forgive me, I will never attempt to be more than a plain gentlewoman again." The contrast in tone between the end of this play and The Country Wife is the measure of the mid-eighteenth-century attitude toward fashionable society. But while Fielding exposes Miss Lucy, he restores her to country life and his farce is not a dramatic satire.

What Fielding did for the country wife, Garrick did to expose the man of fashion. Lord Chalkstone in Lethe boasts of not living with his wife and also of betting that his mother's death will occur before that of the aged relatives of his friends; he is callously certain that he will receive his inheritance first. Garrick also has the Lord replan Elysium to conform with the fashionable mode of eighteenth-century landscaping. Lord Chalkstone begins by criticizing the river Styx. "Why 'tis as straight as Fleet-ditch—You should have given it a serpentine sweep, and sloped the banks of it." Chalkstone does admit that the place has very fine "capabilities," undoubtedly Garrick's deliberate poke at the popular landscape architect nicknamed "Capability" Brown. Still the Lord would clear the grove to the left a little and clump the trees to the right. "In short, the whole wants variety, extent, contrast, and inequality." Finally Chalkstone stops suddenly, and then, approaching the orchestra, he looks into the pit. "Upon my word, here's a very fine hah-hah! and a most curious collection of ever-greens and flowering shrubs."[15] Thus Garrick makes use of the playhouse and audience to spin out his victim's taste to the point of absurdity.

Robert Dodsley used the device of The Toy Shop (1735) to ridicule fashionable taste as artificial, inane and capricious. His Preface, "Author's Epistle to a Friend in the Country," quotes a letter from Pope commending his form of dramatic satire. We can easily imagine Pope's approval of the fourth lady who enters the toy shop to buy a mask, but who is told by the master that he does not keep such trifles. "The People of this Age are arrived at such perfection in the Art of masking themselves, that they have no occasion for any foreign Disguises at all" (sc. ii). The most curious object the master possesses is a chimerical instrument (called a Distinguisher) which obstructs all falsehood, nonsense and absurdity. But when these are removed from fashionable conversation, he admits that nothing remains. "I have sat in a Coffee-House sometimes," he claims, "for the Space of Half an Hour, and amongst what is generally called the best company, without hearing a single word" (sc. ii). Even the epilogue to this short satire derides the fickleness of fashionable taste. The speaker in the Epilogue has warned the author that his play will never please polite society:

    And did he think plain truth would Favour find?
    Ah! 'tis a sign he little knows mankind!
    .   .   .   .
    But tho' we told him, —Sir, 'twill never do—
    Pho, never fear, he cry'd, 'tho grave, 'tis new:
    The Whim perhaps, may please, if not the Wit,
    And, tho' they don't approve, they may permit.

The instability of taste, in other words, will even permit
satire if the method is a novelty. Dodsley's method is at
least as old as Lucian's sale of philosophies, but his adaptation to social satire is ingenious. In fact his "distinguisher" looks ahead two centuries to the "commercial si-
lencer" of our TV sets.

    The dramatic satirists also argued that court life and
fashionable society produced effete and worthless citizens
who frittered away their lives in foolish flirtations. The
author of an anonymous play, Bickerstaff's Unburied Dead
(1743), for example, made a scrutinizing criticism of the
uselessness of fashionable society. This two act play which
Genest called "a moral drama" (IV, 48), depicted Bickerstaff
sitting in judgment on people of both sexes who led ineffectual lives. They were not, of course, all from the ranks
of polite society, yet the majority did belong to the upper
class. Frequently such anonymous plays satirized the fatuous flirtations which had so delighted Restoration audiences but now seemed a customary mark of the behavior of a
prodigal society. A ballad opera, The Wanton Countess, or
10,000ь for a Pregnancy (1733) claimed to be founded on the
"true secret History" of a specific scandal. And The Intriguing Courtiers (1738) was based also on the secret history of several prominent persons in the court circle whose
amorous intrigues were scarcely "secret." The dramatic satirist, in other words, turned a middle-class morality on the
intrigues and scandals of the class above him. If he did not
condemn the fatuous flirtations, he at least treated them
farcically as did John Sturmy in The Modern Wife (1744),
where only the quick thinking of a footman keeps Lady Modern
chaste, and Sir Humphrey Fat-sides (a burlesque Falstaff)
who pretends to help Sir George Modern trap his wife with a
lover, makes, himself, an assignation with the lady only to
be ignominiously trapped in turn.

    Of all the individual types in polite society, the beau

received the lion's share of criticism and ridicule. He was
represented in almost every comedy, particularly if it had
a London setting, and the references to him were almost universally satiric. His dress, his speech, his taste, his habits, even his walk were objects of ridicule. He is well defined in an anonymous comedy, St. James Park (1733) where
Mrs. Straddle points out a beau strolling in the park:

> I see one yonder, who rises before day to be dress'd by
> twelve, and would as soon go abroad without a Limb, as
> without every particular Hair in his Tupee in the most
> exact Order. One to whom his Parents cou'd give but half
> Gentility, his Tutors but half Education, and, they say,
> Nature but half Manhood; yet values himself so much on
> the Adroitness of his Taylor and Barber, as to imagine he
> is a Match fit for any woman. (III)

The variety of the attacks on this eighteenth-century
hangover from the Restoration fop defines the central kernel
of criticism. The beau, of course, received his education in
France,[16] and, like Lord Modely in John Hewitt's A Tutor for
the Beaus (1737), he returned with only contempt for his
fellow Englishmen. He adopted French customs and taste while
despising the cumbersome crudity of English behavior. Toupet
in James Moore-Smythe's The Rival Modes (1727) has become so
converted to French habits that his servant reflects them as
well as Toupet. He even changes his servant's name from
George to Maquereau to make the transformation more complete.
He insists that it is absurd "to conceive that after one's
travels, not that I pretend to be at all improv'd by them,
that any English Things should make a part in my Dress.
. . ." His dress consisted of a brilliant worn in the shoe,
a patch on the upper lip, a coat with sleeves yellow and
high, a tie wig, and a quantity of lace. That such fashions
changed rapidly is evident when Sir Oliver Bruin, after his
long retirement in the country, returns from a visit to
White's and remarks to one of his cronies, "My Lord here
[Striking Lord Late on the Shoulder] is of Age to remember,
when the Drapery of a fine Gentleman consisted in a huge
Perriwig, a preposterous Muff, a slanting Steinkirk and such
a number of monstrous Trinkums that it would have made a
just Proportion for a full length at Kneller's." Sir Oliver
recognizes that the big wig is outmoded but he does not ap-

prove of the young bloods who now put "their wiggs into such huge Bags" and "their Bodies into coats like Portmantles." Thus Toupet's dress is criticized not only for being French but for the fickleness of fashion.

The beau's speech is ridiculed as much as his dress, for not only does Toupet chatter in French to his servants while he is dressing, but he also rings in a French phrase whenever possible to impress the young lady whom he is courting. The young lady is not impressed; in fact she cannot endure the irritating affectation "of mixing French Phrases perpetually with your English. . . . Pray why does your Lordship fancy it to be Politeness in a Man of Travel, to make use of certain Cant Expressions he has just learned, when the same Custom is thought intolerable Pedantry in a Man of Learning?" The beau in Dodsley's The Toy Shop defines another quality of his speech by asking the shop-master for a snuff-box with some smutty jokes on the lid to help out in witty conversation: "O dear, Sir, yes; a little decent smut is the very Life of all Conversations . . . 'tis the smart Raillery of fine Gentlemen . . . 'tis a Double Entendre, at which the Coquet laughs, the Prude looks grave, the Modest blush, but all are pleased with" (sc. ii).

The most frequent objection to the beau's speech was that it was trite. Such objections took the form of parody in a series of dramatic satires based on Swift's Polite Conversation which was itself adapted for the stage in 1740 with a prologue by James Miller who may have made the adaptation. This is a collection of gossip, stock phrases, cliché metaphors, epigrammatic rimed responses, and trite puns which Swift's ear for idiomatic rhetoric accurately recorded. A sample pun indicates the devastating parody of the vapid conversation of fashionable society:

> (When a young lady asks to see the Colonel's snuff-box)
> Col.: Madam, there's never a C upon it.
> Miss: Maybe, there is, Colonel.
> Col.: Ay, but May-bees don't fly now.

This same device of parody appears in James Ayres' ballad opera, Sancho at Court (1742), and in an anonymous farce by "Timothy Fribble, Esq." entitled Tittle Tattle; or, Taste A-la-Mode (1749) to show how often Swift's raillery was imitated.[17] In the last example, polite society is instructed

"to slide or tatter, not walk; to 'lithp,' not speak; to
stare, not look; to leer, not turn the eye . . . and every
night before soft slumber seizes your Eye-Lids, commit to
your Memories two or three Dozen of the following polite
Phrases" (Dedication).

If French phrases, double entendre, and clichés were
satirized in the beau's speech, it was his vanity which the
dramatist satirized in his behavior. Lord Dapper in Fielding's Historical Register (1737) prefers Lincoln's Inn
Fields among all the theatres because it is the only one
that contains a full length mirror in which he can catch his
reflection as he passes. Kitty, the barmaid in James Miller's The Coffee House (1737), sneers at the beau who makes
love to nobody but himself and stands for hours simpering
"at his own Stupid Face in the Glass." And Toupet in Moore-
Smythe's The Rival Modes (1727) twists every question directed to him into a compliment. When a young lady asks him
politely whether he is fond of quadrille, Toupet immediately
whispers in an aside, "so she's inquiring into my conduct
already. I never knew a woman that was not as fond of me at
first sight as afterwards" (Act III).

The beau was vain and selfish, but he was also a coward
as he is portrayed on the stage. Mr. Trippet in Garrick's
The Lying Valet (1741) begs off when there is danger of a
fight, swearing that he has given an oath not to draw a
sword though in reality he is only too glad to escape to the
card room. Another braggart beau, Flash in Garrick's Miss in
her Teens (1747), proves as great a coward as his rival, the
ladylike Fribble, when a duel is threatened between these
fashionable adversaries. Garrick's cowardly beaux follow a
whole series of such characters in earlier plays: "Powder-
puff/Puffpaste" in Charles Coffey's The Female Parson; or,
Beau in the Sudds (1730); Dapper in the anonymous The Woman
of Taste (1738) attributed to Joseph Dorman; Sir Fopling
Conceit in Joseph Paterson's The Raree Show, or, The Fox
Trapt (1739); Modish in Henry Ward's The Happy Lovers, or,
The Beau Metamorphos'd (1744). The list could be easily extended.

Yet Garrick brings a more serious charge than cowardice
against the beau, a charge that is at the heart of all the
satire on the world of fashion. Fribble (Miss in her Teens)
condemns himself with a description of fops. "There is a
club of us, all young bachelors, the sweetest society in the

world; and we meet three times a week at each other's lodg-
ings, where we drink tea, hear the chat of the day, invent
fashions for ladies, make models of them, and cut out pat-
terns in paper" (II, i). Garrick's Fribble is matched by
many similar characters such as the beaux in Kelly's The
Levee who only attend a statesman's levee to be seen and to
take snuff from a Lord's box (I, iv). Sir Charles Raymond in
Edward Moore's The·Foundling (1748) is the most savage of
all the beau's critics. "Thy life," he tells the disreputable Faddle, "is a Disgrace to Humanity—A foolish Prodigality
makes thee needy—Need makes thee vicious, and both make thee
contemptible. Thy wit is prostituted to Slander and Buffoonery—And thy Judgment, if thou hadst any, to Meanness and
Villany. Thy betters that laugh with thee, laugh at thee—And
who are they?—The Fools of Quality" (IV, iii). Thus middle-
class morality by mid-eighteenth-century turns satire of the
beau from parody and wit to sheer invective.

As satire on fashionable society developed in the plays
of this period, it identified the vices common to the whole
as well as attacking individual types like the beau. Card
playing, for example, is ridiculed as both extravagant and
a waste of time. The two games most often mentioned, in comedies of manners as well as dramatic satires, were whist and
quadrille. Lady Towneley in Colley Cibber's comedy, The Provoked Husband (1728) quarrels bitterly over her debts con-
tracted at the whist tables in assemblies. She justifies
herself with the argument that she is only complying with
the fashion, but this fails to appease her husband who re-
gards card playing as an extravagant waste of time. Such
comments about card players were turned into action in dramatic satires. In Fielding's satirical Historical Register,
for example, the audience is presented with a scene of female "politicians" seated at a card table and hears the in-
anity and vulgar gossip of their conversation (II, i). Sir
John Loverule in Charles Coffey's The Merry Cobbler (1735)
describes quadrille as "only a fashionable sort of game
amongst the Quality, which bewitches them out of their Money
and Senses and often occasions them to sacrifice their Virtue to a Debt of Honor" (sc. iv). It was obviously not so
much the game as the idle gossip and constant gambling which
accompanied it that offended the middle-class dramatist. In
1743, the anonymous play, The Humours of Whist, attacked
this game for reasons similar to those for Coffey's thrust

at quadrille, while the subtitle, <u>As it is Acted every Day at White's and other Coffeehouses and Assemblies</u>, indicates that card playing had extended beyond private drawing rooms and the large assemblies such as Ranelagh and Vauxhall to the coffeehouses. This play which burlesques several habitual players at the various gaming tables was not intended, for this reason according to the <u>Biographia Dramatica</u>, II, 134, for the stage. Like an earlier anonymous ballad opera <u>Colonel Split-Tail</u> (1730), it is evidence that single references to card playing no longer sufficed and entire plays were devoted to the subject. <u>Colonel Split-Tail</u> was a scurrilous piece about a specific gambler, the notorious Colonel Charteris, or Chartes, who was drummed out of his regiment for cheating at cards while he was still only an ensign. In this play he is a Don Juan-like character attended by a chorus of satyrs reminiscent of Greek comedy. Harlequin and Scaramouche from the pantomime stage are added to its bawdy attack on gaming tables, and when the hourglass runs out at the end of the second and final act, Colonel Split-Tail and his attending satyrs descend like Don Juan (into hell?) to the accompaniment of thunder and lightning.

Colonel Charteris' career did not end with cheating at cards, but took on grotesque proportions. He was expelled for thievery from a Dutch foot regiment, and when his father purchased a Colonel's commission for him, he was tried shortly afterwards for receiving money from tradespeople who enlisted to save themselves from arrest. He finally abandoned the army and devoted himself to pure gambling. The money he won was in turn lent at exorbitant interest to spendthrifts of his acquaintance. By seizing their estates when they defaulted on payments, he eventually acquired an income of ₤7000 a year in addition to the ₤100,000 which he held in stocks (See the <u>DNB</u>, X, 135-36). Thus his career became a focus for the dramatist's objection to gambling as a mark of degeneracy. Peggy Ambler in Odell's <u>The Smugglers</u> voiced the theme when she sang "The World's all a Cheat, and Business Deceit" and Vulcan in the same play calls gambling "a touch of the times truly" (II, v). Certainly dramatists extended the vice beyond smugglers trying to run goods past the customs' officers. For Moses Mendez' play, <u>The Double Disappointment</u> (1746), has a "gentleman" who gambles on his ward, Isabel; he promises her to a French Marquis and an Irish gentleman in return for the guarantee of a thousand

guineas from each, but in the end his gambling brings him
nothing at all because the Marquis proves to be a valet and
the Irish gentleman a stable boy. The play which came closer
to the career of the gambler Colonel Charteris was Michael
Clancy's The Sharper (1738). Like Colonel Split-Tail it presented the gambler as a profligate Don Juan as he appears in
Plate I of Hogarth's Rake's Progress, and pursued his money-
lending schemes to point a moral which Swift approved (See
Biog. Drama., III, 202-3). Clancy's play illustrates well
the Epitaph of Colonel Charteris that appeared in the Gentleman's Magazine, II, 711, at the time of his death (1732)
wherein he is celebrated as the only person of the age who
cheated without the mask of honesty.

Another popular vice related to gambling was the lottery and this too was attacked by dramatists. How the South
Sea Bubble at the beginning of this period stimulated attacks on this form of gambling was described in the previous
chapter. But lotteries did not cease with the panic following the Bubble, and Fielding's The Lottery (1732) exposed
the same vice. Mr. Stocks, in this play, hears of a young
lady just come to London and he whispers to Jack Stocks that
he will see the lady's fortune made in the lottery if Jack
will marry her. That Mr. Stocks is an experienced hand in
conducting lotteries is made clear in the first scene when
he lists the variety of means by which he cheats the public.
It is therefore no surprise when the young lady's ticket
comes up blank; since she is now worthless as a wife, young
Jack Stocks sells her in scene three to her former lover for
Ł1000. Thus the satire dissipates into the resolution of
comedy.

The lottery scene in Fielding's play is, however, viciously satiric. Each one who frequents the place distrusts
the operators, yet each continues to buy in the vain hope
that some day he will win. Mrs. Sugarsops is paid Ł20 one
day to entice her into buying more on the following days.
Thus she is kept dangling from day-to-day while her fortune
is gradually sucked into the hands of the projectors. Fielding's treatment of the lottery is matched in an anonymous
ballad opera, The Footman, of the same season (1731-1732)
where a footman wins Ł10,000 in a lottery and becomes a gentleman. This elicits a sardonic comment, "Nay as to that, a
Footman has generally the advantage in point of Education,
and I believe there is not much difference in the Blood"

(III, iii). The sale of worthless stocks of projects and projectors could ruin a lady and turn a footman into a gentleman. The lottery was thus an extension of gambling as dramatic satirists made clear.[18]

Another foible of polite society was its taste for auctions. Fielding's card-playing "lady politicians" in The Historical Register, for example, disband as soon as news is brought to them of an auction nearby (II, ii). They have no intention of buying but they desire to be seen at a place where everyone of importance is certain to be present. The art of the auctioneer made auctions a good show, and Fielding's auctioneer, Christopher Hen, is undoubtedly Christopher Cock, one of the most popular of the profession. Mr. Hen, in the play, auctions an allegorical assortment of objects which ridicule this frivolous but fashionable pastime. In a parody of Lucian's sale of philosophers, Mr. Hen finds no bidders for a remnant of political honesty, nor for a piece of patriotism, nor for three grains of honesty. But he does sell a bottle of courage to an army captain badly in need of it, although he cannot sell all the wit of Hugh Pantomime of Mr. William Goosequil, a composer of political pamphlets in defense of the ministry. Interest at court he sells for ₤1000, but the ten cardinal virtues bring a bid of only 18d from a gentleman who mistakes them for a Cardinal's virtues, a great rarity. Here Fielding seems to be imitating the ironic sale of abstractions in Dodsley's The Toy Shop which had appeared three years before his Historical Register.

Conolly's The Connoisseur (1736) gives a better hint why auctions were popular, a hint which Fielding's scene, because of the crowded satire, fails to make clear. Like the gentleman who desired the unusually rare Cardinal's virtues, most of the fashionable patrons of auctions were in search of rarities. Sir Godfrey Trinket in The Connoisseur is typical of the upper-class gentleman in search of the rare objet d'art, but Sir Godfrey is also a dilettante who cannot distinguish false from true rarities. He therefore falls victim to Cheatly who sells him worthless trifles.

Samuel Foote also included a burlesque of the auctioneer, Christopher Cock, in his Auction of Pictures (1748). According to the Biographia Dramatica (I, 444), Cock was a very clever man. It is doubtful whether even the desire for rare trinkets would have attracted the continuously large

audiences at these auctions had there not been the fine show
which Cock and his successor, the dramatist Abraham Langford,
were able to provide. Their wit and ingenuity in the rapid
fire comments which accompanied their sales made excellent
entertainment. Thus the auctioneer comes off better than
polite society when auctions were satirized on the stage.

Apparently drinking did not excite eighteenth-century
dramatic satirists as much as the other popular vices. It is
true that Fielding pokes fun at Puzzletext, the four bottle
clergyman in The Welsh Opera, and that Coffey has Jobson in
The Devil to Pay declare, "I am a true English heart, and
look upon Drunkenness as the best part of the liberty of the
subject." (II, ii). But even Garrick's naming the drunken
fellow in Lethe Mr. Riot does not indicate any deep-seated
criticism of drinking. The strong opposition to Walpole's
halfhearted attempt to limit the number of gin shops in 1736
(see Chapter 1) is further proof that there was little articulate criticism of drinking as a moral or economic problem.[19]

Finally, the bulk of the dramatist's social satire was
concentrated not so much on card playing, gambling, lotteries and auctions as it was on sexual immorality. The Restoration delight in clandestine assignations had given way to
sentimentality about proper conduct, and this sentimentalism in turn was translated into "a kind of mildew" which
spread over the surface of literature at this period "to indicate a sickly constitution."[20] Sentimentality is hardly
the proper tone of satire; in fact it is antithetical to the
cynicism and critical, ironic tone of the satirist. The impression of sentimentalism is easier to describe than to define. Why was it that England became supersensitive about
morals accepted fifty years earlier without a wink? What was
the origin of the "man of sentiment"? Apparently he was the
product of a combination of ingredients. The anti-Hobbes,
anti-Puritan, anti-Stoical sermons of the late seventeenth-
century Latitudinarians are in part responsible for him.[21]
The philosophy of the third Earl of Shaftesbury with its
conviction of the inherent goodness of human nature, is another ingredient.[22] Undoubtedly there were others in the
books of Courtesy and in the general reliance in the eighteenth century upon common sense as the proper guide of conduct. But to explain the crystallization of the orgy of
sentiment into the "man of feeling," it is necessary to turn

to social historians. The inefficient and corrupt prison
system, the harsh criminal code, and the dangerous life of
an unpoliced and unlighted London have already been mentioned. In addition, unemployment and poverty were common in
the city while eviction and hunger were stark and immediate
problems of rural areas still undergoing the process of en-
closure.23 It is not surprising, then, if, by a certain combination of social conditions and common-sense morality, benevolence became synonymous with virtue. The "man of feeling" could satisfy both his moral and social obligations by
relieving the distress he saw around him. So distinct was
the pleasure he derived from having fulfilled his obligations to society that benevolence became a luxury and weep-
ing even took on a moral tone.

The theory that human nature is perfectible by an appeal to the emotions or the sensibilities of man is reflected in two dramatic forms that developed in this period,
the sentimental comedy and the domestic tragedy. Authors of
the two forms felt it their mission "to moralize the stage,"
as Richard Steele's Prologue of The Conscious Lovers (1722)
put it. This impulse to use the drama for the encouragement
of virtue was reinforced by the clergyman, William Law, who
in 1723 violently attacked the theatres in The Absolute Un-
lawfullness of the Stage Entertainment fully Demonstrated
(See Law's Works, [London, 1742], II, 7). Such criticism
justified the sentimental dramatist in hounding immorality
off the English stage. Furthermore other critics claimed
that "a good play, by having the advantage of action, may
emulate to virtue, with more efficacy very often than well-
wrote treatises. . . ."24 The "man of feeling" readily accepted the invitation to employ the stage for propaganda
against vice, and the particular objects of his attack were
the rake, the courtesan, the unfaithful wife, and her equally
unfaithful husband—in other words, the type characters of
Restoration comedy. But the form of his attack was not dramatic satire. In fact the dramatist often enjoyed having his
cake while he ate it too since he rarely punished infrac-
tions of sexual morality until the second or third scene of
the last act. After so many scenes of profligacy and assignations, his conversions at the end of the play were no less
than miraculous. Thus his comedies remained comedies of manners with a new twist to the denouement rather than contrib-
uting to the form of dramatic satire.

The unfaithful married couple was the most popular subject of such <u>sentimental</u> social criticism. In Colley Cibber's <u>The Provoked Husband</u> (1728) the wife misbehaves. Lady
Towneley spends all her time at assemblies and keeps such
boisterous company and late hours that she has not time to
talk to her husband for days at a time. Of course she re-
pents in the end. Instead of turning her into the street,
Cibber has her reform, which his Foreword admits is a soft-
ening of the play which Vanbrugh had begun. There is a parallel situation in the play between Sir Francis Wronghead
and his wife who has just arrived in London. Cibber makes
Lady Wronghead more ludicrous than Lady Towneley, since the
newcomer piles up huge debts by her lavish attempts to ape
the fashionable wives, and she almost marries her daughter
to a gambler and her son to a cast-off mistress, before she
discovers her folly and departs again for the country. But
here too repentance saves the day. Cibber seems content with
the exposure of vice and mild, if improbable, propaganda for
virtue. He still employs the form of Restoration comedy of
manners while he modifies the denouement in the direction of
sentiment, not satire.

Benjamin Hoadly's <u>The Suspicious Husband</u> (1747) refines
the Restoration marriage scandal to the extent that Strickland, for whom the play is named, has not even grounds for
his suspicion. Yet the situations and dialogue of his play
are filled with echoes of Restoration comedy. Thus his play
is another of those strange mixtures which pretend to punish a vice that the author is quite willing to exploit.
Strickland, of course, since he has no grounds for his suspicion, is himself an object of ridicule, but at best this
situation is but flabby irony without the bite or direction
of satire.

John Gay was more successful at the ironic reversal of
satire when he made the Peachums object to Polly's <u>marriage</u>
to Macheath in <u>The Beggar's Opera</u>. Again in <u>Polly</u> he treats
married fidelity lightly, for Mrs. Trapes urges Ducat to
buy a mistress by telling him, "Though you were born and
bred in the <u>Indies</u>, as you are a subject of Briton, you
should live up to our customs. . . . Your luxury should distinguish you from the vulgar. You cannot be too expensive
in your pleasures" (I, i). For Mrs. Trapes, then, a mistress
is a sign the man is both wealthy and fashionable, but Gay's
audience would have remembered Mrs. Trapes as a demimonde

character from The Beggar's Opera. Mrs. Trapes's advice is
therefore akin to the behavior of young Lady Languish in
John Mottley's The Widow Bewitch'd (1730) who is so eager to
conform to fashion that she does not even wait to verify the
story of her husband's death before she admits the atten-
tions of her suitors.

Fielding weakened his most bitter attack on scandalous
marriage relations in his comedy The Modern Husband (1732)
by also adding a sudden conversion at the end. Much of the
plot is devoted to Mrs. Modern who has had affairs with
practically every man in the cast of characters, a fact that
her "modern husband" overlooks because he needs money. This
satiric situation loses its force when Bellamont, a reformed
philanderer, returns to his wife's arms vowing, "My future
days shall have no wish, no labour, but for thy happiness;
and from this hour I'll never give thee cause of a complaint" (IV, x). Although Fielding later expressed contempt
of such sudden conversions in comedy (Tom Jones, Book XVII,
Chapter I), here he falls into the language of the sentimental dramatist. If he intended this conversion in The Modern Husband as an ironic denouement like that of The Author's
Farce where Luckless is suddenly proclaimed the King of
Bantam, it is less clear.

Charles Coffey is a more successful satirist in his
travesty of the usual marriage scandal in The Devil to Pay
(1731). By a trick of magic the wives of Sir John Loverule
and a loutish cobbler, Jobson, are made to exchange houses
but not beds. Since the real Lady Loverule was a shrew, the
false one charms the servants as well as Sir John by her
mild manners. Meanwhile Jobson does not fare as well when he
attempts to tame Lady Loverule by his customary technique of
beating his wife. Eventually the magic is explained after
both Jobson and Lady Loverule are somewhat chastened by the
experience. In the sequel, The Merry Cobbler (1735), Jobson
again resorts to beating his spouse since he now mistakenly
assumes that Sir John made him a cuckold during the exchange
of wives. Jobson's unsuccessful attempt to get revenge by an
affair with Lady Loverule exposes him to the ridicule of everyone in the play. Thus by means of a mock marriage scandal
based on magic rather than fact, Coffey undertook to laugh
immorality off the stage.

Dodsley's dramatic satire, The Toy Shop (1735) neatly
defined the gentleman's ambiguity about marriage. A young

man enters the shop to inquire about a plain gold ring (sc. ii):

>   Master: A Wedding Ring, I presume?
> Y. Gent.: No, Sir; I thank you kindly; that's a toy I
>   never design to play with.

But after the master eloquently defends marriage, the young gentleman admits it is a wedding ring which he desires:

> Y. Gent.: Well, Sir, since I find you so staunch an advo-
>   cate for Matrimony, I confess it is a Wedding
>   Ring I want; the Reason why I deny'd it, and of
>   what I said in Ridicule of Marriage, was only to
>   avoid the Ridicule which I expected from you
>   upon it.

Not all satire on sexual immorality was aimed at the married couple. The rake and the courtesan came in for their share as well. Young Wilding in Fielding's The Temple Beau (1730) is a typical rake who attempts to carry on intrigues simultaneously with both Lady Gravely and Lady Lucy. But while he flatters the ladies by putting on "as hypocritical a countenance as a Jesuit at confession" (III, i), he cannot convince his father that he is studying law even by capital-izing on Pedant's library to make a good impression. Field-ing's purpose in exposing the rake is evident in Veromil's sentimental speech about virtue. "Virtue may indeed be un-fashionable in this age; for ignorance and vice will always live together. . . . Virtue is a diamond, which when the world despises, 'tis plain that knaves and fools have too much sway within" (II, xii). This moralizing and the saccha-rine way he has of forgiving the disloyal Valentine, mark Veromil as a genuine "man of feeling." Again as in The Mod-ern Husband Fielding dilutes his criticism of immorality by joining the sentimentalists.[25] If his political satire had been as flaccid as his social satire, Walpole would have had little to fear from Fielding's plays.

George Lillo's Sylvia (1730) also presents a dissolute rake, Sir John Freeman, who at the beginning of the opera has already debauched Lettice and Betty, and is ready to se-duce Sylvia also. Although she proves her moral fibre by re-fusing him, Sylvia freely admits she loves the rake and will

consent to an honorable marriage. When the plot reveals that
she and Sir John were exchanged as babies and that the Freeman fortune is rightfully hers, Sir John, now a reformed
reprobate, is, very quickly, as elaborate in his contrition
as the rake in Cibber's Love's Last Shift. He says of Sylvia,
"I have not so ill-profited by her bright example, as to
repine at a change of fortune, so just, and so much to the
advantage of this wondrous pattern of all that's excellent
in womankind" (III, xxi). Sir John clearly knows on what
side his bread will be buttered. Thus Lillo's attack on
the rake is so weakened by this absurd repentance that it
is sentiment rather than satire.

Another play with confused purpose is Thomas Southerne's
Money the Mistress (1726). The author claims in the dedication to Lord Boyle that he has "punished infidelity in the
lover and falseness in the friend." This is correct since
Mourville, the faithless rake, deserts one lady to marry
another whose fortune appears larger, and then ends by heaping himself with self-abuse (V, ii). Yet while justice triumphs, humor is provided by scenes straight out of Restoration comedy. Don Manuel, for example, pretends he is in a
fit when his wife unexpectedly surprises him prostrated at
another woman's feet (IV, iii). Thus Southerne's claim that
he is punishing infidelity lacks conviction. He too is willing to exploit clichés of Restoration comedy while claiming
to disapprove of its morals.

Theophilus Cibber's The Lover (1730) presents the hypocrisy of the rake. Granger in this play has seduced his
ward, Eustacia, and seized her fortune, but he is prompt
and regular in his attendance at church, and his virtue is
accepted as beyond reproach by all his neighbors. Not until
he plots to have Eustacia murdered to make way for another
victim does this so-called comedy reveal Ranger's hypocrisy.
Again the rake is exposed by "sentiment," not satire.

One of the least attractive rakes in the plays of this
period is young Belmont in Edward Moore's The Foundling
(1748) who may have been suggested by Lovelace in Richard-
son's Clarissa Harlow which appeared in 1747-1748. Belmont
has stolen Fidelia from her guardian and carried her off to
his home, but once there she is so well protected by his
sister he is unable to seduce her. Thereupon, he decides on
a monstrous scheme to disgrace her in his family's eyes so
that after she is turned out of the house she will be en-

tirely dependent on him. Throughout the play he boasts of
his lack of moral scruples until suddenly, at the end, he is
converted—to the extent that he wants to marry a penniless
girl. "And now, Fidelia, what you have made me, take me—a
convert to Honour! I have at last learned that Custom can
be no Authority for Vice; and however the mistaken World
may judge, He who solicits Pleasure, at the Expense of Innocence, is the vilest of Betrayers" (V, v). Again by sudden conversion the rake turns moralist and the social satirist dissolves into sentimental reformer of sexual immorality.

Millwood, the prostitute in George Lillo's tragedy The
London Merchant (1731), is the bleakest portrait of the female counterpart of the rake. Her sole motivation for the
crimes to which she drives George Barnwell, the young ap-
prentice, is her desire for money. "I found it necessary to
be rich" (IV, ii) she says, for with money she can buy her
way into the fashionable world. Yet despite her ruin of
young Barnwell, she is completely cold to his intense re-
morse. "I can't repent, nor ask to be forgiven" (V, iii). In
making Millwood the unrepentant antagonist of his tragedy,
Lillo damned the greed and ruthlessness of the female rake,
but Millwood is not a satiric figure; she is a figure of
tragedy. Had Lillo made her foolishly repentant like Sir
John Freeman in his Sylvia, Millwood would have lost all
her force as tragic antagonist.

In two plays, Gay's Polly (1729) and Miller's Art and
Nature (1738), the noble savage is introduced as a technique to criticize the corrupt morals of English society.
Pohetohee, in Polly, is a West Indian chieftain who cannot
understand the Europeans' ethics when they invade his land.
His fiercest criticism is of Ducat who will not fight when
his home and liberty are in danger from pirate invasion:

> How different are your notions from ours? We think virtue,
> honour, and courage as essential to man as his limbs, or
> senses; and in every man we suppose the qualities of a man
> 'till we have found the contrary; but then we regard him
> only as a brute in disguise. How custom can degrade na-
> ture!
>
> (III, i)

Gay had hit upon an ideal vir bonus or stable norm for his

satire by introducing the outsider to comment on English society, but his technique was not controlled so that the
criticism becomes preachy and dogmatic, as in Act II, xi,
where the chieftain's son, Cawwawkee, lectures Polly on the
morals of her society which he has never seen. Gay was not
skillful enough to give such sermons the bite of the King
of Brobdingnag commenting on Gulliver's description of his
homeland.

James Miller's Art and Nature uses the noble savage
more successfully as satire when he has Truemore return
from the West Indies bringing the Indian Julio with him. By
introducing the savage to the conventions of London society
Miller satirizes by action rather than sermon. Both Truemore and Julio are shocked by the contrast of London and
the place from which they came. Truemore reacts by exposing
the hypocrisy of Courtly who lives by flattery. But Julio is
arrested when he beats a bookseller attempting to fleece him
and Julio becomes the scapegoat of the comedy.

Thus the device of the noble savage only increases the
middle-class social criticism of fashionable society without becoming satire. It is clear that the dramatist as social satirist identified himself with the middle class to
which he belonged. He rarely satirized the middle-class
merchants; in fact he dignified them in domestic tragedy.
He did attack professions—rascally lawyers, quack doctors,
and particularly such dissenting clerics as Quakers and
Methodists. But the bulk of his social satire was on the low
standard of morality and the individual vices and customs
of the upper class whose useless existence he challenged.

While politics stimulated the dramatists of this period
to develop the satiric genre for the stage, social criticism diffused and weakened the development of dramatic satire. The ridicule of society's folly and affectation dis-
solved in the sentimental comedies into the didactism of
direct statement which was antithetical to satiric irony.
The result was a modification of the comedy of manners but
not in the direction of satire. The sudden conversion of
the rake or the wanton wife in the last scene of such "comedies" pulled the rug out from under satire leaving only
sentimentality. Such converted characters, saved from debauchery, were neither realistic nor satiric but evidence
of the author's intention to arouse "feeling." Conversely in
a domestic tragedy such as Lillo's The London Merchant,

Millwood, although she is more realistic as a consistently
unrepentant courtesan, is not ridiculed but used as foil to
the tragic hero in Lillo's attempt to evolve a social problem play out of the conflict between the morally weak ap-
prentice and his consistently immoral mistress. Thus both
the new developments, domestic tragedy and such sentimental
comedy of manners as Cibber's The Provok'd Husband, were
detrimental to dramatic social satire.

The ballad opera was the new form better adapted to social satire. It offered a popular medium for parody and burlesque action, satiric strategies both, to ridicule everything from Quakers to "Polite Conversation." When it was
also combined with fantasy as in Coffey's The Devil to Pay
or The Merry Cobbler, it expanded the technique of satire by
the magic of switching wives between social classes. The
irony of a cobbler behaving toward a Lord's lady as he would
to his own wife was a good technique for the social satirist.
Dodsley expanded the use of fantasy in social satire by the
sale of trifles to which ironic values were attached and underscored (The Toy Shop). Fantasy was also exploited by Garrick's Lethe with its Lucian-like descent to the underworld
and by the author of Colonel Split-Tail when satyrs appear
and devils carry the dissolute gambler (Colonel Charteris)
off the stage. Foote's Auction of Pictures exploited the
short scenes made popular both by ballad opera and pantomime in a series of satiric skits, thus extending the hodgepodge technique of Fielding's rehearsal-type satires (The
Author's Farce, Pasquin) or his reportorial, journalistic
technique (The Historical Register) of scenes of card playing and an auction, where the sale of abstractions is reminiscent of Dodsley's The Toy Shop.

Finally the social satirist recognized the value of the
outsider as norm for the satiric criticism of society. While
Fielding had used a fictional character in Don Quixote in
England to criticize English elections, he did not exploit
the mad knight as a norm for social satire. The naive foreigner, or noble savage, brought to England and confronted
with English society was a better norm in Miller's Art and
Nature. Julio's outraged reaction to London creates better
social satire than Gay's indignant West Indian chief (Polly)
who only hears about English society because Julio can act
out his indignation without preaching about what he finds
wrong in the new scene. Yet Julio is a scapegoat who is

beaten when he opposes the unfamiliar mores. Miller's play,
despite Julio, remains a comedy like Fielding's Don Quixote
in England.

The social satire of the dramatists of this period is
more interesting as an indication of a shift in values than
as experiment in dramatic satire. By identifying with the
rising middle class, the dramatist reformed the rakes of
Restoration comedy just as he scolded unfaithful husbands
and wives into repentant fidelity. Frivolity (cards, gambling, lotteries, auctions, masquerades) was exposed and
parodied. Country life by contrast with urban society was
idealized in Pastorals (by Ramsay and Lillo) as implied
criticism only. Professions such as law, medicine and church
were criticized by stock characters who, the dramatists made
clear, were no reflections on honest lawyers, competent
doctors, or good Church of England clergymen.

What seems to distinguish social satire from political
satire in drama is that it is less particular and more concerned with the habits of society than with individuals.
Card playing is a satiric target, for example, more often
than a specific gambler like Colonel Charteris. Auctions
are ridiculed as foolish behavior. Affectation, hypocrisy
and aberrant behavior cause general comic criticism which
only occasionally amounts to satire on a specific scandal,
a specific quack doctor such as Misaubin or Ward, or a specific Catholic priest such as Father Girard. While most of
the dramatists included their social criticism in comedies
and farce rather than creating dramatic satire, they did
develop some new techniques (fantasy, plotless skits, the
noble savage as a moral norm) of dramatic satire. Finally,
the content of their middle-class oriented attacks on society is more interesting than its form.

CHAPTER 4

LITERARY SATIRE

We oft, 'tis true, mistake the Satirist's Aim,
Not Arts themselves, but their Abuse they blame.
                    —William Whitehead, An Essay on Ridicule (1743)

Satire is a witty and severe Attack of mischievous
Habits or Vices.
                    —Corbyn Morris, An Essay toward Fixing the
                    True Standards of Wit, Humour, Raillery,
                    Satire and Ridicule . . . (1744)

Misconduct will certainly be never chas'd out of the world
by satire, if no satires are written.
                    —Edward Young, Preface to Love of Fame
                    (1728)

THE EVIDENCE in the two preceding chapters makes clear that
the political satirist contributed more consistently to the
form of dramatic satire than the social satirist. His targets were more easily identifiable in Walpole, his ministers, and Whig policy, and when he used the ballad opera or
rehearsal play to attack these targets, he was capable of
wit, ironic inversions, parody, burlesque, grotesque hyperbole and considerable imaginative fantasy. The social satirist was less skillful in using these tools of satire. When
he attempted to adapt the Restoration comedy of manners[1] to
satire, he either produced sentimental comedies antithetical
to satiric tone or buried his social criticism in domestic
tragedy. The same dramatists who were successful political
satirists, like Gay and Fielding, were diffuse and diluted
social satirists. Gay, for example, began well in Polly with

Mrs. Trapes's advice to Ducat, but Gay's social satire fal-
tered in the preachy West Indian noble savages who criticized English society. And Fielding is a better satirist of
corrupt elections in Pasquin than he is of marriage scandals
in The Modern Husband.

THE AUTHOR'S WORLD

The transition between social dramatic satire and literary dramatic satire is best traced in the satire on
the dramatist's world of patrons, audience, theatre
managers and authors. Much of what follows in this section
is also social satire but is so intimately related to the
dramatist's milieu that it seems better to consider it sep-
arately before discussing the specific literary satire on
form and theory later in this chapter. Much of this transi-
tional material records a kind of grumbling malaise about
the necessity of a patron to succeed as a dramatist or about
the low taste of audiences who preferred the new pantomime
and opera performances so popular in the early 1720's. As
such this grumbling criticism is scarcely distinguishable
from criticism of society except that it is closely associated with the profession of the dramatists who, with few
exceptions, needed patrons. The poverty of the dramatist is
referred to in countless Prefaces, Prologues, Epilogues, and
plots in this period. Playwrights are presented as penniless
writers (Gay's beggar poet in The Beggar's Opera) who must
pawn all their possessions (Luckless in Fielding's The Author's Farce) or sit in their rags before a blinking taper
in the worst garret (Tragedo in Odingsells' Bayes's Opera).
Their poverty necessitates groveling and fawning for the
favor of a patron. To survive as a dramatist Witmore says
in The Author's Farce you must "get a Patron, be a pimp to
some worthless man of quality, write panygerics on him,
flatter him with as many virtues as he has vices. Then perhaps you will engage his lordship, his lordship engages the
town on your side, and then write till your arms ache, sense
or nonsense, it will all go down" (I, v). Authors, like Fustian in Pasquin who vow to scorn all flattery of patrons,
yet write hypocritical dedications informing their benefac-
tors "You have more wit, sense, learning, honour, and humanity than all mankind put together" (III, i).
The dramatist frequently satirized the instability of

the patron's support. The favor of a patron was a will-of-
the-wisp affair and thoroughly unreliable. The Lord in
Kelly's The Levee rewards his dependent author only by wishing him increased sales on his next book. Unfulfilled ex-
pectations were the dramatist's fate as the anonymous Bickerstaff's Unburied Dead solemnly proclaimed. Much of the
criticism of patronage seems a contempt for Grub Street hack
writers and the dramatist's fear that he must join these
parasites unless he wishes to starve. For there would always be a few scurvy fellows like Fustian willing to flatter
his patron.

Patrons clearly reflected what the dramatist considered
the low taste of the audience. Yet without the backing of an
influential patron the playwright was dependent on this
false taste which, as Fielding's Witmore proclaims bitterly
(The Author's Farce, I, v), cannot distinguish sense from
nonsense. From the anonymous Modern Poetasters (1725) to the
also anonymous Marforio, being a Comi-tragical Farce call'd
The Critick of Taste or, A Tale of a Tub (1736), dramatists
bewailed the decline of poetry in drama and the strangle-
hold of Grub Street on popular taste. Odingsells' Bayes's
Opera traced the low ebb of poetry to that time "ever since
Sound got the upper Hand of Sense." The dramatist thus was
trapped between the fickle patron, the poor taste of his
audience, the decline in style, and the rising importance of
the actor.[2] Epilogues resounded with preachments against the
"senseless ribaldry" which "disgrac'd the stage" (Miller's
Mahomet) and called for a reform of corrupt taste:

> Rouse, Britons, rouse, this modish Taste despise,
> And Let good Sense to its old Standard rise.
>   (anonymous Tittle Tattle, 1749)

Audiences were described as interested only in novelties
(Dodsley's The Toy Shop) or the acrobatic dancers of the
pantomime stage. When Lucy arrives in London in Fielding's
farce Miss Lucy in Town (1742), she wants to know what the
fashionable people do at theatres and Tawdry tells her,
"Why, if they can, they take a stage-box, where they let the
footman sit the first acts, to show his livery; then they
come in to show themselves, spread the fan upon the spikes,
make curtzies to their acquaintances, and then talk and
laugh as loud as they are able."

First night audiences were notoriously fickle and were
satirized as erratic and unreliable. In Eurydice Hiss'd or A
Word to the Wise (1737) Fielding left a biting testimony to
the first night performance of his failure, Eurydice. Eurydice Hiss'd which again uses the rehearsal format for dramatic satire, has a scene in Spatter's comedy where the
author bribes various actors to applaud his play on the
first night. The scene is intended, says Spatter, as a warning to all future authors "against depending solely on a
party to support them against the judgment of the town."
Honestus is the only one who refuses the bribe and he is
also the only one who, on the night of the opening, stands
by the author. The others desert so completely that Spatter
refuses to show the interior of the playhouse. "No, sir, it
is a thing of too horrible a nature; for which reason I
shall follow Horace's rule and only introduce a description
of it." Fielding thus at his own expense ridicules the whims
which governed a play's reception. He had good reason since
Miller's The Coffee House and Captain Boaden's The Modish
Couple had also been hissed off the stage by hostile audiences. But Genest also records how a packed house could
smother a first performance with too much applause; when
Benjamin Martyn's Timoleon (1730) was played in January at
Drury Lane, the author's friends were so enthusiastic that
scarcely a word was heard, and even the candle snuffers were
applauded while a couch made its entrance amid riotous ac-
claim (Genest, III, 252).

If patrons and a claque were necessary to the success
of a play so were favorable critics. Yet critics too were
satirized as nit-pickers or so wedded to Rules with a capital R that they damned a play before hearing it to the end.
The discussion of the dramatic satire on the Ancients and
Moderns controversy belongs to the following section, but it
should be pointed out that the rehearsal type satire was
filled with such critics as Sneerwell (Fielding's Pasquin)
who interrupt the play-within-the-play by foolish questions
or ironically literal interpretations. Frame plays such as
The Beggar's Opera also gave the satirist an opportunity to
ridicule critics who cry reprieve for Macheath. One of the
best formulas for satirizing foolish critics is to be found
in an afterpiece by Charles Macklin near the end of the period. Picking up on Fielding's allegorically named Sneerwell, Macklin's The New Play Criticiz'd (1747) has quibbling

critics named Nibble and Trifle. They assemble at the house
of Lady Critick after a performance of Hoadly's The Suspicious Husband to give the disgruntled Canker their judgment
of his rival dramatist. Yet the best Trifle and Nibble can
do is to argue at length that The Jealous Husband would be
a better title. Their major criticism beyond this distinction with no difference is that Ranger's hat is laced
against "all the Rules of Criticism." While much of Macklin's afterpiece is social criticism of first night audiences, he also makes fun of those who write by Rules to
please the critics. Heartly, the hero, states Macklin's
norm: "Well, for my Part, I shall always prefer the irregu-
lar Genius who from mere Affection compels me to laugh or
cry, to the regular Blockhead who makes me sleep according
to Rule." Macklin's invention of tying to an actual performance (Hoadly's play ran at Covent Garden on the same
nights, March 24 and April 30, that Macklin's afterpiece
appeared at Drury Lane)[3] his satire on carping critics who
raise trifling, nonsensical objections was an ingenious
formula for dramatic satire. In fact it is one of the best
for topical satire to emerge in the thirty years covered by
this study.

Finally the dramatist's relation to the theatre itself—
the production staff, the managers and the actors—was satirized. Dramatists were in many cases managers and even
more often actors; thus their proximity to theatrical affairs made them both objects and agents of satire. There
seems to have been little specific satire on the production
staff although Fielding did take a poke at the Dutch scenic
artist when he mentioned Mynheer van Bottom-Flat as the
"prodigious scene painter" in his burlesque pantomime, Tumble Down Dick (1736). But theatrical managers were continuously under attack, especially John Rich (Lun), Charles
Fleetwood, and the Cibbers—father and son. John Rich was
frequently attacked as in James Miller's satiric poem, Harlequin Horace (1735), for corrupting the stage by encouraging
Harlequins and entertainments degrading to drama. Fielding
made the attack more personal in the Dedication of his Tumble Down Dick (1736) by claiming that Rich was responsible
for the indifference shown to one of his plays which he had
offered to Drury Lane, an indifference which Fielding says
"immediately determined me against any farther pursuing that
project." He then continued by audaciously thanking Rich

"for that satire on Pasquin [Rich's "Marforio a Theatrical
Satyr" unpublished] which you was so kind to bring on your
stage. . . . I own it was a sensible pleasure to me to observe the town, which had before been so favorable to Pasquin at his own house, confirming that applause by thoroughly condemning the satire of him at yours."[4] Fielding's
quarrel with Rich is more personal than most of the satire
which condemns Rich as responsible for the vogue for pantomime, but the attack on pantomime as a debasing of dramatic
form will be discussed more fully later.

Charles Fleetwood, the manager at Drury Lane, was satirized most notably by Mrs. Charlotte Charke, the actress
daughter of Colley Cibber. Her quarrel with Fleetwood grew
out of his refusal to assign her the parts she wanted in the
1735 season. The result was her satiric Art of Management or
Tragedy Expell'd (1735) performed at the York buildings as a
bitter denunciation of her former manager. Fleetwood was so
enraged by her attack that he attempted to buy up all the
printed copies of her play and destroy them (DNB, X, 66).
Actors were not the only ones to complain about Fleetwood's
management. James Ayres complains in the Preface to his comedy Sancho at Court (1742) that a friend showed the play to
William Chetwood who urged cutting it to one act but that
subsequently Fleetwood proceeded to lose the copy. The Preface then concludes bitterly "for as things are now circum-
stanced, viz., the Approbations of the Players, the Licensing Office, and the ill-natured Critic, not to say anything
of the Publick, an Author has but a small chance of succeeding."

The satire on Fleetwood's management was, however, mild
by contrast to that on Colley Cibber and his son Theophilus.
Perhaps because they were not only managers but actors and
authors they drew more varied fire and inspired dramatists
to many-faceted complaints. Colley Cibber was the butt of
the satirist almost from 1720 on; Theophilus came under attack after a managerial quarrel in the season of 1732-1733.
It was the complex relationship of dramatist, actor and management that was the subject of a satire in dramatic form on
the elder Cibber in 1723. It was entitled lengthily, To Diabouloumenon or the Proceedings at the Theatre Royal in
Drury Lane occasioned by the death of Sir Harry Wildair with
an Apotheosis spoken on that Occasion and a Tragi-Comi-
Farci-cal scene call'd Love and Friendship, or, the Rival

Passions, as it was acted before the 3 Mock Kings, Phyz,
Trunk, and Ush. Faithfully collected from the original Mss
and Journals of the House at their Majesties Command, by the
Rt. Hon. Baron Bungey, Sec. of State to their Majesties.
London 1723.[5] This anonymous satire was apparently elicited
by an advertisement in the Daily Advertiser, April 16, 1723,
which stated that Wilkes would act Sir Harry Wildair in The
Constant Couple for the last time at the Drury Lane perform-
ance of April 18.[6] Thus the satire mentions in its preface
that Wildair "expir'd at a quarter after Nine" on April 18,
1723, and that their Majesties "conven'd a Cabinet Council."
What follows at the Council of the three kings in the Green
Room identifies "their Majesties" as the three patentees of
Drury Lane—Cibber, Wilkes and Booth—and it contains a parody
of Marc Antony's funeral oration to be spoken over the dead
Wildair. The parody oration is used to point ironically to
Cibber's improvements on Shakespeare (not "Lend me your
ears" but "Pray, let me borrow your ears") and to show Cibber's conceit when Phyz (Cibber) condescends to admit that
Shakespeare was "certainly a fine writer for the times he
liv'd in . . . but all the World must allow, he fell infi-
nitely short of the Delicatesse and Belle Air of my Language" where "every Word is Bullion." Despite this boast,
Phyz later admits that he "wrote not one word of my C[are-
less] H[usband]." The satire cuts many ways by mentioning
actors, managers and writers in cross-reference to plays
both at Drury Lane and at Lincoln's Inn Fields for the 1723
season. It demonstrates effectively the dramatist's complex
relationships with theatre management, but its topicality
quickly limited what interest it had as satire on Colley
Cibber. As a sustained allegory, it is both an effective and
unusual format for dramatic satire, and the mock-laureate
oration might well have been revived when Cibber was appointed poet laureate seven years later.

Cibber's appointment to the new honor in 1730 generated
a flood of personal satire on this less than distinguished
poet. A new scene was added to Fielding's Tom Thumb, for example, satirizing the selection of the new laureate. Called
The Battle of the Poets by Scriberlus Tertius, supposedly
Thomas Cooke,[7] the scene burlesques the choice of a poet to
succeed Eusden. It is tied to the plot of Fielding's play by
having King Arthur call for the poet laureate to write an
epithalamium for the marriage of Tom Thumb and Huncamunca,

whereupon he is told that the laureate is dead. The remainder of the scene concerns the choice of a successor from the "tribe of Rimesters" standing about the King's door. The contestants who present sample poems are Sulky Bathos (Dennis),[8] Comment Profound (Lewis Theobald), Sir Fopling Fribble (Colley Cibber), Noctifer (James Ralph), and Flail (Stephen Duck). All but the last of these candidates were connected with the theatre which made the epithets and abuse by Scriblerus Tertius, whoever he was, apt though bitter. The tone is more scurrilous than the tone of Fielding in the rest of the play which suggests that Fielding is not the author of this satiric scene.

Not that Fielding did not satirize Cibber; he did as early as 1730 in his play The Author's Farce but he does so with humor. In a burlesque of Cibber's custom of pruning the plays that were submitted to his management, he has Marplay Senior and Marplay Junior (Theophilus Cibber) listen to Luckless read his play which they constantly interrupt with suggested emendations more ridiculous than the already bad blank verse. Marplay Junior even describes how he and his father cut a play before it is produced; "When a play is brought to us, we consider it as a tailor does his coat; we cut, sir, we cut it; and let me tell you, we have the exact measure of the town, we know how to fit their taste" (I, vi).

This catering to public taste may well have irritated Fielding, but The Author's Farce also hits at Colley Cibber's poetry. Charon tells the poet in Luckless's play that in order to gain entry to the court of the Goddess of Nonsense he should have a certificate from the Goddess's agent, "Mr. What d'ye call him, the gentleman that writes Odes so finely!" The pregnant pause before the ironic praise "so finely" indicates that the quarrel between Fielding and the Cibbers, begun in 1730 by some disagreement with the elder Cibber over his failure to produce one of Fielding's plays, soon moved on to an attack on the style of the new poet laureate. Yet for two years (1731-1733) Fielding was reconciled to father and son and returned to Drury Lane. He even complimented the Cibbers as actors in the Preface to his Molière adaptation, The Mock Doctor (1732). However, this was a short-lived truce; he again quarreled violently with them in 1733, and this time the breach was never healed.

Fielding nursed three objections to the Cibbers: first,

their managerial policy; second, Colley Cibber's poetry; and
third, Theophilus' bombastic style of acting. In Pasquin
(1736) he sharply ridicules Colley Cibber's poetry in the
play-within-the-play; Lord Place, in Trapwit's comedy, The
Election, finds a voter who likes sack and promises to make
him poet laureate if he wins the election (II, i). The voter
protests he cannot write poetry, but Lord Place assures him
that if he can write odes he will make an excellent laureate
even if he cannot write poetry. Fielding then followed this
up by writing a parody of Cibber's annual New Year's Ode in
the dedication of his Historical Register for the year 1736
(1737). The parody is underscored when it appears in the
play where Medley, Fielding's satiric norm, calls it "the
very Quintessence of the Odes I have seen for several years
past" (I, i). There could be no doubt about the satiric intention of such false praise, and this is six years before
Cibber was honored at the court of Dulness in Pope's final
version of The Dunciad (1743).9
    In the Historical Register Fielding also pokes fun at
Cibber's alterations of Shakespeare, for Ground Ivy (Colley
Cibber) tries to prevent the bastard son of Apollo from assigning the parts in King John until he has had time to re-
write the play; Ground Ivy proclaims "Shakespeare was a
pretty fellow, and said some things which only want a little
of my licking to do well enough; King John, as now writ,
will not do" (III, i). Here Fielding extends his former
charge of managerial pruning and rewriting beyond his earlier attack in The Author's Farce; now that his quarrel with
Cibber has been renewed, he makes Cibber as ridiculously
conceited as did the author of To Diabouloumenon. In the
same scene he burlesques the acting of Theophilus Cibber who
rushes in so boisterously that he knocks Ground Ivy down.
"Pox on't," says Ground Ivy, "the boy treads close on my
heels in a literal sense." Thus Fielding's earlier praise
of Cibberian acting in the preface of his Mock Doctor is now
changed to ridicule of the mad Pistol (Theophilus) who
shouts with gusto his lines to the crowd that has followed
him along the street while Medley assures the audience "I
warrant we don't over-act him half so much as he does his
parts."10 Fielding is thus scarcely less harsh on the son
than on the father. Nor did his enmity stop when his theatrical career came to a close but extended later into his
novels and journalistic writing.11

Theophilus Cibber attracted dramatic satire distinct from that on his father when he became involved in a managerial quarrel at Drury Lane in the season of 1732-1733. The cause for the quarrel, according to Genest, III, 373, was the complicated joint ownership of the patent for this theatre. Theophilus Cibber had acquired a part while Highmore also inherited a part on the death of Booth. The younger Cibber soon became exasperated with Highmore's inexperience and accompanied by most of the actors he left Drury Lane for the Haymarket between 1733 and 1734. Almost immediately an anonymous play The Stage Mutineers; or A Playhouse to be Lett (1733) appeared at Covent Garden. In this satire, again a rehearsal-type format, Crambo is rehearsing a play of his own, but he can please none of the actors with their parts. Each finds fault with the lines or the costume until the manager declares "This is Pistol's work who has spirited them up to this contumacy." Since Theophilus Cibber was well known for his acting of Pistol in Henry IV, II, the identification of the rebellious actor-manager-playwright is clear. Furthermore, the wardrobe keeper in enumerating the articles in his custody, mentions Apollo's withered crown of Bays which the manager commands that he keep: "let that be laid aside for Mr. Pistol; he may claim it by hereditary right." Fielding also made reference to this quarrel in his 1734 version of The Author's Farce when at the last moment before Luckless's play is to be performed, the manager comes in despair to Luckless and tells him the actors do not like their parts "and threaten to leave the house, some to Haymarket, some to Goodman's Fields, and others to set up two or three play houses in several parts of the town" (III, i). As late as 1743 the younger Cibber's withdrawal from Drury Lane was reflected in the fictitious name of the author "Fitz-Crambo" (clearly borrowed from The Stage Mutineers) in another satiric play Tyranny Triumphant and Liberty Lost; the Muses Run Mad; Apollo Struck Dumb and All Covent Garden Confounded. By this time T. Cibber was involved in a paper war with Thomas Sheridan and a new actor-manager quarrel had arisen between Charles Macklin and the rising David Garrick.[12]

Quarrels between dramatists, actors[13] and managers continued throughout the period 1720-1750, but they did little to affect the form of dramatic satire. Often they were reflected only in Prefaces and Dedications where the drama-

tist's chief complaint was his failure to get his play accepted for production. When he tried to translate quarrels
into dramatic satire, he usually resorted to farce or comedy of manners with the life of the theatre as content.
Macklin's innovation of tying a satire, The New Play Criticiz'd, to a specific play being performed was an effective
satiric use of the afterpiece. To Diabouloumenon with its
combination of allegory and parody was also an interesting
variation on the usual satiric format, and even the much
criticized pantomime was used to satirize the quarrels of
the theatrical world (see note 13). However, To Diabouloumenon was apparently never acted and thus was only influential as part of the paper warfare between actors, playwrights and managers: Macklin's innovation coming late in
this period was not imitated.

Of the major nondramatic Augustan satirists, Alexander
Pope was the chief target of dramatic satire. Perhaps this
is to be expected since his Dunciad, appearing first in
1728, had pinned so many writers to a wall of Dulness in its
catalogue of incompetent authors. Why Jonathan Swift escaped after his scathing attack on modern hacks in A Tale of
a Tub is not clear. Perhaps the stir that Swift generated in
1704 was too far in the past or he was too isolated by his
residence in Ireland. At any rate his Polite Conversation
was imitated by the social satirists[14] as were some of the
devices of Gulliver's Travels, but he himself was not satirized on the stage. Pope, however, did not escape so easily. He was close to many dramatists, and if we can believe
Benjamin Victor, he frequently advised such dramatists as
Aaron Hill and James Thomson on revisions of their plays besides his close association with John Gay's What D'Ye Call
It (1715), the farcical afterpiece that had earlier attacked Cato.

Satire on Pope was aimed both at his personality and
his scholarship, especially his translations of Homer. He
was first attacked on the stage by John Mottley and Thomas
Cooke (Hesiod Cooke) in a little known ballad opera Penelope (1728) which, according to its Preface, was inspired to
parody Pope's translations of Homeric epics. The authors
complain that Pope made Ulysses "a Figure a little below
Comedy" and as proof they cite his lines about the returning
hero:

> Propt on a Staff a Beggar old and bare
> In Rags dishonest, flutt'ring in the Air.

"We should be very glad," Mottley and Cooke comment sarcastically, "to know whether he or his Rags were dishonest. Poor King!"

Penelope is a well sustained parody of The Odyssey but written in heroic couplets to mock Pope's style. The authors thus combine the ballad opera which Gay had introduced just a few months earlier with the mock-epic technique of Pope's own satire in The Rape of the Lock. Ulysses or "Uly" is transformed in this reductio ad absurdum to a British sergeant returning from his adventures in the wars in the Lowlands to his faithful Penelope, proprietess of an ale house in London. The sign over her shop reads:

> This is the Royal Oak, the House of Penn,
> With Entertainment good for Horse and Men.

The fickle maids of Ulysses's home are condensed into a single barmaid, Dolly, who plays Penelope's suitors (Thimble, a tailor; Cleaver, a butcher; and Hopkins, a parish clerk) off against each other while accepting bribes from them all. Dolly's own heart belongs to Cleaver who boasts of the hecatombs of beef he has killed. "Tely," the son, gives a ha'penny to the strange beggar before discovering his father's Regimentals under his rags. "Uly" is identified by a mole on his toe instead of a scar on his knee. Thus the entire epic is reduced to comic parody and burlesque action. After Ulysses drives out the suitors with the help of Minerva who arrives in a burst of lightning (thereby extending the burlesque to pantomime tricks), he embraces his wife while singing her praises for not wasting her time in his absence on ombre and quadrille:

> Marbro I envy not thy mighty name
> Eternal Glory Thine, give me my Dame.

What is significant about Mottley and Brooke's Penelope is that while intended as satire on Pope's Homeric scholarship, it uses the Popian mock-heroic technique to sustain the ballad opera. What it seems to indicate is a suggested satiric

parallel between their comic parody and Pope's serious
translation of Homer. Homeric similes are thus wittily fitted by these satirists to characters who utter them. Thimble,
for example, chides Penelope by saying her heart is "stiffer
than buckram" and he professes to love her more permanently
than "staytape on a bill." Thus the style makes clear the
author's objections to Pope's inflated phrases and the
heavy Latinate diction of his Greek translations.

What motivated Mottley and Cooke to satirize Pope as a
Homeric scholar might be Cooke's self-confidence that he was
the better Greek scholar, but the real motivation is more
probably a line in the 1728 Dunciad: "Cook shall be Prior,
and Concanen, Swift" (II, 1.130). This seems borne out by
The Dunciad Variorum Pope published in April, 1729, for in
the Remarks on this line in this subsequent Catalogue of all
of his enemies, Pope identifies Cook as the author of The
Battle of Poets, "wherein our author was attack'd in his
moral character, in relation to his Homer and Shakespeare:
He writ moreover a Farce of Penelope, in the preface of
which he was also squinted at."[15] Thus Pope leaves no doubt
that the Cook of The Dunciad, Book II, line 130, is Thomas
Cooke, the co-author of Penelope which was acted at the Haymarket theatre as early as May 8, 1728.

Pope was also ridiculed in two later comedies, Mr.
Taste (1732) and The Man of Taste (1733) which appear to be
different printings of the same play.[16] Both bear the subtitle the Poetical Fop and the words on the title page "as
it was acted near Twickenham." The cast of characters in
each contains Mr. Alexander Taste who is described as "a
Poet who in spite of Deformity imagines every woman he sees
in love with him and impudently makes addresses to Lady
Airy."[17] Mr. Taste is vain and self-important in every scene
in which he appears and is viciously attacked behind his
back as "crooked in Mind and Body" (III, ii; V, iii). Taste
shows his conceit especially in raillery against contemporary authors: "Our present Sett of authors are despicable
Creatures, they have neither Genius nor Learning; and yet
are too proud to be instructed: I have given them the true
Standard of Poetry in all my Performances, but to no purpose;
for instead of endeavouring to Imitations, they rail at my
Works because they are above their Understanding" (III, ii).
This sour portrait of Pope is embellished by the other characters who describe him as a "vain, empty Fool," ignorant of

Greek, who impudently attacks all who befriend him. It is acknowledged that "the Poetical Fop" has "a good deal of ready Wit, and People laugh at the ridiculous Pictures he draws of them, without considering 'twill be their turn the next Company he comes into" (V, iii). Genest says the Taste play was the result of Pope's poem on Taste published in 1731 (X, 157-58), probably referring to the first of his Moral Epistles which appeared in that year as "Of Taste" then as "Of False Taste" and finally as "Of the Use of Riches." Pope's "Pictures" of the tasteless nouveaux riches added to those of the early Dunciad (1728) and The Dunciad Variorum (1729) might well have provoked this 1732 stage satire.

Mr. Taste's conceit is also used to raise the same objection to his Homeric translations which Mottley and Cooke had raised in Penelope, but this time the satire is more direct. Taste himself asks what the others think of Pope's Homer and then is forced to listen to Mr. Briton's sneering reply: "'Tis indeed an English Poem . . . and I aver, Sir, that it is no more a translation of Homer than the good old Ballad call'd The Siege of Troy is one." Sir Harry Oldcastle adds that it is "a Piece of Patch-Work" whose very best lines are stolen from Dryden verbatim (IV, i). Having the character who is Pope both ask for and listen to such damning criticism of his own work is an ingenious device for personal satire. However, the play ends with a farcical trick played on "the Poetical Fop" and a stern warning to him when Taste vows revenge: "forbear to asperse People's characters, and everybody will be willing to forget your past Follies: your works will be read with Pleasure and your Person respected" (V, iii). Thus when the author of the Taste play attempts to correct the satirist Pope with his own weapon, the sharp pen, his cleverness dissipates into didacticism at the final curtain. Mottley and Cooke had the better formula for beating Pope at his own game in the mock-epic Penelope.

THEORY AND FORM

Most of the dramatic satire on literature itself in this period was less concerned with theory, at least with theory of satire, than with form. As I explained in Chapter 1, very little theory of satire existed before

1750 and what did exist considered satire to be verse satire
in the classical tradition—satura or medley, a collection of
satiric targets brought together by the satirist whose only
distinctive quality was in the tone of his ridicule. Should
the satirist be genial in tone or abusive? Should he imitate,
in other words, Horace or Juvenal? As the attack on Pope indicates (in the Taste plays discussed earlier in this chapter), abusive, ad hominem attacks were generally disapproved
as circular or self-defeating because they ultimately reflected back on the satirist himself.

A few plays did consider the broader question of the
rationale for satire. Momus Turn'd Fabulist (1729), for example, acknowledged the risk of the satirist by threatening
to banish Momus from the skies if he did not stop his attack on the Gods. The threat is ignored by Momus who, like
Aesop, ingeniously makes up fables about birds and beasts to
fit his characters. Another anonymous play, Lethe Rehearsed
(1749), undertook a critical examination of the satire in
Garrick's Lethe to determine whether his satire was justified. The question of Garrick's satire is never settled in
the diffuse consideration of dramatic satire as a whole. No
consideration is given to the form of dramatic satire—its
peculiar rhetoric, its problems of plot, or even the distinct advantage of showing a satiric character in action on
the stage.

This questioning of the satirist on moral rather than
aesthetic grounds is typical of references to satire in
drama during the period of my study. The argument about
whether the satirist is justified in his choice of targets
indicates an uneasiness about the satiric method and an un-
derlying distrust and disapproval. The satirist's response
was apologia, which in fact was self-justification, claiming that he attacks only when it is necessary and that the
guiltless are never hurt by the attack. Gay offered such a
justification in the Introduction to Polly where he argued
that it is the dramatist's privilege to attack vice "however dignified and distinguished." The first player then
asks how the author can hinder the malicious application of
satire to persons. Gay's reply is typical of the satirist
shifting responsibility: "Let those answer for them who
make them. I aim at no particular persons! My strokes are at
vice in general! but if any men particularly vicious are

hurt, I make no apology, but leave them to the cure of their
own flatterers." Gay's defense is echoed by Fielding when
he was attacked for holding nothing sacred in his dramatic
satires. His Eurydice Hiss'd, for example, was criticized
in the Daily Gazeteer of May 7, 1737, for suggesting that
"all Government is but a Farce." There are things, Fielding's critic claimed, "which from the good they dispense,
ought to be sacred; such are Government and Religion. No Society can subsist without 'em; To turn either into Ridicule, is to unloose the fundamental Pillars of Society, and
shake it from its Basis." To this charge Fielding replied
with the example of Aristophanes who never hesitated to
lash at vice; exposing corruption, Fielding argued, is actually a service to the state (Common Sense, May 21, 1737).
In The Champion for January 3, 1740, Fielding argued for
the use of wit in defense of country or friend: "But when
the Defence of one's Country, or Friend, hath flowed from
Valour; or when Wit hath been used, like that of Addison or
Steel, to propagate Virtue and Morality; when, like that of
Swift, to expose Vice and Folly; it is then only, that these
become commendable, and truly worthy of our Praise and ad-
mirations." In some recently discovered verse written in defense of his cousin Lady Mary Wortley Montagu, Fielding dis-
tinguishes, further, satire which is justifiable from that
which is not:18

> Satire, the Scourge of Vice, was sure design'd
> Like Laws, to profit, not to hurt mankind.
> Nay gentler and more friendly is it's Course.
> It cures you by Persuasion, not by Force.
> Laws, while the bad they slay, the good defend,
> But Satire teaches ev'n the bad to mend.
>   (ll.72-77 of "An Epistle to Mr. Lyttleton . . .")

After chastising Pope for too personal attacks ("The
injur'd Sappho's wrongs to Verse provoke/And bid me for
a-while lay by the sock" ll.16-17), he turns to an analogy
of law, the "Knight of Post" or swearer of false evidence:
"Thus runs some little cur along the Streets/And barks, and
snaps at evr'y one he meets" (ll. 166-67). Both the verse
definition and the denunciation of Pope as a swearer of
false evidence seem to indicate that Fielding is shifting
from his satiric plays with their personal attacks to his

"Comic prose epic" novels where he claims to have "endeav-
oured to laugh mankind out of their favorite follies and
vices" (Dedication to Tom Jones).

Thomas Cooke in a preface to The Mournfull Nuptials
(1739) made a sharper defense of satire. His preface Con-
taining some Observations on Satire, and on the Present
State of our Public Entertainments declared that satire was
a touchstone of truth since "whoever endeavours to render
truth ridiculous, supposing him armed with the keenest
weapons to attack it, will lose by the assault, and go
wounded from the engagement" (p. v). In words reminiscent of
Gay's, Cooke claims only the guilty are hurt by the satirist, while "they whose abilities and manners shield them
from the point of satire are never offended by those who
scourge vice severely, and correct error gently" (p. vi).
This moral justification of satire differs little from
Shaftesbury's doctrine of corrective laughter, but satirists
have traditionally claimed moral purpose whether the cor-
rection provided is a gentle hint or a corrosive lash.

The Rev. James Miller, another prolific though less
successful satiric dramatist, added somewhat more specific
advice on the technique of satire in a long preface to his
Harlequin Horace:

> Who'er would Comedy or Satire write
> Must never spare Obscenity and Spite.
> A quantum sufficit of Smut will raise
> Crowds of Applauders to the dullest Plays;
> Whilst gross Scurrility, and pure Ill-Nature,
> Are found the best Ingredients for Satire.
>
> (4th ed., 1735, pp. 29-30)

Miller obviously followed his own advice in many of his own
plays such as Vanelia on a court scandal, The Camp Visitants
on army life, and Mr. Taste on Alexander Pope, if this un-
signed play is his. What is interesting is that he makes no
distinction between comedy and satire (a confusion shared by
most of the dramatists of this period) and that the ingredient he mentions as essential is the use of scurrility. Scurrility or billingsgate, the eighteenth-century term since
Steele's Spectator No. 451, had become the chief objection
to satire since it was thought to degrade genteel comedy.
It was an eighteenth-century reaction to the license of Res-

toration comedy of which all satirists in the 1720-1750 period were conscious. That Miller should pay lip service to
this common objection to the risqué and then employ what he
derides, and that he should speak of comedy and satire in
the same breath (or sentence) illustrates well the lack of
distinctions in theory of satire.

Miller was undoubtedly reflecting the obviously self-
conscious middle-class morality of the eighteenth century
in protesting the popularity of obscenity and scurrility in
satire. The same objection that was made to Swift's scatology could easily be applied to dramatic satire such as The
Golden Rump (on Walpole) or Colonel Split-Tail (on Colonel
Charteris) or To Diabouloumenon (on Colley Cibber), or his
own Taste play (on Pope). The live presentation of scatology
or billingsgate on the stage would be more evident and
therefore even less acceptable than on the printed page.
The problem of the dramatic satirist was to construct a format that could withstand repeated performances and not al-
ienate the audience at least until the author's benefit
night. The audience, not the bookseller, was the dramatist's
bread and butter. The dramatist in the anonymous The Author's Triumph (1737), for example, cautions his valet who
has been belaboring the Poet Laureate, "Hold, hold—you grow
rude—" (Preface) while Mecaenas later lectures the Managers
and Players to choose authors who avoid obscenity. "Your
Satyr must be levell'd at Vice alone, for personal abuse is
Cruelty. . . . Wit must be ever attendant on good Manners"
(sc. iv).

In the neo-classical argument over rules for the drama,
the dramatic satirists were more consistent and more specific. The crux of the argument for this period shifted emphasis away from the difficulty of fitting Shakespeare's
plays to the unities of time, place and action. Dryden had
already established in An Essay on Dramatic Poesy that there
was something to be said for Shakespeare even if he did not
conform to classical measurement. It is, therefore, in the
tradition of Dryden's emancipating criticism that eighteenth-century dramatic satire on the rules takes its stand.
The emphasis for this period is whether rules are necessary
at all.[19]

Dramatic satirists after 1720 did not often suggest a
complete overthrow of classical models but in this extension
of the quarrel between the Ancients and the Moderns that had

engaged Wotton, Bentley, Temple and Swift, their attacks
were usually the expression of a middle position that respected the ancients but did not hold their rules sacred.
Charles Johnson is a good example of this middle position.
It was not his wish to shelve the classicists and trust entirely to individual judgment. In the prologue to his play
The Female Fortune Teller (1726), he did satirize slavish
adherence to rules as amounting to absurdity and boasted
that in his play he had broken them all. Few would disagree
with him. Henry Carey's Hanging and Marriage (1721) had already burlesqued the unities by designating time, place and
action, "Time even with the action, Place a little country
village, Action as follows." Dramatists appeared to wish to
advertise their knowledge of Aristotle, Horace or Boileau
rather than to follow their rules.

Fielding attacked the close adherence to rules in his
Covent Garden Tragedy (1732). The play is a ridiculous jumble of nonsense in which people supposedly dead appear again
at the end and the "tragedy" concludes with a dance. While
it is also a satire on heroic tragedy, as will be discussed
later, the essential satire is directed to the pseudo-classical. In the Prolegomena Fielding pretends to quote from a
critic who has analyzed his tragedy. This mock critic examines the play and gives a definition of tragedy that is an
absurd travesty of classical criticism: "a Tragedy is a
thing of five acts, written dialoguewise, consisting of several fine similes, metaphors, and moral phrases, with here
and there a speech upon liberty . . . it must contain an action, characters, sentiments, diction and a moral." Yet the
mock critic is made an ignorant lout who misspells the ancients as Aristutle and Horase and recommends that Fielding
read the "Tragedies of Plautus" to find a model for the sentiments of love. Fielding here seems to be hitting more at
the ignorance and misinterpretations of those critics who
are rigidly tied to the classics than at classical rules
themselves.

In a later play like Pasquin (1736) with a rehearsal
formula, Fielding provided himself with a better opportunity of satirizing rules when Trapwit and Fustian, the two
playwrights, offer frequent criticisms of each other's plays
as they watch the double rehearsal. It is Trapwit's comedy
that receives the bulk of the satire. Fustian asks what the
fable or design is, and Trapwit replies, "Oh, you ask who is

to be married! Why, sir, I have a marriage; I hope you think
I understand the laws of comedy better than to write without
marrying somebody" (I, i). But Fustian cannot understand how
the previous scene is conducive to marriage, and he continues to question Trapwit about the motivation. Thereupon.
Trapwit declares he is no shallow modern writer who pub-
lishes all the banns of the couples in the first act. Instead he does it in one stroke at the end, and until that
time, "I defy you to guess my couple till the thing is done,
slap, all at once." Trapwit exposes more than his plot and
motivation to ridicule. Fielding also uses him to satirize
the rule about offstage action. When Fustian objects to Miss
Mayoress saying she has used her lover ill, since she has
never before spoken to him, Trapwit justifies himself by
claiming the lovers have spoken many times before, "behind
the scenes, sir. What would you have everything brought
upon the stage? . . . I have Horace's advice on my side; we
have many things both said and done in our comedies which
might be better performed behind the scenes" (III, i). Thus
Fielding satirizes rules by having Trapwit pull a rule out
of the hat to justify his worst inconsistencies.

In his prologue to Lillo's <u>Fatal Curiosity</u> (1736) Fielding openly showed his scorn for slavish imitation of the
classical rules. The prologue approves Lillo's choice of a
character from the middle class, even if the choice is not
in accordance with the classical concept of the tragic
hero.[20] In Lillo's play, Fielding assured the audience,
there would be no "royal robes" nor would the tragic muse be
degraded to suit the author's "language or his wit." Lillo,
then, will avoid the fault of pseudo-classical writers in
whose plays "Fine things are said," yet any one of the characters "might speak them all." Thus Fielding's direct statement that Rules are to be used with caution and good sense
is consistent with the irony of his satire in <u>Pasquin</u>.

Frequently Fielding and other dramatists extended their
satire on slavish imitators of the classics to include imitation of French authors. Fielding, for example, despite his
own adaptations of Molière's <u>The Mock Doctor</u> (1732) and <u>The
Miser</u> (1733), has Trapwit in <u>Pasquin</u> justify his ridiculous
comedy as a "play consisting of humour, nature, and simplicity; it is written in the exact and true spirit of Molière"
(I, i). He would thus seem to be condemning Trapwit for a
habit to which he was himself addicted. But Trapwit also

points out that he is not beginning his play, "like most of
our modern comedies, with three or four gentlemen who are
brought on only to talk with." It was this trite practice of
stealing jokes from wits and calling it comedy which caused
Fielding to adapt Molière's The Miser as a change for the
dull fare of:

> A dull collection of insipid jokes,
> Some stale from conversation, some from books.
>
> (Prologue)

In other words Fielding offered in 1733 the same justification for copying from the French that he has Trapwit offer
in 1736. Yet Fielding is not as inconsistent as this seems,
nor is he allowing himself to do what he ridicules in others. It is Trapwit's misunderstanding of Aristotelian unities and his citing of Molière's authority for the wrong
reason—a sop to Frenchified taste[21]—that Fielding is satirizing. Thus it is not classicism or neo-classicism that
Fielding attacks but the abuse of such models.

David Garrick, early in his career, joined Fielding's
attack on mediocre imitations of the French. In an epilogue
written for James Ralph's The Astrologer (1744), he chas-
tized dramatists for borrowing models from across the chan-
nel:

> Long have our senseless playwrights, void of spirit,
> From Molière's humour pilfer'd all their merit;
> Our author scorn'd in foreign climes to roam,
> He thought some merit might be found at home.

Undoubtedly a strong argument against imitation of the
French was the neglect of "merit" which might be found in
English drama. Yet English drama did not conform to classical rules as French drama did. In the contest of patriotism
with classical rules, both Garrick and Fielding opposed
slavish imitation of the French and joined the tradition of
Dryden who refused to throw out English drama that did not
fit rules.[22] Significantly, none of the dramatists' satire
on rules contributes to a theory of dramatic satire. No distinctions are made between comedy and satire to distinguish
the separate modes. Thus the Ancients versus Moderns controversy as reflected in the drama of this period is only a

decorative reflection of the larger neo-classical controversy.

In 1729 Samuel Johnson of Cheshire brought out a
strange anomaly that profoundly stirred the theatrical
world, Hurlothrumbo, in which Johnson himself acted the part
of Lord Flame. It is composed of so great a jumble of fine
sentiments and unintelligible rant that it is practically
impossible to tell the author's intention. Nevertheless
this confused production was given almost daily in its first
season and the credit for its immediate success apparently
was due to Johnson's acting as Lord Flame (Biog. Dram., I,
402-3, reports he walked on stilts, played a violin, sang
lustily, danced with mincing steps, all the while proclaim-
ing nonsense which no one could understand). The difficulty
in determining whether this play is satire is that it is
not certain whether this Samuel Johnson was sane. It was
suspected by Fielding and others from the rival company at
the Haymarket where Hurlothrumbo was acted that Johnson's
wild raving was only an outlet for a tortured imagination
(he appears in The Author's Farce saying his name is "Hurlo
borumbo-rumbo-Hurloborumbolo," III, 1), yet if it is not entirely a product of madness, it is possible that Johnson's
play was intended to expose the completely false taste for
drama.23 If Johnson's purpose was to ridicule dramatic taste,
his play was the most wholesale condemnation of drama to appear in this period. For its implication is that all drama
is nonsense or the half-mad raving of a lord on stilts,
playing a violin while he pours out fustian and bombast.
Johnson's play, therefore, would go far beyond satire on the
rules of the Ancients; it would suggest that all drama is
inexcusable folly.

Usually, as I indicated at the beginning of this section, the dramatic satirists were much more specific in
their criticism of form than they were of theory. Some of
the newer forms such as ballad opera and domestic tragedy
escaped almost unscathed but pantomime, sentimental comedy
and Italian opera were not so fortunate. Of the older forms
heroic tragedy bore the brunt of dramatic satire although
there were also hits at Dedications, Prologues and Epilogues.

The only popular new dramatic form of which there seems
to have been no articulate criticism was domestic tragedy.
One explanation is that Fielding, the sharpest dramatic satirist after 1730, was sympathetic to the form.24 Another explanation is that the form was not yet well defined. Profes-

sor Ernest Bernbaum in his study (The Drama of Sensibility,
1915, pp. 163 ff.) points out the lack of definite leadership for sentimental or domestic tragedy during the years
1732-1750, and Arthur Sherbo (English Sentimental Drama,
1957) agrees that its development was greater after 1750.
Before that date the plots of domestic tragedy are divided
between the tragedy of fate and the tragedy of character,
while the development of such plots into the problem play
would come much later. There was also variety in the style.
Lillo wrote The History of George Barnwell (1731) in prose,
but John Hewitt used blank verse in The Fatal Falsehood
(1734). Domestic tragedy was not, therefore, well enough
established in either plot or style to elicit parody or
satire on its form. Furthermore its subject matter lent dignity to the middle class with which the dramatist was by
this time identified. Thus just as the dramatist curbed his
social satire on this class, so he also spared the dramatic
form which most elevated the middle class.

The meteoric success of John Gay's The Beggar's Opera
(1728) that marked the beginning of the popularity of another new form, the ballad opera, was initially hailed as
salutary for the English stage. The prologue to Colley Cibber's Love in a Riddle (1729) celebrated the return to
English songs:

> If songs are harmless Revels of the Heart
> Why should our native Tongue not bear the Part.

Genest even credits The Beggar's Opera with driving Italian
opera out of England for a season (III, 222-23). Yet The
Beggar's Opera, while it produced many imitators, did not
establish a single form. Nicoll (p. 239) lists a variety of
imitations extending from farce to pastoral and sentimental
ballad operas. It is obvious from such an extensive list
that ballad opera implied only a dramatic entertainment composed of a series of popular airs accompanied by a running
text of prose, rhymed verse, or occasionally even blank
verse. With such diversity there was little definite about
its form for the satirist to attack. The form might vary
from Essex Hawker's mock pastoral, The Wedding (1729) to
George Lillo's painfully sentimental pastoral, Sylvia (1730).
With no dominant form as target, the satirist hit at its
popularity or influence.

A few sentimentalists, for example, attacked Gay's The Beggar's Opera on the grounds that it encouraged thieves,[25] but these were moral essayists not dramatic satirists. Anthony Aston's short play, The Fool's Opera (1731), was a satire on Gay's personal success,[26] but Gabriel Odingsells in the Preface to his farcical Bayes's Opera (1730) disclaimed any intention of satirizing Gay. In fact he asserted that in no instance was his burlesque aimed to expose the celebrated author of The Beggar's Opera. And while the inclusion of Mr. Ballad in the cast of James Ralph's The Fashionable Lady or Harlequin's Opera might appear as criticism of the form, the same cast included Harlequin and other stock characters of pantomime so that the emphasis does not fall on Mr. Ballad. Thus most of the dramatic satire on ballad opera was incidental or in Aston's play, personal, while the charge against its influence as an encouragement to pickpockets and highwaymen came chiefly from outside the theatres.

The fact that ballad opera was little criticized by dramatists seems logical when it is recognized that The Beggar's Opera itself was in part a satire on a rival form of entertainment, the Italian opera. Every loyal Englishman would be likely to criticize Italian opera before ballad opera with English songs. The testimony of the welcome which dramatists extended to the new form is to be found in the long list of ballad operas written especially in the middle years of this period, 1728-1738. Furthermore the structure of this type of musical comedy was so pliant, so capable of infinite variations that it was difficult for the satirist to isolate glaring absurdities as characteristic of its style. Obviously it was too successful a form of dramatic satire in itself for the satirist to attempt to drive it off the stage.

With pantomime, however, the dramatic satirist was not so lenient because it was considered an innovation that definitely debased drama. While ballad opera was indigenous, pantomime, like Italian opera, smacked of foreign influence. Unlike ballad opera, which offered possibilities of humor and originality to the ingenious satirist, pantomime was regarded as derivative and a perversion of taste. First it was a crowding together of tricks of staging, of dancing, singing, and occasional dialogue into a haphazard entertainment. Secondly it brought a flood of foreigners to compete with

English actors since French dancers were more popular than
native talent.27 However, its amorphous structure and its
encouragement of French performers did not prevent pantomime from becoming popular. Managers were sympathetic because it increased the size of their audiences. Genest records (III, 158) that the price of a box rose from four to
five shillings because the managers were able to demand
more from a public which eagerly attended the performance of
pantomime. It was facts like these which the dramatic satirist seized upon in ridiculing this dramatic form.

The appearance of Harlequin Dr. Faustus and The Necromancer at John Rich's theatre in the season of 1723-1724
forced pantomime into prominence. Almost immediately there
was a satiric reaction to it. The anonymous farce, The British Stage (1724), attacked it for its continental influence.
The title page explains that The British Stage is presented
"as it was performed by the Company of Wonderful Comedians
at both Theatres, with Universal Applause; with all its
Original Songs, Scenes, and Machines. Design'd as an After-
Entertainment for the Audiences of Harlequin Dr. Faustus
and The Necromancer." However the satire of this farce was
not all aimed at the distasteful foreign flavor of pantomime. It also exaggerated into absurdity all stage directions to illustrate the extravagance of the stage business
of pantomime performances. The dragon comes on spitting
fire; there is a dance of ghosts and devils; and one stage
direction reads, "enter Windmill."

In 1727 Lewis Theobald devoted his pantomime opera,
The Rape of Proserpine, to satire on this form. In the Dedication to Thomas Chamber, Esq., Theobald acknowledged the
popularity of pantomime while he also insisted that when
public taste returns to drama as opposed to this foolish
entertainment, "no one shall rejoice more sincerely than
myself." The structure of Theobald's play satirized the particular form of pantomime most popular on the English stage—
alternations of serious mythological scenes with grotesque
scenes of Harlequin and his companions. After scene three,
the play switches from the Ceres-Proserpine plot to a
farmyard where, according to a stage direction, "the grotesque part begins." Some of the "grotesque part" is then
inserted after each of the three succeeding scenes. At the
end of scene six there is a nonsensical raree-show in which
the actor recites dialect verse in the broad accent of a

Frenchman—proof that an important objection was the importation of foreign actors:

> De first ting be de true Picture of de great magnificent
>   city of Londre,
> Dat fill every Part of de Vorld vid surprize, Pleasure
>   and Vondre;
> Here de cunning French, de vise Italian, and de Spaniard
>   rumre,
> And vere can dey go else, marbleau, to get von Quarter of
>   de Money.

There is also reference in these verses to a French actress, Mme. Violante, who can "jump upon de Rope ten stories high and never break her neck," and the actor concludes, "so prodigious Entertainment vil never be again dis tousand year!"

Immediately following the exaggerated horseplay of this raree-show, the scene again turns back to the serious, a "solitude" where Jupiter restores the raped Proserpine to earth for half of every year. In these serious mythological scenes Theobald is mocking the theory of John Weaver, a dancing master, who argued for classical pantomime as opposed to the horseplay of the spoken French and Italian varieties.[28] Thus the last scene closes with the dancers miming the marriage of Pluto and Proserpine, and Theobald out-mixes the mixture.

Gabriel Odingsells' Bayes's Opera (1729) offered even sharper satire on pantomime as a form of stage entertainment. Odingsells to make his purpose clear takes the reader into his confidence in the Preface to his play. It was not his intention to satirize the ballad opera; instead, he says, "It was my view to alarm Men of Sense to a care of the Liberal Arts, which seem to languish, and, at their last Gasp, invoke their Assistance to raise them." In order to demonstrate the perversion of taste, Odingsells used the Buckingham rehearsal formula which Fielding was to adopt a year later. The plot of Bayes's opera is an allegory of Pantomime capturing the throne of Wit; the action is explained from time to time by the author for the benefit of spectators watching the rehearsal. At the beginning the throne of Wit is already occupied by a usurper, Cantata, but with the aid of Harlequin and Lord Briton, Pantomime is able

to depose even Italian opera and seize the coveted place of
honor. Lord Briton claims to represent the voice of a brave
and witty people as he joins the forces of General Pantomime
(II, i). Odingsells thus places the blame for the success
of pantomime on the shoulders of all Englishmen who are
corrupt enough in taste to become followers of this new
foreign form of entertainment.

   Odingsells uses his allegory also to satirize the origin of Pantomime who is discovered in a cobbler's stall.
Bayes explains that this "shows you that Prince Pantomime
and his ancestors have hitherto lived in obscurity—the Idol
only of the Dregs of the People, Cobblers and Tinkers. Here
it is that British wisdom finds him out, and weighing his
merits, exalts him to the throne of Wit" (II, i). A value
judgment on pantomime as opposed to virtue and good sense is
added when Arabella, one of the spectators, asks Bayes why
all the characters that stand for sense and virtue have extremely short roles or appear only as objects of contempt.
Bayes claims to have many reasons for this structural device. "In the first place, I know the genius and Temper of
my Audience; and know 'tis my Business to make them laugh
and not to make them wise. . . . The chain of my allegory
. . . oblig'd me to represent 'em such, in order to display
the more lively contrast of Pantomime" (II, ii). Finally
Odingsells hits at the lack of organization that reduced
plot in pantomime to a cipher. For when Belinda apologizes
to Bayes for interrupting his play as she is abruptly called
away from the rehearsal, Bayes claims that it makes no difference:

   I can break off my Affairs as abruptly without any detri-
   ment to Plot or Conduct in any Particular. For in this new
   art of Wit, where we are confined to no Dramatic Rules, we
   are allowed the same liberty that is us'd by the Heros at
   Figg's Theatre—we can represent our Gods and Demons on the
   stage, make 'em flourish their several Ensigns, play their
   Bouts and retire.
                                                    (III, i)

   Odingsells' satiric voice was soon joined by others.
James Ralph, in his Prologue to Fielding's The Temple Beau
(1730), objected to the popularity of pantomime on the
grounds that it was banishing wit and humor from the stage.

Now, he says, only show will go down, "And Harlequin's the
darling of the Town." And Fielding in a song at the end of
his burlesque pantomime, <u>Tumble Down Dick; or, Phaeton in
the Suds</u> (1736), also testified to the universal taste for
the antics of Harlequin:

> From Fleet Street to Limehouse the City's his range
> He's a saint in his shop, and a knave on the Change.
>
> (Air V)

In fact this entire play is a satire on pantomime as the
burlesque full title makes clear; Fielding called his hodgepodge "a Dramatic Entertainment of Walking in Serious and
Foolish Characters. Interlarded with a Burlesque, Grotesque,
Comic Interlude, called <u>Harlequin a Pick-Pocket</u>. As it was
performed at the New Theatre in Haymarket. Being ('tis
hoped) the last Entertainment that will ever be exhibited
on any stage." Thus Fielding declares in the title his intention of satirizing pantomime out of existence.

Here again Fielding uses the rehearsal format. Machine,
the author of this ambitiously ridiculous "Entertainment,"
orders the Prompter to cut Acts I and V of <u>Othello</u> in order
to provide sufficient time for his afterpiece. When Fustian
objects to mangling Shakespeare for this "trumpery," Fielding has the Prompter reply with the telling argument, "Sir,
this gentleman brings more money to this house than all the
poets put together" (sc. i). Also satirized are the ambitious pretensions of the pantomime author who wants to justify his work on the authority of the Ancients. Machine,
for example, lets Harlequin escape after much buffoonery because, "Aristotle, in his book concerning entertainments,
has it laid down as a principal rule, that Harlequin is always to escape" (sc. iii). Furthermore Machine makes a stud-
ied attempt to write as unnaturally as possible. When it is
suggested that it would be more natural to have the gods in
his play speak in heroic couplets and Clymene, the oyster
wench, in prose, Machine replies, "You think it would be
more natural; so do I, and for that reason have avoided it;
for the chief beauty of an entertainment, sir, is to be un-
natural" (sc. vii).

Machine's entertainment is thus a parody of the standard pantomime performance. It begins with the mythological
story of Phaeton, the son of Phoebus and Clymene, a Grecian

oyster wench, with grotesque scenes of Harlequin inserted
into the middle. Like Odingsells, Fielding places pantomime's origin in a cobbler's stall. But the mythological
story in this instance is scarcely dignified because Phaeton
is taunted by all the "parish boys" with the story of his
illegitimate birth. Fielding also seized the occasion of
Phaeton's destruction of his father's "lanthorn" to satirize
a popular pantomime stage trick. For Jupiter, now that the
sun has been destroyed, does not want another one; he says
there are already two at Drury Lane and one at Covent Garden
that hatches an egg with Harlequin inside.[29] Thus by fusing
mythology with the tricks of actual stage production Fielding ridiculed the sensational staging that was responsible
for much of the success of pantomime. The Prompter (April 2,
1736) commended "Mr. F---d--g" for coming to the defense of
common sense in this play where his burlesque is not only a
satire on the form of pantomime but a condemnation of the
public who craved novelty at the expense of quality on the
stage. He had previously hinted at his distaste for pantomime by making Monsieur Pantomime one of the contestants
for the rank of poet laureate at the Court of Nonsense (The
Author's Farce) and he continued his attack through Pasquin
where the Queen of Ignorance is made the patroness of Harlequin and his fellow performers. When the London theatres
send hostages to this new Queen of Ignorance, she replies
that if they come from Sadler's-Wells, "then are they indeed foes to Common Sense"—her enemy.[30] With Pasquin and
Tumble Down Dick appearing in the same year (1736), Fielding
deservedly earned the praise of The Prompter for defending
common sense. Tumble Down Dick is a consistent and effective
satire on pantomime.

Sarcastic references to John Rich, or to his stage
name Lun, are too frequent to list, but they reflect, as
the previous section of this chapter suggests, the dramatists' scorn for the man they considered chiefly responsible
for promoting pantomime by hiring conjurors, foreign dancers, or designers of new stage tricks to attract audiences.
However, the continuing objection to the formlessness of
pantomime was a more significant subject of dramatic satire.
John Kelly's one-act ballad opera, The Plot (1735), satirizes the structure of pantomime by including two Harlequins, one English and one French, to emphasize the debased
plot of pantomime. Another anonymous play, Harlequin Student; or, the Fall of Pantomime: With the Restoration of

the Drama, was performed several times as an afterpiece at
Goodman's Fields in 1741.[31] This mock-pantomime ended with
a representation of Shakespeare's monument and attempted to
drive pantomime off the stage by its tribute to the genius
of Shakespeare.[32] Finally, David Garrick, in a prologue at
the opening of Drury Lane in 1750, closes the period by adding his voice to the dramatists' plea to preserve the English stage against spectacle and pantomime. The same prologue advocates a return to English tragedy as opposed to
the debased fantasies from foreign sources. Thus it is evident that from The British Stage; or, The Exploits of Harlequin (1724) to Garrick's prologue in 1750 dramatists ridiculed pantomime as non-English and therefore fit only to be
banned from native drama. The mock-pantomime was the most
effective satiric form because very little exaggeration was
needed to prove that lack of structure was the chief dramatic weakness of pantomime. The appeal to common sense as
the enemy of pantomime is consistent from Odingsells
through Fielding and Kelly to Harlequin Student. By 1750
there is some evidence that the public was beginning to
tire of the perpetual theatrical devices to attract their
attention to the pantomime stage. A poem On a Late Action at
the Haymarket Theatre appeared in the Universal Magazine in
1749(IV, 41) which cried shame on theatrical managers who
enticed their audiences by "giddy lies in public papers."
This poet particularly points to false promises made in ad-
vertisements for pantomime:

> no, let me speak in brief,
> The Audience fools, the Conjuror's a Thief.

The dramatic satire on Italian opera resembles that on
pantomime in that both reflect the element of loyalty to native English drama. While commedia dell'arte, classical
myths, and Italian and French performers were all attacked
by satirists of pantomime, the influence of foreign musi-
cians was strongest in the foreign operas introduced into
England in the first decade of the eighteenth century.[33]
The stage satirists early in this period were not always
clear on the object of attack. If a dramatic form was French,
it was bad; if it was Italian, it was very bad, and satire
on pantomime and opera is sometimes almost indistinguishable
in the same play. A play attributed to Thomas D'Urfey, The

English Stage Italiniz'd (1727), illustrates this confusion. It is undeniably a satire on pantomime since it consists of five acts with no dialogue; only stage directions
are given. The title also indicates a burlesque of pantomime, for it is called a New Entertainment called Dido and
Aeneas: or Harlequin, a Butler, a Pimp, a Minister of State,
Generalissimo, and Lord High Admiral, dead and alive again,
and at last crowned King of Carthage by Dido. All the ingredients are present for a satire on pantomime. Yet the advertisement at the end of the play introduces another satiric purpose. There it proclaims that "For the Benefit of
the English Quality, and others who have forgotten their
Mother-Tongue, This Play is translating into Italian by an
able Hand." This thrust at the Italianization of the English
upper class appears to be satire on Italian opera. The Introduction further illustrates the confusion. Here the author, addressing his readers, says "you are not insensible
to what a pitch of Perfection we have brought the Italian
opera here in England. The Italian language will be either
totally introduc'd in England, or the English tongue taught
to Italian comedians." The satirist is clearly more worried
about the dilution of the English stage language than he is
about the consistency of his attack.

Of course not all dramatists confused their satire on
pantomime with satire on Italian opera. The opera presented
difficulties that were peculiar to itself, and in these distinguishing characteristics the satirist found most of his
ammunition just as he eventually, with Gay's direction,
found a new vehicle in the ballad opera. One reason for the
dramatists' hostility was that Italian opera was expensive
to produce. Its scenery was elaborate and its properties infinite as Addison had already pointed out when he sarcastically told of canaries released on the stage. Furthermore
the singers who drew large salaries were chiefly Italian.
Finally the emphasis in an opera was on music at the expense
of plot or libretto style. It was, therefore, considered degrading to English drama. Plainly there were sufficient in-
centives for satire on opera in addition to the purely pa-
triotic argument that it was foreign.

Dramatists were never able to conceal exasperation with
English taste which fostered Italian opera. Henry Carey, for
example, in his poem, A Satyr on the Luxury and Effeminacy
of the Age, blamed the affectation of the age on the taste

for singing in Italian.[34] Colley Cibber, who also complained
of the "gothic taste" which encouraged spectacle and song,
was certain that polite society might have been better
pleased with his Caesar in Egypt (1724) "had Caesar been
sung." (Prologue) But it was John Gay who established the
precedent for satirizing the plot of Italian opera in dramatic form. Gay had complained of the popularity of Italian
opera as early as his play, The Captives (1724), in an acid
epilogue:

> Ev'n in this house I've known some tender Fair,
> Touch'd with meer sense alone, confess a Tear.
> But the soft voice of an Italian Wether,
> Makes them all languish Three Whole hours together.
> And where's the wonder? Plays, like Mass, are sung,
> (Religious drama) in an unknown tongue.

Other dramatists added their objections to Gay's. Sagely,
in James Moore-Smythe's The Rival Modes (1727), complained
that "the composers of our operas scorn to call in the Assistance of good Poetry that they may show how the science
of Musick can shine by itself" (Act I). And Lewis Theobald,
in the Dedication of his Rape of Proserpine (1727), explained that good poetry was at a premium in opera because
of the expensiveness of the productions; with the cost of
hiring foreign voices, poetry must suffer. Then Gay by using
English airs in his Newgate opera to mock the musical taste
of his countrymen found the most effective formula for satirizing Italian opera in The Beggar's Opera (1728). From the
Introduction when the Beggar poet makes clear his intention
to parody the operatic style ("I have introduced the similes that are in all your celebrated operas: the swallow,
the moth, the bee, the ship, etc.") to the end when the
Player objects to hanging Macheath "because an opera must
end happily" Gay maintains his satire of Italian opera. The
Beggar gives in to the objection about the hanging: "Your
objection, sir, is very just; and is easily remov'd. For you
must allow, that in this kind of drama, 'tis no matter how
absurdly things are brought about—so you Rabble there run
and cry a Reprieve—let the Prisoner be brought back to his
wives in Triumph" (III, xvi). In the quarrel between Polly
and Lucy he also burlesques the rivalry of the two most
prominent operatic stars, Faustina and Cussoni. Recent

scholars have also found parodies of several of the leading
operatic composers in bravura passages.[35] Thus mixed with
his political satire and his social satire, Gay folded in
great variety also in his satire on Italian opera.

Henry Carey shared Gay's contempt for the plot structure of Italian opera, but he satirized it through fantasy.
In two of his ballad operas he burlesqued the usual serious
plot which involved great and noble action at the expense of
logical and effective dramatic organization. In The Dragon
of Wantley (1737) it is a huge dragon who is at the center
of the plot. This monster has been bothering Wantley and
adjacent districts of Yorkshire. When the citizens apply to
Moore, a valiant knight, to relieve them of this scourge,
he refuses to undertake the task until he has been promised
Margery as a reward. The plot goes berserk when he has to
postpone his fight with the dragon in order to prevent Maux-
alinda, a former mistress, from killing Margery with a bod-
kin. After this comic juxtaposition of heroic battle and a
lover's jealousy, the dragon is finally slain and the play
ends happily while Gublins proclaims:

> The Loves of this brave Knight, and my fair Daughter
> In Roratorios shall be sung hereafter.   (Act III)

In the sequel, The Dragoness or Margery (1738), Carey again
burlesqued operatic plot. Here Margery, now Lady Moore, has
become a termagant, and the "valiant knight" has returned to
his former mistress. Again there is a happy ending to an improbable situation. That Carey's satire is intentional is
evident from constant reference to opera, as when Gublins
says:

> What are your Operas to me? . . .
> No Musick under the Sky
> Can equall the Hounds at full cry. (II, ii)

Despite the satire of Gay and Carey, the taste for
opera continued. William Havard's friend who wrote the prologue to Havard's tragedy, King Charles I (1737), did not
expect the play to win favor because:

> Our bard, as then, despises song and dance,
> The Notes of Italy, and jigs of France.

Perhaps the most damning satire on the elitist taste for
opera is to be found in Francis Lynch's The Independent Patriot (1737) where "at Musick's trunk the furious Ax he
drives." (Prologue) Dulcissa, the foolish woman of fashion
in this play, cannot endure English music. Nothing pleases
her unless it is Italian. "My poor Mama took me once to see
the filthy Beggar's Opera, thinking to reconcile me to English Musick; but she heartily repented her; for I sicken'd
of the Small-pox that very Night" (II, i). Anyone who prefers comedies or tragedies to opera is, in the opinion of
this silly young lady, a stranger to politeness. Yet despite
her passion for opera, Dulcissa has no ear and screams
shrilly when she is learning to sing. Her most absurd error
is mistaking a song sung in Irish dialect for one of her be-
loved Italian arias (III, i). Yet Dulcissa is presented as
typical of the fashionable ladies who encourage opera as if
Lynch were saying, "See, Gay's Beggar's Opera failed to
drive Italian opera off the stage."

Fielding, as might be expected, agreed with Havard and
Lynch about the perversion of taste which was responsible
for the popularity of opera. The author in Eurydice (1737)
speaks for him, "Why sir, for an English people to support
an extravagant Italian opera, of which they understand nor
relish the sense nor the sound, is as heartily ridiculous
and much of a piece with an eunuch's keeping a mistress"
(sc. iii). His coarse joke about eunuchs is repeated in Medley's play-within-a-play, The Historical Register (1737),
where the ladies make a snickering reference to the wax
children of the famous Italian castrato singer, Farinelli,
and Medley as author underscores the satire by calling this
"the most extraordinary accident" if Farinelli has children,
for as he says, "if we go on to improve in luxury, effeminacy and debauchery, as we have done lately, the next age,
for aught I know, may be more like the children of squeak-
ing Italians than hardy Britons" (II, i).

The Italian castrati were frequently the butt of dra-
matic satire. Fielding punned on the name of Farinelli as
Squeakaronelly, but he also added a symbolic Signior Warb-
lerini in Tumble Down Dick, and Signior Cantileno in Miss
Lucy in Town (1742). Treblini in the anonymous Cupid and
Psyche (1734) and Signior Dorima in Lewis Theobald's The
Happy Captives (1741) are similar examples. Fielding even
had the audacity to ask another male Italian singer (Miss

<u>Lucy in Town</u>) what use he would have for a mistress. Thus
the dramatists joined the journalists (see the <u>Universal
Spectator</u> for October 5, 1735) and artists (see Hogarth's
"The Opera House or the Italian Eunuch's Glory") in capi-
talizing on the popular belief that the unnaturally high
Italian male voices were possible only in eunuchs. The fact
that Farinelli's salary of Ł1500 for 1734-1735 was increased
by Ł5000 in gifts from his admirers, undoubtedly increased
their asperity.[36]

In one of his last plays, <u>The Wedding Day</u> (1743),
Fielding ridiculed the taste for opera by suggesting it was
chiefly the taste of butlers and valets. Brazen, a servant
to Millamour in this play, begins a soliloquy:

> [<u>alone with an opera book in his hand</u>] Well I can not come
> into the opinion of the town about this last opera. It is
> too light for my gout. Give me your solemn, sublime music.
> But pox take their taste: I know scarce five footmen in
> town who can distinguish. The rascals have no ear, no
> judgment. I would as soon ask a set of country squires
> what they liked. I remember the time when we should not
> have suffered such stuff as this to have gone down. Oh
> dear, <u>si caro</u>.
>
> (III, viii)

and he goes off singing.

Most of the dramatic satirists would have followed
Fielding in consigning Opera to be a follower of the Goddess Nonsense (as he did in <u>The Author's Farce</u>). Its poor
plots, debased poetry, and highly paid performers equally
offended writers for the stage. Thus they had little pa-
tience for the singers' quarrels and irritability. An anonymous play, <u>The Contre Temps: or Rival Queens</u> (1727), laid
the scene of the quarrel between "Queen" Faustina and
"Princess" Cuzzoni, which Gay referred to in <u>The Beggar's
Opera</u>, in the Hall of Discord where the High Priest of Discord meets with the Professor of Harmony and the Choir Director to settle the dispute. It is a form of satire anticipatory of Fielding's allegorical plays-within-plays. But
whether satire on opera took this allegorical form or the
burlesque form of Gay's <u>Beggar's Opera</u> or Lynch's <u>The Independent Patriot</u>, it is evident that opera next to pantomime united dramatic satirists. Of all the reasons for the

decadence of the English stage in this period, it was the
popularity of these two forms that was most often attacked
as the responsible factor.

Another relatively new dramatic form that aroused satire was sentimental comedy. It is not difficult to understand why this new development in comedy should stimulate
satire. For sentimental comedy was based on a theory vastly
different from the classical concept of comedy as essen-
tially laugh-provoking. Nor was it developed from the Aristotelian theory that humor is caused by the spectator's
perception of incongruity. In fact sentimental comedy had
very little to do with humor. It was, as the Tatler No. XXI
made clear, intimately concerned with the necessity for the
comic writer to achieve a reformation of the audience by an
irresistible appeal to the heart. This appeal, it was suggested, could be accomplished by the juxtaposition of right
against wrong. Thus the opposition of right and wrong and
the ultimate triumph of virtue was said to be the true
source of the comic spirit. Richard Steele, in describing
the purpose of sentimental comedy, even defined virtue as
"that agreeableness of behavior, with the intermixture of
pleasing passions which arise from innocence."[37] This emphasis on the "pleasing passions," on agreeable behavior, and
on innocence provides the tone of this moral comedy. That so
great a distortion of the theory of comedy should cause a
reaction is not remarkable; on the contrary, it seems almost
inevitable that a form of comedy which inspired tears instead of laughter, should be the butt of dramatic satire.
What is remarkable is that it produced relatively little
stage satire, as opposed to that on other new dramatic forms
such as pantomime and Italian opera.

The attack on Sir Richard Steele's The Conscious Lovers
began offstage when this sentimental comedy appeared in
1722. John Dennis expressed his contempt for Steele's definition of comedy in a tract entitled A Defense of Sir Fopling Flutter . . . In which Defense is shown . . . that he
has been barbarously attack'd by the Knight his Brother in
the 65th Spectator. By which it appears that the latter
Knight knows nothing of the Nature of Comedy. Dennis followed this in 1723 with another publication of more specific
criticism of Steele's play, Remarks on a Play called The
Conscious Lovers. However, the attack on sentimental comedy
begun by critics like Dennis, did not spread to the theatre
for several years. When Fielding revised his The Welsh

Opera into The Grub Street Opera (1731), he seemed to be
writing a satiric parody of Lillo's sentimental opera Sylvia
(1730). Fielding's plot, like Lillo's, has a nobleman pursuing a country maid. But unlike Lillo, Fielding fails to
emphasize the young lady's indelible virtue. Instead he has
Molly parody an oration to her pursuer with ridiculous analogies on his lack of virtue. "Henceforth I will sooner
think it possible for butter to come when the witch is in
the churn, for hay to dry in the rain, for wheat to be ripe
at Christmas, for cheese to be made without milk, for a
barn to be free from mice, for a warren to be free from
rats, for a cherry orchard to be free from blackbirds, or
a church yard to be free from ghosts, as for a young man
to be free from falsehood" (II, ii). This preposterous list
of analogies together with the ostentatiously didactic prologue which announces that the play

> Teaches that virtue is the maid's best store,
> Teaches all these, and teaches nothing more.

would appear a conscious burlesque of the dreadful serious-
ness of sentimental comedy. For the author, Scriblerus Secundus, says in the Introduction, that his "opera was writ,
sir, with a design to instruct the world in economy.—It is a
sort of family Opera. The husband's vade-mecum; and it is
very necessary for all married men to have in their houses."
Undoubtedly Fielding was screening his political satire in
this play under the heavy smog of didactic "family instruction." The extravagance of style is also anticipatory of another Fielding parody of the sentimental—Shamela.
    It is also possible that Fielding was poking fun at
Theophilus Cibber's sentimental The Lover (1730) in his own
play, The Author's Farce (1730). Ernest Bernbaum says (The
Drama of Sensibility, p. 148), that Marplay junior's speech
about his recent play is a reference to the exaggerated
pathos of The Lover: "Besides, sir, there was one scene of
tender melancholy conversation, enough to have melted a
heart of stone; and yet they damned it" (I, vi). Captain
Charles Boaden's play, The Modish Couple (1732), also provoked Fielding's satire on sentimentalism. Boaden's play,
modelled on the Cibberian plot, is assigned in Pasquin to
the patronage of the Queen of Ignorance. She hands the play
to her company of actors with the instructions:

          Take this play . . .
          There is not in it either head nor tail . . .
          The Modish Couple is its name; myself
          Stood gossip to it, and I will support
          This play against the Town (Act V)

That Fielding held Colley Cibber responsible for the weak
dialogue of all "genteel" comedy is evident from the Preface to his and the Rev. Young's translation of Plutus (1742)
where Fielding quotes The Provok'd Husband to illustrate
how the wit of Wycherly has declined in Cibber. But while he
indicates that sentimentality is antithetical to comedy,
Fielding's satire on sentimental comedy is neither as sustained nor as inventive as his satire on heroic tragedy.
That his final thrust at sentimentalism in his translation
of Aristophanes should come so near the end of this period
is appropriate. For sentimental comedy, which had remained
quiescent after 1730 in the decade of intense political satire, was experiencing a revival at mid-century, stimulated
by new interest in the "man of feeling."[38]
     Unless the cheerful realism of Gay's The Beggar's Opera
(where the Peachums regret Polly's marriage because she will
no longer be their "key" to the gang of thieves) is considered as a deterrent to sentimentality, Fielding is almost
the only dramatist to ridicule sentimental comedy. Whatever
new forms the dramatists felt strongly about—pantomime or
Italian opera—as degrading to their craft they did not hesitate to attack, but they were not usually critical of sentiment. Satire and sentimentalism are both emotional; satire
is, however, critical emotion, while sentimentalism is not.
Sentimental comedy appears to be a new form more imitated
than criticized in the period 1720-1750. Of the other form
of sentimental drama new in the period, domestic tragedy,
not even Fielding was critical, as I have already indicated.
     Heroic tragedy, an older form established by Dryden,
Lee, Banks and Otway on the Restoration stage, was not so
fortunate. The bombastic style and poorly organized structure of this form of tragedy Addison had tried to correct
in Cato by a return to classicism, and Lillo in 1730 replaced the unrealistic heroes and exotic plots with The
London Merchant. But neither a revival of classicism nor the
beginning of domestic tragedy drove heroic tragedy off the
stage. In fact an examination of the performance records of

The London Stage for the beginning of this period, 1720-1727,
reveals numerous performances of Dryden's Don Sebastian, The
Indian Emperor, The Spanish Fryar, and The State of Innocence; Lee's Caesar Borgia, Mithradates, The Rival Queens,
Sophonisba, and Theodosius were also acted frequently as
were Banks's The Albion Queens, The Unhappy Favorite, and
Virtue Betrayed. The list could be further extended by the
tragedies of Otway, Ravenscroft, Tate and Sir Robert Howard.
Thus the dramatists of the 1720's were thoroughly familiar
with the characteristics of heroic tragedy—the high moral
sentiments, the double and triple plots, the flamboyant
melodrama, the extravagance of style, and the unmotivated
action. These were all characteristics which lent themselves
to the burlesque and parody of satirists.

Henry Fielding first burlesqued heroic tragedy in Tom
Thumb (1730) which he expanded a year later into The Tragedy of Tragedies: or, the Life and Death of Tom Thumb the
Great.[39] Abandoning the rehearsal formula of The Author's
Farce, he permitted the play to stand alone as satire on
the plot, character and style of this popular form of tragedy. Tom Thumb is a miniature hero in a grand scale heroic
tragedy. In fact size is used throughout to add to the ludicrous situation. Glumdalca is a giantess who speaks of herself in the plural: "We were yesterday both queen and wife"
or "twenty whereof were wedded to ourself" (I, ii). In addition to this skillful Swiftian use of scale (the name
Glumdalca may well have been suggested by Glumdalclitch), he
ridicules the type characters of heroic tragedy throughout
the entire cast. Because the characters of heroic tragedy
were the embodiment—almost the personification—of some great
and noble passion, love, honor, revenge, or jealousy, Fielding attaches comic labels to his dramatis personae to satirize the unreality of the traditional heroic figures. King
Arthur is described as "a passionate sort of King." Tom
Thumb is called "a little Hero with a great Soul, but sometimes violent in his Temper." And the same ridicule is extended to the ladies who were, in heroic tragedies, spotless
characters. Queen Dollalolla is, therefore, called "A Woman
entirely faultless, saving she is a little given to Drink."
And Princess Huncamunca is called a lady "of a very sweet,
gentle, and amorous Disposition."

Fielding also built the action of The Tragedy of Tragedies to burlesque the plots of heroic tragedy which were

filled with violence leading to wholesale slaughter. Thus
Fielding's play begins with Tom Thumb's return from a successful war against the giants while the succeeding action
is motivated by jealousy, love and revenge. It is action
filled with unmotivated violence as in the scene where Tom
kills the bailiff and his follower without a moment's hesi-
tation (II, ii), or as in the scene where Tom is swallowed
by a cow (III, x). Finally the play ends with a house-that-
Jack-built slaughter that involves seven homicides and a
suicide.

   The verse of Fielding's play is his most effective satire on the style of heroic tragedy, for in the extended
version he carefully points out the parody in the notes of
"H. Scriblerus Secundus," thus adding a burlesque of the
pedantic critic while simultaneously calling attention to
his parody of lines from Dryden, Lee and Banks.[40] Nor did
he limit his parody to tragedies from the Restoration stage.
He also illustrates the popularity of heroic tragedy in his
own day by ridiculing the style of such contemporary dramatists as Charles Johnson, Mallet, Thomson, Gay, Young, Theobald and Dennis, who wrote in the bombastic style of heroic
tragedies.[41] The technique of Fielding's parody is worth examining. He not only misquotes lines out of former plays,
but he is apt to begin in the serious style and then extend
an epic simile to the point of absurdity. For example, he
begins a parody of lines from Sophonisba when King Arthur
asks:

                  Ha, what wrinkled sorrow
      Hangs, sits, lies, frowns upon thy knitted Brow?

But he extends this ridiculous metaphor into a ridiculous
simile:

   Whence flow these tears fast down thy blubber'd cheeks
   Like a swoln Gutter, gushing through the Streets? (I, ii)

   Fielding also ridiculed by exaggeration the hyperboli-
cal rant characteristic of such heroic puppets as Myron in
Young's Bursiris who exclaims:

   For oh, I burn, I rave, I dye with love!

This is transformed in <u>Tom Thumb</u> into Lord Grizzle's extravagant promises:

> I'll swim through Seas; I'll ride upon the Clouds;
> I'll dig the Earth; I'll blow out ev'ry Fire;
> I'll rave; I'll rant; I'll rise; I'll rush; I'll roar;
> Fierce as the Man whom smiling Dolphins bore
> From the Prosaick to Poetick shore. (I, v)

There is no lack of variety in Fielding's parody of the style of heroic tragedy. In fine irony the Queen equates her virtue with Tom Thumb, a midget (I, vi). Ridiculous metaphors abound (Lord Grizzle's reference to Huncamunca's "pouting breasts" is a prime example, II, v), and Fielding even provides a catalogue of the elaborate similes, introducing them with the characteristic, "So have I seen. . .":

> So have I seen the Bees in Clusters swarm,
> So have I seen the Stars in frosty Nights,
> So have I seen the Sand in windy Days,
> So have I seen the Ghosts in <u>Pluto's</u> shore,
> So have I seen the Flowers in Spring arise,
> So have I seen the Leaves in <u>Autumn</u> fall,
> So have I seen the Fruits in <u>Summer</u> smile,
> So have I seen the Snow in Winter frown.
>
> (III, ii)

The note by "Scriblerus Secundus" to this passage emphasizes the satiric intent by a cryptic comment, "a String of Similes (says one) proper to be hung in the Cabinet of a Prince." Prince of satirists Fielding certainly was when he deflates rant by introducing a comic image into a series of exclamations. Huncamunca's "I've sighed, I've wept, I've gnawed my Sheets" (II, iv) and Glumdalca's "Confusion, Horror, Murder, Guts and Death" (II, vii) are characteristic examples.

In <u>The Covent Garden Tragedy</u> (1732) Fielding again let burlesque action stand by itself without a rehearsal format. The plot laid in Mother Punchbowl's house of ill-fame is only an apparent tragedy for like the many heroic tragedies with inexplicable happy endings, all the supposedly dead lovers, killed in duels of jealousy, turn up alive before

the final curtain. Again Fielding parodies the bombastic
verse as in the grotesque promises Lovegirlo makes to Kissinda:

> Thou shalt wear forms and houses in each ear,
> Ten thousand loads of Timber shall embrace
> Thy necklac'd neck. . . . (II, vi)

But he also adds a new device when he imitates the distorted
word order of heroic verse which sacrificed sense to produce an end pause, as in the line, "I through the Coat was,
not the body, run" (II, xiii). The distorted syntax is a
clever addition to the high-flown sentiments and stock similes, yet this play was not as popular as Tom Thumb which
ran to 33 performances in 1730 alone.[42]

Henry Carey also satirized heroic tragedy in Chrononhotonthologos (1734) but his method was slightly different.
First, his satire on style was more general and less tied
than Fielding's to parody of actual lines out of previous
plays. Yet his satiric intent is still evident since he always employs the grand style in a ludicrous situation. Besides Carey used the special trick of emphasizing hyperbole
by the incongruity between realistic fact and extravagance
of a character's speech. The king, for example, is awakened
by some "rough music" made with "salt-boxes, rolling pins,
grid-irons and tongs, sow-gelder horns, marrow bones and
cleavers." Yet the king, apparently impervious to dishar-
mony, exclaims:

> What heavenly sounds are these that charm my ears!
> Sure 'tis the music of the tuneful spheres. (sc. v)

The same trick is used when the queen dances off the stage
while commanding her ladies-in-waiting, "Come, ladies, let's
to prayers" (sc. ii). Carey's mismatching of words and action increases the ridicule and adds an additional effect
that The Tragedy of Tragedies did not possess.

The names of Carey's characters are another satiric device. The characters of heroic tragedy had long, elaborate
foreign names whose resounding syllables were intended to
convey the dignity and nobility of the characters. Dryden's
heroic tragedies are filled with examples. Zempoalla in The
Indian Queen, Porphyrius in Tyrannic Love, Nourmahal in

Aureng Zebe and Almahide, Almanzer, Abdelemech and Lyndaraxa
in The Conquest of Granada are good illustrations of this
passion for elaborate proper names. Carey plainly had this
in mind when he named his characters Bombardian, Rigdum
Funnidos, Fadladinida, and Tatlanthe, but when he blessed
the king with the mouth-filling appelation, Chrononhotonthologos, and then conjured up the monstrous Aldiborontiph-
oscophornio, and, with this one name, filled a ten syllable
line, it is apparent that his burlesque is intentional ridicule. (Fielding in Tom Thumb, by contrast, had stuck to
allegorical names like Grizzle, Noodle and Doodle [other
than his Swiftian Glumdalca], depending on the name of a
folk-hero King Arthur or Tom Thumb to provide ironic contrast. In Covent Garden Tragedy, his names were again allegorical: Kissinda, Stormandra, Lovegirlo and Captain Bilk-
um.)

The plot of Carey's play combines the slaughter of Tom
Thumb and the happy ending of Covent Garden Tragedy. For
while there are three murders and a suicide in Queerumania,
the play does not end with the sudden and unpredictable mas-
sacre. Carey follows the precedent of the heroic tragedies
which, though filled with blood and violence, permit the
hero and heroine to escape romantically to each other's arms
when the violent action has ended. Carey's conclusion bor-
ders on the ludicrous when the queen forgets her grief and,
unable to choose between two candidates for the murdered
king's bed, decides to marry them both. By turning the sudden happy ending into a farce, Carey effectively burlesques
the sudden shifts in tone of heroic tragedy.43

Two other dramatic satires attempted to improve tragedy
by allegory. Mrs. Hoper's Queen Tragedy Restor'd (1749)
lacked the inventiveness of Fielding and Carey. Her satire
is distinguished only by its sincere desire to purge tragedy
of the "heroic" elements inconsistent with tragic nobility.
Thus her attack is didactic and lacks the humor and sharp
bite of the two preceding burlesques. There is no apparent
parody of a particular play or style; her method is diffuse
rather than specific. A contemporary reviewer mentions this
play as "a farcical burlesque on some modern plays [though
without particularly pointing out any] and on the reigning
taste for stage representations."44 Queen Tragedy, in the
play, is in very poor health and various allegorical characters attempt to restore her. Dr. Doleful would make her
well by introducing her to a somber and exaggerated false

dignity. Dr. Doleful thus seems to represent Mrs. Hoper's
conception of the ill effects of heroic extravagance, and
he not surprisingly is unable to restore the Queen to
health. Dr. Drollery then introduces humorous pantomimes to
cheer the invalid queen, but is equally unsuccessful. It is
only the genius of Shakespeare, whose ghost appears at the
end of the play, that is sufficient to cure the queen's ill-
ness. In other words, Mrs. Hoper would abolish both heroic
tragedy and comic afterpieces (especially pantomime) and
return to Elizabethan models. Her dramaticized criticism is
both too serious and too dull to contribute much to the
form of dramatic satire.

In a less serious allegory than Mrs. Hoper's, Aaron
Hill wrote The Snake in the Grass as a dramatic satire on
tragedy.[45] While Tragedy is struck dumb and buried alive,
Hill crowds his scene with so many other characters such as
Comedy "set upon her Head, and her wrong End turned upper-
most," that his satire is dissipated into farcical tricks
and weak criticism of the stage in general. Fightfashion,
the author, is told by the Genius of the Stage that his
tragedy will not succeed because it lacks humor and a dancing cat or two. Lady Tragedy is said to be "losing her
voice" season after season as a result of "wooden swords,
wooden heads, wooden management" (p. 98). Although Hill's
satiric exercise is an essay in dramatic criticism and reflects his own difficulties with theatrical management, it
is closet drama and ineffective as stage satire.

The role of the dramatic satirists in driving heroic
tragedy off the stage can easily be exaggerated, but the
fact remains that at the end of this period it was a less
popular form of tragedy. By contrast with the frequent performances of heroic tragedy from 1720 to 1727, it represented only 3.7 percent of the tragedies performed per season from 1747 to 1776 according to the calculation of Professor George Winchester Stone.[46] What replaced it was what
he calls "pathetic" tragedy (19 percent) and Shakespearean
tragedy (17 percent). Were the stage satires on heroic tragedy in the 1730's and 1740's merely a reflection of this
change in taste or did they help to form the taste? It could
be argued that Henry Fielding and Henry Carey in the 1730's
were effective enough satirists to help mold taste. Mrs.
Hoper and Aaron Hill are undoubtedly only a testimony to
change.

There are also several examples of satire on Prologues,

Epilogues, Dedications, and other extraneous material attached to plays although most of these examples are too
brief to affect the form of dramatic satire. The Prologue
spoken by Macklin, for example, before Fielding's The Wedding Day (1743), is a good-natured burlesque of the usual
introductory verses. The actor claims he has forgotten the
real prologue. All he can remember is the usual harangue
about a justification by the rules of the Ancients, about
the low taste of the age, and about the author's fear for
the success of his play:

> Then there was a good deal about Rome, Athens and Dramatic
>   Rules,
> And characters of knaves and courtiers, authors and fools,
> And a vast deal about critics—and good nature—and the poor
>   Author's fear;
> And I think there was something about a third Night—hoping
>   to see you here.

Thus he gives the content while pretending to have forgotten
it.

Epilogues, however, were more often satirized than Prologues, probably because they traditionally preserved the
Restoration delight in the risqué. It was a common practice
for even a sentimental comedy to close with a "luscious dialogue" spoken by the actress who had throughout the play
been a model of chastity and virtue (See Nicoll, pp. 49–50).
The incongruity of such comic epilogues was of course fair
game for the satirist. In Fielding's revision of The Author's Farce, four poets are unable to write an Epilogue after a half-hour of tedious labor; when they give up, the
author calls in a cat to speak one. Trapwit in Pasquin also
has difficulty with his Epilogue. First he can get no ac-
tresses to speak it because it contains insufficient double
entendres. He then goes home and reads all the Epilogues of
Mr. Watts, a prominent printer, and as a result he has too
many double entendres, so that even the actress's taste is
offended. Thus Fielding acknowledges the popularity of the
risqué Epilogue, but at the end of Pasquin, he says that
since his play was in jest, his Epilogue will be serious,
thereby inverting the usual practice. Indeed it is serious,
for it begs the audience not to let poetry starve for music.

While most of the satire on Epilogues is an extension

of satiric plays, occasionally the Epilogues of tragedies
attacked the degrading effect of comic Epilogues on tragedy.
James Miller's Mahomet the Imposter (1744) has such an Epilogue:

> How have I blushed to see a tragic queen
> With Ill-time mirth disgrace the well-wrote scene,
> From all the sad solemnity of woe,
> Trip nimbly forth to ridicule a beau;
> Then as the loosest airs she had been gleaning
> Coquette the fan, and leer a double meaning.

The Epilogue of another tragedy, Thomson's Tancred and Sig-
ismunda (1745), begins in the usual humorous vein, but is
interrupted by the tragic muse who has come to take her
stand in Britain, "Freedom's noblest seat," and she protests
an Epilogue which taints the effect of five acts of tragedy
with a "wretched jest" in the concluding verses.

While satiric Prologues and Epilogues could be effective on the stage, Dedications, Prefaces and other extraneous appendages were, like the annotations of "Scriblerus
Secondus" in The Tragedy of Tragedies, only effective in
the printed form of dramatic satire. They could be used
like the Prolegomena of Fielding's The Covent Garden Tragedy
to present a mock-critic's misunderstanding of the play:

> The characters, I think, are such as I have not yet
> met with in Tragedy. First, for the character of Mother
> Punchbowl; and, by the way, I cannot conceive why she is
> called Mother. Is she the mother of any body in the play?
> No. From one line one might guess she was a bawd. Leather-
> sides desires her to procure two whores, &c, but then is
> she not continually talking of virtue?

Thus Fielding extends the satire of the play to the dull
critic who measures every play by "Aristutle and Horase" or
by his own stupidity. Or a Dedication could be used to burlesque a fawning dedication as Fielding does when he dedi-
cates his satiric pantomime, Tumble Down Dick, to John Lun,
"vulgarly called Esquire." In a triumph of false praise,
this dedication applauds John Lun (or Rich) for his introduction of "that sort of writing which you have pleased to
distinguish by the name of Entertainment"—the form which

Fielding, in fact, was himself satirizing in this very play.
This dedication concluded with heavily ironic flattery: "I
will therefore desist, though I can affirm, what few dedi-
cators can, that I can, and perhaps may, say much more; and
only assure you that I am, with the sincerity of most of the
foregoing lines, your most obedient and humble servant, Pasquin." Concealing this threat of future satiric attack in
the parody of a dedication is a technique worthy of Swift
whom Fielding again echoes by writing both a Preface to the
Dedication and a Dedication to The Historical Register. By
this proliferation of prefatory material, Fielding appears
to recall A Tale of a Tub, especially when, in a humorously
extended analogy, he likens the choosing of a patron to the
choosing of a godfather to a child. Thus by false praise,
heavy irony and attacks on pedantic critics Fielding, in
Prefaces and Dedications as well as annotations, effectively
extended the dimensions of satire in his printed plays.

To summarize the dramatic satire on literary theory and
form, the validity of classical or neo-classical rules for
drama was the main subject of satire on theory. Here the
dramatists took a middle position satirizing slavish depend-
ence on rules and pedantic critics, but simultaneously attacking such forms as pantomime for disregarding rules entirely. As for new dramatic forms, they commended ballad
opera and domestic tragedy and saved their satiric fire for
pantomime, Italian opera, and to a more limited extent, sentimental comedy. Heroic tragedy was the chief target among
older dramatic forms, although the comic Epilogue attached
to tragedy and the fawning Dedications to a patron also
came under fire.

CHAPTER 5

THE FORM OF DRAMATIC SATIRE: 1720-1750

Some, to whom Heaven in wit has been profuse,
Want as much more, to turn it to its use;
For wit and judgment often are at strife,
Though meant each other's aid, like man and wife.
                    —Alexander Pope, Essay on Criticism (1711)

The one thing these works have in common, no matter
what their authors hope for, is to state magnificently in
imaginative form the values which their authors held.
    —W. O. S. Sutherland, Jr., The Art of the Satirist (1965)

WHAT EMERGES from the prior chapters is the conclusion that
dramatic satire did not take one form but several: one, the
rehearsal, a revival of Buckingham's Restoration technique;
two, the mock-epic; three, the satiric allegory; four, the
burlesque parody; and five, the ballad opera. Dramatic satire's aim was the same as that of all satire—to expose by
the use of irony, grotesque fantasy, wit and ridicule the
folly of man, not nature. It is man's criticism of men,
whether it is aimed at political corruption, social follies,
or literary theory or form.

Before examining the merits and limitations of these
forms of sustained dramatic satire, several summary observations are appropriate. For one thing, the dramatic satirists
often contributed to the poor quality of drama written in
this period of experimentation and fluctuating taste. Particularly when they wrote too hastily to capitalize on a
court scandal or a managerial quarrel or a bill before Parliament, they sacrificed quality to expedience. The sati-

rist's insistence on being heard often caused him to throw
together a satiric afterpiece which only compounded the confusion of dramatic form in a period of instability and
changing modes.

Secondly, dramatists were often content to insert their
digs and barbs in other dramatic forms. Veiled references to
ministerial mismanagement thus appeared in such political
tragedies as Thomson's Edward and Eleanora or the anonymous
Majesty Misled. Direct satire on persons such as the attack
on Alexander Pope was dissipated in the farce of The Man of
Taste or Mr. Taste. Satiric characters often appeared in
comedies where they were discredited before the final curtain as was Wilding in Fielding's The Temple Beau. As long
as satiric bits and pieces were buried in tragedy, farce or
other forms of comedy they limited the development of dramatic satire. Isolated bits of satire are interesting for
what they tell us about the political, social or literary
history of this portion of the eighteenth century, but they
should not be labeled as satire per se. The distinction I
made earlier between the adjective satiric and the noun satire is appropriate to recall here.

Third, topical satire did little to affect the form of
satire because the more direct the play was, the less chance
it had of appearing on the stage. Only one of the plays on
the South Sea Bubble—Odell's The Chimaera—was performed, for
example; none of the five ballad operas on the Excise Act
found their way to the stage in 1733; only one play on the
proposed Gin Act was performed—The Deposing and Death of
Queen Gin—and that for one night on August 2, 1736 (See Pt.
3, LS, I, 593). Such satiric plays were, therefore, more a
part of the paper warfare than an aid to the development of
a dramatic form for satire.

Finally, much of the dramatists' problem with the form
of dramatic satire is the result of critical confusion.
From Dryden's Discourse on Satire (1693) to Dr. John Brown's
An Essay on Satire (1745) critics were primarily writing
about verse satire, not dramatic satire—Dryden distinguishing between Roman verse satirists and Brown extending the
discussion to such Augustan satirists as Alexander Pope.
Dramatists lacked definitions to distinguish dramatic satire from verse satire as well as to distinguish dramatic
satire from comedy and farce. As I pointed out in Chapter 1,
Corbyn Morris in his essay, Toward Fixing the True Standards

of Wit, Humour, Raillery, Satire, and Ridicule . . . (1744)
did attempt to separate wit and humor in English comedies
(pp. 23-25) but he used classical verse satirists as models
to do so and he failed to recognize that wit is only one
ingredient of satire.[1] The critical muddle of attempting to
fix "True Standards" for English comedy and satire by examples from Roman verse satirists helps explain why the
dramatists of this period took over the definition of satire
as satura, a medley or hodgepodge; it also helps explain why
they filled their plays with characters named Medley, Pasquin, or Marforio and why they labeled their plays as Mis-
cellanies or mixed forms ("A Tragi-Comical Farce" for Exchange Alley) rather than satire.

Critics and dramatists of the eighteenth century cannot be blamed for their failure to distinguish satire from
comedy or other dramatic forms when there is still no agreement among critics on the difference between satire and comedy or satire and farce or even whether satire is a genre be
it prose, poetry or drama. Allardyce Nicoll's bemused question, "What, after all, are we to make of Fielding's The
Historical Register, for the Year 1736?" (A History of English Drama, 1660-1900, II, 261) indicates a distrust of
satura satire translated to the stage when there is "no
clear plot" but a miscellany of political satire (Quidam
equals Walpole), social satire (auctions, card playing, the
quarrel of the two Pollys) and literary satire (Colley Cibber and his son Theophilus). I would suggest that what we
make of Fielding's play, to answer Nicoll's question, is
that it was an attempt to develop a dramatic satire out of
journalistic Registers of events of the day. The Mr. Medley
who puts the scenes together in this plotless play is proof
of Fielding's understanding of satire as mixed, a miscellany
of targets, or in other words, satura. But as I mentioned in
Chapter 1, other literary historians and critics ask not
only questions like Nicoll's, What are we to make of this
play? but also state the problem of separating satire and
comedy as insoluble as W. K. Wimsatt does in The Idea of
Comedy (p. 88). His statement is worth quoting more fully:

> English comic writers, from the time of Ben Jonson, had
> steadily protested the moral intent of their ridiculous,
> sometimes scandalous, scenes. Thus they tended to assimi-
> late comedy to satire—making an equation which may tempt

purists in genre criticism to object, but which is difficult enough to refute, for in truth <u>it would seem impossible to draw a hard line between the two aims and forms</u>.
(Italics are mine.)

Wimsatt's acknowledgement of the blurred distinction
between comedy and satire is shared by many modern critics.[2]
I have adopted the definition that satire is the use of grotesque fantasy or exaggeration, wit and irony to ridicule
and expose human folly—a definition I think applies to dramatic satire as well as to verse or prose satire. Wit and
ridicule do appear to ally satire to comedy, but a distinction can be made in that comedy works toward a resolution;
satire does not.[3] The resolution of satire, as I said earlier, is the author's own catharsis and not one that is nec-
cessarily shared by the audience which may go away angry,
stirred up, or chuckling, depending on how well they agree
with the author's judgment of what is folly. Satire is also
distinct from farce which plays a joke for what it is worth,
but once the joke is over, there is no lasting overtone of
meaning, which explains why the plot of a farce is so hard
to remember. Laughter for the sake of laughter is not necessarily critical which is what satire demands that it be.
The satirist not only wishes to stir up his audience by his
wit, but to shake him into an awareness of the folly exposed.
(Frye, p. 223, calls satire "militant irony" to distinguish
the satirist's intention.) Farce is entertainment with no
catharsis for either the author or the audience beyond the
pleasure of laughter. While the satiric dramatists of this
period did not make such critical distinctions between comedy, farce, and satire, they did develop some satiric forms
for the stage as I suggested at the beginning of this chapter.

The rehearsal format used by Gabriel Odingsells in
<u>Bayes's Opera</u> (1729) traced its ancestry back to Bucking-
ham's <u>The Rehearsal</u> (1671) by borrowing the name of Bayes
for the author of the opera-within-the-play. It also reflected the immediate popularity of the ballad opera after
Gay's success early in 1728. The advantage of the rehearsal
format for the dramatic satirist was considerable as Fielding illustrated in <u>The Author's Farce</u> (1730), <u>Pasquin</u> (1736),
<u>The Historical Register</u> (1737) and <u>Eurydice Hiss'd</u> (1737),
for it provided a built-in commentator on the play-within-

the-play. The commentator could be a straight man like
Fielding's Medley (The Historical Register) who thus provides the norm for the real author, or he could himself be
the object of satire like Trapwit (Pasquin) who dredges up
rules for the stupidities of his interior play. By adding
spectators and critics to discuss the play in rehearsal,
the real author could also underscore points and provide a
guide to his satire both for those on stage watching the rehearsal and for the audience in the theatre. Another advantage was that the format reduced the necessity for plot.
The play-within-the-play was necessarily composed of short
scenes, interrupted frequently by comments of the spectators;
there need be no sustained allegory, for example, in the
battle between Common Sense and Ignorance in Fustian's tragedy, nor any concern for story-line in the election scenes
of Trapwit's comedy. By playing out some scenes and interrupting at will, Fielding, as author, could engage in what
Robert Charles Bennett has called a "satiric dance."
("Fielding and the Satiric Dance," unpublished doctoral
thesis, University of Pennsylvania, 1969).

There were also disadvantages to the rehearsal format
in that it tended toward hodgepodge, a miscellany of satire
with too many objects of attack. The author, the critic,
the audience, the players, when they are all targets, diffuse the satire and scatter it beyond the ability of the
audience to concentrate. Parts cancel parts. Perhaps this is
why the formula was little used for topical satire, though
the anonymous The Stage Mutineers: or a Playhouse to be Lett
(1733) on Theophilus Cibber's managerial quarrel with Highmore is an exception to such a generalization. As though the
dramatists were conscious that the rehearsal format was
close to satura satire, most of the rehearsal-type plays
were literary satires on bad dramatists, poor acting, ter-
rible poetry, pedantic critics or the low state of theatrical taste. Trapwit's interior comedy, The Election, in Pasquin is subordinate as political satire because Fielding is
also ridiculing Trapwit as playwright. Thus the rehearsal
form almost automatically exploited the ingredients of drama
—authors, managers, actors, critics and audience—at the expense of other themes.

The mock-epic formula was a promising formula for stage
satire but little used. It allowed for parody of style as in
Penelope (1728) where Pope's translation of Homer's Odyssey

was under attack. It also allowed for considerable wit and
inventiveness in translating Ulysses' adventures into eighteenth-century terms. It might well have served as a model
for political satire. "Sturdy beggars" opposing the Prime
Minister were good material for a mock-epic plot if the
dramatists were clever enough to reduce important issues to
trivialities as in The Rape of the Lock; no end of invention was possible if the regiments of political parties were
translated into the supernatural. Yet when dramatists made
use of classical mythology, they more often used the Gods
for burlesque (Theobald's The Rape of Proserpine or Fielding's Tumble Down Dick: or Phaeton in the Suds) or farce.
The advantage of a mock-epic was a consistent and known plot
which could unify the occasional jabs and pokes into the
genre of satire. The epic was already at hand; the dramatist
had only to exercise enough inventiveness to translate his
own period by exaggeration, wit, and irony into the mock-
heroic mold. Gay may have attempted to copy the technique of
Penelope when he chose a comic portion of a classical myth
for his posthumously performed Achilles (1733), but except
for Achilles' long strides and oaths when he was disguised
in girl's clothing, Gay was not successful in exploiting
myth to produce a mock-epic satire.

Allegory proved a more popular form with these dramatic
satirists. Because it avoided censure by the Licenser after
1737 and allowed for witty invention, it was used for political satire such as The Congress of Beasts on the treaty
of Aix la Chapelle, Fortune's Tricks in Forty Six on the invasion attempt of 1745, and The Northern Election or Nest of
Beasts on the Scottish support of the Stewart invasion. It
was also used for personal satire on theatre managers (To
Diabouloumenon) and to bewail the low quality of tragedy and
comedy (Mrs. Hoper's Queen Tragedy Restor'd and Aaron Hill's
Snake in the Grass) and to present the Court of Discord
where rival opera singers are tried (The Contre-Temps or Rival Queens). Its advantage was that it concealed the identity of anonymous authors and distanced them from the allegory. The difficulty with the form was that satiric allegory was not easy to sustain beyond overt suggestions in a
title; thus it often was used only in short scenes like
Fielding's play-within-the-play (Pasquin) where Ignorance
and Common Sense contend for supremacy in Fustian's tragedy.
The one-to-one relation necessary for consistent allegory

requires invention in developing a sustained metaphor which
does not limit the plot. Dodsley's The Toy Shop, for example, is a metaphor which suggests that the social value of
the objects for sale is all of the miniature scale of toys,
yet his play is not an allegory but a jumble of annotated
sales of abstractions with no controlling metaphor. The toys
for sale are interesting only for the value which the characters assign to them; the result is a miscellany of characters assigning a miscellany of values (again satura).
While Dodsley has abundant opportunity for irony, he does
not exploit his implied metaphor into a consistent allegory.
The beast fable remained the most viable form of satiric allegory for the stage, yet it never produced a sustained
metaphor such as Swift's horses and Yahoos or Robert Down-
ey's modern example of men locked in a trap as in his play
The Pound.

Burlesque/parody was more effectively exploited for
dramatic satire, especially for literary satire of heroic
tragedy and pantomime. Little exaggeration was necessary to
burlesque the action and plotlessness of pantomime, and
when Fielding added parody of style to the burlesque action,
he found an excellent formula for ridiculing heroic tragedy
in his Tragedy of Tragedies and Covent Garden Tragedy. The
form allowed for great variety. Carey's mismatching of words
and action in his Chrononhotonthologos or his use of supernatural fantasy to ridicule Italian opera in The Dragon of
Wantley are examples of the satirist's range of imagination.
Fielding's annotations to the expanded Tom Thumb play (The
Tragedy of Tragedies or Tom Thumb the Great) also increased
the potential of satire in the printed play. H. Scriblerus
Secundus can justify any line in the burlesque tragedy by
proving that it had an antecedent in previous tragedies, as
though that were proof of quality. The specious editor thus
adds greatly to the irony of Fielding's satire. Burlesque/
parody of pantomime was even used successfully for political
satire in Harlequin Incendiary or Columbine Cameron on the
Stewart invasion attempt, and in Politics in Miniature on
Walpole's resignation. And Kelly used burlesque tragedy to
satirize Walpole's Gin Act in The Fall of Bob.

An advantage of burlesque/parody was the pre-existence
of models (heroic tragedy, pantomime, operatic plots) out-
rageous enough in themselves so that an audience could easily detect a parody. Thus the invention of the satirist was

freed to add new satiric devices of style (ironic juxtaposition, long lists with a disparate equivalent, comic mixed
metaphors, ten-syllable names). He could exaggerate action
to the grotesque (Tom Thumb swallowed by a cow) or reduce
it to the ridiculous (a queen dancing off to prayers). The
use of the burlesque/parody thus greatly increased the variety of style in dramatic satire and helped separate it
from comedy and farce. While many of the burlesque/parodies
appeared as afterpieces, the number was sufficient enough
and the performances were numerous enough to balance the
tears of sentimental comedy and keep laughter alive on the
stage in this period.

Of the new dramatic forms which appeared in these decades the most promising formula for dramatic satire was the
ballad opera as initiated by Gay in The Beggar's Opera. Its
scenes were short, it was enlivened by music familiar to the
audience, and it offered a variety of attack useful for topical satire (the ridicule of Italian opera; the extended
metaphor that all politicians are thieves; the irony of in-
verted social values in the highwaymen's code of honor; the
"polite conversation" of trollops; the Peachums' scoff at
marriage; the alias names for Robin of Bagshot which applied to Robert Walpole). Such variety was unequalled by any
of the other forms of dramatic satire, and in Gay's model
the variety was not just a miscellany of satire because it
was held together by the great vitality of the central character, the rogue-hero Macheath. Thus it was the most multidimensional of the five forms which I listed at the beginning of this chapter.

Unfortunately Gay was unable to hold on to his formula.
When he added other techniques of satire such as the vir
bonus or satiric norm in the person of a West Indian chief
in his sequel, Polly, the added device for commenting on the
social follies of the English led to deadly didacticism
which killed the wit and reduced the vitality of his satire.
His imitators and successors among the dramatic satirists
went in all directions in their use of the ballad opera.
Mottley and Cooke used it for a mock-epic (Penelope); Fielding as a burlesque of a sentimental pastoral and a political
allegory (The Grub-Street Opera); the anonymous author of
Colonel Split-Tail for coarse personal satire on the gambler
Colonel Charteris. But the form has survived into the twenti-
eth century as the social satire of Brecht's Three Penny

Opera has proved. Because of the great popularity of ballad
opera in the 1730's and 1740's, particularly between 1728
and 1738, it was the form of dramatic satire most often combined with the other forms—the rehearsal format, the mock-
epic, the burlesque/parody, and even allegory. Its influ-
ences extended as far as European theatres where performances of English ballad operas have been cited as influenc-
ing German Singspiel. English dramatists, as I have indicated, did not always use Gay's model of ballad opera for
satire. It was also used by writers of sentimental and pastoral comedies and for reworked plots from Restoration comedies. However, in the hands of Mottley, Coffey, Carey,
Dodsley, Fielding, Thomas Walker—the original actor of Macheath—and numerous anonymous dramatists, its potential for
dramatic satire was both realized and supplemented.

Thus while the dramatist from 1720 to 1750 was undoubtedly hindered by the lack of critical distinctions between
satire and comedy and by his confusion of dramatic satire
with classical verse satire (satura or medley), he continued to write what he labeled as satire even after the Licensing Act of 1737. Some of the plays in this study surmounted
the adjective satiric and developed into definite forms of
dramatic satire. The rehearsal form was not new, but the
mock-epic, the allegory, the burlesque/parody and the ballad
opera were innovations for English stage satire. Medley and
hodgepodge were conceptions the dramatist inherited from the
verse of Horace and Juvenal and its Augustan imitators,
while fantasy and the sale of abstractions were borrowed
from the prose satire of Lucian. From Pope he borrowed the
idea of a mock-epic and The Dunciad's technique of distinguishing Common Sense from Nonsense—a suggestion for al
legory. From Swift he adopted the idea of scale to aid in
ridicule and the use of prefatory material and annotations
to reinforce the satire of the printed text. He was still
experimenting with dramatic satire at the end of this period as Macklin's The New Play Criticiz'd (1747) illustrates.

If the dramatist lacked models for stage satire except
for Aristophanes, Ben Jonson's humours comedy, Buckingham's
rehearsal play and Molière's satiric characters, at least he
recognized the stage as potential for satire and borrowed
hints from his contemporaries, the nondramatic Augustan satirists. Folly in action on the stage is convincing as Field-

ing pointed out as early as 1734: "examples work quicker and
stronger on the minds of men than precepts," Fielding wrote
in the letter to Lord Chesterfield as his Dedication to Don
Quixote in England. Certainly for Fielding, the most prolific and ingenious of these dramatic satirists, the stage
was the public forum where he polished the irony and witty
inventiveness that was to distinguish him later in another
genre, the novel.[4]

For all these dramatic satirists the stage offered an
advantage over journalism by distancing the author as satirist from the plays and by presenting satire in action. It
also offered an advantage over visual arts such as caricature because the dialogue of drama sustained the satire beyond the single point which the caricature made. William
Hogarth in such conversation pieces as "The Rake's Progress"
came closest to the advantages of the stage by showing in
several related prints the progression of folly, yet his
visual art was a series of static statements. Satiric
drama could animate these "stills" by scene, voice, music
(in ballad opera) and action. The vitality of dramatic satire is great as modern revivals of The Beggar's Opera have
demonstrated. If the mode of contemporary literature is
irony as Frye and others have suggested, contemporary dramatists might do well to take some hints from these eighteenth-
century plays.

N O T E S

Introduction

1. Aristotle, _Poetics_ 4. See the discussion of Aristotle's statement in Cornford, _The Origin of Attic Comedy_, p. 214. (Note: for complete citations of authors listed in Selected References, see pp. 179-183.)
2. Pp. 49-200 discuss curses and magic spells from the work of the anthropologist, Jane Ellen Harrison.
3. John Harold Wilson, _A Preface to Restoration Drama_ (Boston: Harvard University Press, 1965), argues that most Restoration playwrights "lacked the indignation requisite for satire," p. 165. Robert D. Hume, "Diversity and Development in Restoration Comedy," has spelled out the variety of Restoration comedy.
4. _The London Stage 1660-1800_, Pt. 3, I, cxxx.
5. The author is indebted to the Newberry Library and to the Henry E. Huntington Library for summer grants to continue this study begun as a doctoral dissertation at the University of Wisconsin.

Chapter 1

1. Edward W. Rosenheim, _Swift and the Satirist's Art_ limits the satirist to an attack on "Discernible, historically authentic particulars" (p. 25) which gives him trouble with the Fourth Book of _Gulliver_ moving, he says, "beyond the satiric spectrum" (p. 167).
2. Martin Price, _Swift's Rhetorical Art_ (New Haven: Yale University Press, 1953); Glenn W. Hatfield, _Henry Fielding and the Language of Irony_ (Chicago: Chicago University Press, 1968); William B. Ewald, _The Masks of Jonathan Swift_ (Cambridge: Harvard University Press, 1954) for example.
3. University of Wisconsin, _Language and Literature Studies_, Number 7.
4. Pope generated most of the negative criticism of

153

satire from 1720 to 1750; see Cooke, The Battle of the Poets
(1725, but revised in 1729 to attack The Dunciad); Edward
Ward, Durgen, or, a Plain Satyr upon a Pompous Satyrist
(1729); Walter Harte, An Essay on Satire (1730); George
Lyttleton, An Epistle to Mr. Pope (1730); and Aaron Hill,
The Progress of Wit (1730) and Advice to the Poets (1730).

    5. Prose satire, usually traced to Lucian or to Menip-
pus whose satires survive only in Lucian's imitations of
him, has been labeled Menippean by Frye (pp. 309-12) and Elliott (pp. 186-88) and cited as a source for the form of
Swift's Gulliver's Travels. Moses Haddas suggests that Me-
nippus of Gadara influenced Semitic short stories or novella
called maqama. (Hellenistic Culture, New York: Columbia
University Press, 1959, p. 111.)

    6. "Modern Satire: A Mini-Symposium."

    7. I have argued elsewhere ("Modern Satire: A Mini-
Symposium") that eighteenth-century satire has an established norm based on man's capacity to act rationally and is
thus Frye's satire of the "low norm" closest to comedy.
Frye's "high norm" satire closest to tragedy I find a more
accurate description of modern dramatic satire—the theatre
of the absurd or the theatre of violence where the satirist
does not take the norm from the past nor from what man is
capable of—i.e., something to return to—but from the apocalyptic assumption that life is absurd. The separation of
Frye's "high norm" satire from tragedy should emerge from a
study of twentieth-century dramatic satire.

Chapter 2

    1. Robertson, England under the Hanoverians, pp. 52-
53; 83.

    2. Biographia Dramatica: Or, A Companion to the Play-
house. . . . ed. David E. Baker, Isaac Reed, and Stephen
Jones. James Ralph was pensioned off because of his attacks
on the ministry, I, 588-89. James Moore-Smythe was paymaster
to the Gentleman Ushers, I, 678-79. John Gay held a minor
post from the government until he refused the post of Gentleman Usher to the youngest Princess. See The Correspondence
of Jonathan Swift, ed. F. E. Ball (4 vols., London: Long-
mans, 1912), III, Gay to Swift, 427.

    3. Biog. Dram., I, 119, 746.

    4. Ibid., I, 350, 480, 615, 711. This includes David

Mallet, Dr. John Hoadly, Lacy Ryan, and James Thomson, although Captain Charles Boadens should also be mentioned. Cf.
Woods, "Captain B------'s Play."

    5. Biog. Dram., I, 576, 743.

    6. Ibid., I, 757-58.

    7. Ibid., I, 688.

    8. The list of dramatists compiled from Genest, Some
Accounts of the English Stage, III and IV; Biog. Dram.;
Nicoll, Early Eighteenth Century Drama 1700-1750, Appendix
C; and the Larpent Collection of the Huntington Library,
shows approximately 160 dramatists writing from 1720 to
1750, twenty-three of whom were in the service of the government or the opposition.

    9. John Kelly was not exaggerating the vagaries of a
politician when the Duke of Newcastle, for example, vacil-
lated for two years before granting a minor pension to
Charles Jenkinson. See Namier, England in the Age of the
American Revolution, pp. 85-86.

    10. Biog. Dram., II, 339.

    11. Edward W. Rosenheim, Jr. Swift and the Satirist's
Art, p. 25.

    12. One scholar argues that it was the intensity of po-
litical turmoil in the seventeenth century that caused formal verse satire to disappear. Cf. Alden, "The Rise of Formal Satire in England under Classical Influence," pp. 244-
45.

    13. Robertson, p. 39, and Lecky, A History of England
in the Eighteenth Century, pp. 348-51 (quoted from Macpher-
son's Annals of Commerce).

    14. The Catalogue of Prints and Drawings in the British
Museum, Div. I, Political and Personal Satires, Vol. II
(London, 1873), 412 ff, gives an extensive list of English,
Dutch, French and German prints satirizing the South Sea
Bubble. This collection is a useful parallel of the politi-
cal satire in the plays of this period. The print of The
Golden Rump, for example, gives evidence of the content of
the missing play which allegedly caused the Licensing Act
of 1737.

    15. Robertson, p. 40. No one doubted Stanhope's honesty,
but Sunderland, despite his acquittal, was forced by the
strength of public opinion to resign his office in the Ministry.

    16. The Mississippi scheme in France, formulated by

John Law, was a counterpart to the English financial fiasco,
though it came to an end somewhat sooner. Cf. Robertson, p.
38.

17. F. S. Oliver, The Endless Adventure (3 vols., London: Macmillan, 1930-1935), II, 234.

18. Ibid., II, 263-67.

19. Robertson, p. 68. Satirical drawings on the excise
scheme are listed in the Collection of Prints . . . in the
Brit. Mus., II, No. 1094; II, pt. 1, No. 2025.

20. Biog. Dram., II, 115. LS, Pt. 3, I, 299 mentions a
performance of an afterpiece, The Vintner's Escape, or,
Good Luck at Last, at Haymarket, May 12, 1733, but the anonymous act and a half was never printed after the single performance.

21. Robertson, p. 69. Applebees records that Walpole
was in the audience when an actor in Love Runs All Dangers
made some impromptu remarks on the Excise. Walpole immediately went backstage and determined that the lines were
not in the script and then ordered that the actor omit the
reference. Cf. Pt. 3, The London Stage, I, 280.

22. For a description of the incident, see Charles E.
Mallet, A History of the University of Oxford (3 vols., London: Methuen, 1927), III, 48-49.

23. Lecky, I, 519-20.

24. Pt. 3, The London Stage, I, 299, records another
one act farce, The Vintner's Escape, added as an afterpiece
at the Haymarket, May 12, 1733, probably to capitalize on
Walpole's unpopular Act, though this play was apparently
never published and its contents remain conjectural.

25. The DAB, XLV (1896), 336 suggests Archibald Pitcairne as the author of The Assembly. Pitcairne had strong
Jacobite sympathies, which would explain the satire on Whigs
and Presbyterians.

26. The invasion attempt also revived interest in the
Perkin Warbec story and Charles Macklin hastily put together
a tragedy on this in Henry VII, or the Popish Imposter
(1746). John Genest also mentions two older plays on Perkin
Warbec performed at Covent Garden and Goodman Fields in the
same season as a clear bid, like Macklin's play, for public
approval. (Genest, IV, 178. See also Cat. of Prints, II, pt.
1, 508-45 for satiric drawings on the invasion theme.)

27. London Magazine, 1744, quoted in Genest, IV, 161.

28. Namier, The Structure of Politics at the Accession

of George III, gives a complete analysis of the electoral structure of England in this period.

29. Robertson, p. 39.

30. Namier, I, 97-98.

31. Hogarth's engraving of an election scene (1755) follows closely the practices Fielding satirizes. As late as his farce Miss Lucy in Town (1742) Fielding has Lord Bawble say that he learned how to make love to country ladies at his elections.

32. Robertson, p. 88.

33. Oliver, II, 17.

34. Robertson, p. 73.

35. See Nicoll, pp. 23, 93, and Kern, "The Fate of Thomson's Edward and Eleanora," pp. 100-102 for a full discussion of this play.

36. Woods, "Captain B----'s Play," p. 252.

37. Walpole's modern biographers no longer castigate his conduct of the secret service. He is considered, in the light of a corrupt age, no worse than his colleagues and enemies. He merely employed a technique that was used later to even greater advantage by the Duke of Newcastle and George III. Cf. Oliver, I, 4; Namier, The Structure of Politics, I, 128; Robertson, Bolingbroke and Walpole, p. 209. Plumb, Sir Robert Walpole, The King's Minister is an able recent interpretation.

38. At Walpole's seat, Houghton in Norfolk, he was already collecting his fine gallery of paintings which impressed Arthur Young fifty years later as the best in England outside the royal collection. See Arthur Young, Six Weeks Tour through the Southern Counties of England and Wales (London: W. Straham, 1769). Daniel Defoe, Tour through the whole island of Great Britain (London: G. Straham, 1724), Appendix to Letter I, describes the estate in this period when it was still in the process of construction.

39. See The Correspondence of Jonathan Swift, ed. F. E. Ball, 6 vols. (London: 1910-1914), III, Gay to Swift, Oct. 22, 1726, 352, and Gay to Swift, Oct. 22, 1727, 427.

40. Schultz, Gay's Beggar's Opera, p. 195, claims Macheath's affairs with Polly and Lucy are a reference to Walpole's liaison with Moll Skerrett, which would identify the Prime Minister with the highway robber and leader of a band of thieves.

41. Oliver, II, 17, 56.

42. Loisseau, "John Gay et le Beggar's Opera," p. 6.
Swift thought the scene was an imitation of the quarrel of
Cassius and Brutus. Cf. Swift to Gay, March 28, 1728, Cor-
respondence, IV, 20.

43. W. Coxe, Memoirs of . . . Sir Robert Walpole (3
vols., London: T. Cadell, Jr., W. Davies, 1798), I, 335-36;
Hervey Memoirs, Ed. Croker (2 vols., London: J. Murray,
1848), I, 117n.

44. Oliver, I, 408.

45. Cf. Kern, "A Note on The Beggar's Opera."

46. Hodgart, Satire, p. 212, suggests the modern revue
as one of the best forms of contemporary satire, but curi-
ously traces it to vaudeville and cabaret songs rather than
to ballad opera.

47. Genest, II, 520-22. Cf. Crean, "The Stage Licensing
Act of 1737," and Loftis, The Politics of Drama in Augustan
England, p. 94.

48. An engraving entitled "The Festival of the Golden
Rump" clearly based on the same play shows a part of this
action. See The Catalogue of Prints, III, Pt. 1, No. 2327.

49. Letters and Works of . . . Chesterfield, ed. Lord
Mahon (London: Bentley, 1853), V, 15-16.

50. J. E. Wells, "Fielding's Political Purpose in Jonathan Wild," PMLA, XXVIII (1913), 1-56, suggests Jonathan
Wild may have been intended as a parallel to Walpole, great
statesman, great robber. Cf. Van der Voorde, Henry Fielding:
Critic and Satirist, pp. 135 ff.

51. Medium in this play, bewailing the fact that men
are never what they seem, concludes, "Well, of all Men living, I think a Primier Minister the most wretched—Let his
Intentions be never so upright (Wou'd to Heaven I cou'd say
that was the Case at present) he shall often find himself
oblig'd to practice on the Passions of those whose Duty
'twou'd be to cooperate with him without Gratuity. Miserable
Degeneracy!" II, ii.

52. Kelly had already written his mock-tragedy, The
Fall of Bob, or the Oracle of Gin (1736) which marked him as
a foe of Walpole. See p. 29.

53. Biog. Dram. Companion to the Playhouse (London,
1764), unpaged Huntington Library copy, claims this was
never intended for the stage but as "a Satire on the alterations made in the Ministry." Lord Fardall, the fallen Minister, is brought to trial in this revised play which ends
with a song about party vacillators: "Come follow, follow

me,/All ye that Turncoats be." Thus the efforts to bring the
fallen Walpole to trial seem behind the topical revision.

Chapter 3

1. Plumb, Sir Robert Walpole, p. 241.
2. Biog. Dram., I, 506, mentions Moses Mendez, a Jew,
as the only dramatist of this period who was extremely rich.
3. Loftis, ed., Essays on the Theatre, p. 13.
4. Stuart Miller, The Picaresque Novel (Cleveland:
Western Reserve University, 1967), p. 97, discusses the appearance of parallel types in picaresque novels as symbols
of disorder.
5. Kidson, The Beggar's Opera, Its Predecessors and
Successors, pp. 53-54, finds the moral teaching of an evil
social system more important than the jibes at politics or
Italian opera. Cf. Armens, John Gay, Social Critic, p. 56.
6. See Correspondence of Swift, III, 427, for Gay's
letter, and A. P. Herbert, "The London of The Beggar's Opera," London Mercury, V (1921), 156-71, for an account of
this contemporary document.
7. Belden, "Samuel Foote," pp. 9-10.
8. See p. 56.
9. Fielding's interest in medicine is attested by several books on the subject in his library. For a list of
these, see Ethel M. Thornbury, Henry Fielding's Theory of
the Comic Prose Epic, University of Wisconsin Studies in
Language and Literature, 30 (1931), 168-89.
10. "W. H." could be William Hammond, William Hatchett,
William Havard, William Hawkins, William Hunt or William Hy-
land, all of whom wrote plays between 1720-1750.
11. DNB, XXV, 414-15 (1891 ed.).
12. In the edition of this play by James Plumptre of
1812, Friend Sly was removed because the editor considered
he might be offensive to Quakers. Cf. Editor's Preface, III,
201.
13. See the handwritten note of "JPC" in the Huntington Library copy of Biog. Dram., III, facing p. 40.
14. Both Este's Preface and Wesley's Journal record the
Methodist opposition to Este's theatrical troop. Leo Hughes,
University of Texas Studies in English, 29 (1950), 151-61,
traces the conflict of Este and Wesley.
15. Chalkstone's criticism is based on actual terms of

eighteenth-century landscape gardening borrowed from the
landscape artists it emulated—Lorraine, Poussin and Salva-
tor Rosa. See William Shenstone, Some Unconnected Thoughts
on Gardening, and Horace Walpole's Essay on Gardening for
contemporary doctrine from men of letters.

16. The Italianate Englishman of the Elizabethan age
had been replaced by the Frenchified beau in the Restoration; satire on Italian influence survives in this period
as criticism of Italian opera singers like Farinelli, and
this will be discussed in the following chapter.

17. See George Mayhew, "Some Dramatizations of Swift's
'Polite Conversation'," PQ, 44 (1965), 51-72, for a discussion of what these plays owe to Swift.

18. The most ridiculous catalogue of worthless stocks
is assembled in the anonymous comedy The Projectors (1738).
See pp. 65-66.

19. Even the five-bottle Sir Roger Ringwood of Charles
Macklin's satire, The Covent Garden Theatre (1752) at the
end of the period is more satirized as the loud-voiced,
bluff country squire than as drunkard.

20. Leslie Stephen, History of English Thought in the
18th Century (London: Smith, Elder and Co., 1881), II, 436.

21. See R. S. Crane, "Suggestions Toward a Genealogy
of the 'Man of Feeling'," ELH, I (1934), 205-30.

22. Bateson, English Comic Drama, p. 7.

23. H. D. Traill, ed., Social England (6 vols., London,
etc.: Cassell and Co., Lts., 1896), V, 133-35, makes clear
the cost of poor relief was kept from increasing by the
ruthless enforcement of the Act of Settlement of Charles
II's reign.

24. Universal Magazine, VII (1750), 129.

25. Glenn W. Hatfield, Henry Fielding and the Language
of Irony (Chicago: University of Chicago Press, 1968) underscores the importance of Fielding's plays in developing "the
ironigenic potentialities of corrupt language" in his style
(p. 165), but admits that Fielding does not find human nature corrupt, only language (p. 156).

Chapter 4

1. For a recent (1972) discussion of the diversity of

Restoration comedy, see Hume, "Diversity and Development in
Restoration Comedy, 1660-1679." His argument that the comedy
of manners was slow to develop against the tendency toward
satire and farce indicates that the eighteenth-century mixture of dramatic modes had begun much earlier on the Restoration stage.

2. Gentleman's Magazine, II (1732), 566, criticized
fashionable taste for degrading the poet by honoring the
player. Julian L. Ross, "Dramatist versus Audience in the
Early Eighteenth Century," PQ, XII (1933), 73-81, gives
some evidence that the dramatist thought the degeneracy of
taste was a natural consequence of the degeneracy of society.
Dennis's essay, Remarks on Cato, is a good summary of the
conflict between the dramatist and his audience.

3. See the Augustan Reprint Society edition of this
manuscript play in the Larpent collection, 128 (1967), 69.
The Introduction to this edition by Jean B. Kern gives the
performance record of both Hoadly's and Macklin's plays, p.
iii.

4. Cross, A History of Henry Fielding, I, 189, gives
a more complete account of Fielding's quarrel with Rich.

5. A copy of this play was found at the Huntington
Library, KD 290.

6. See Pt. 2, The London Stage, II, 719. No performance of To Diabouloumenon is listed in The London Stage although it is recorded that Wilkes resumed the role of Wildair at Drury Lane on November 26 of the same year (Pt. 2,
II, 796). Apparently the satire was effective in changing
Cibber's casting policy.

7. See Nicoll, p. 316, and the Hillhouse edition of
this play (Appendix A, pp. 187-89) for arguments about the
authorship of this scene.

8. Biog. Dram., II, 52, identifies this character as
Aaron Hill, but the adjective "sulky" better describes Dennis as Hillhouse agrees, Appendix A, p. 187.

9. Fielding was not the only one to satirize the Cibberian Odes. The Gentleman's Magazine for January, 1732, and
January, 1735, published parodies of the New Year's day
Odes, and Nichols, "Fielding and the Cibbers," records another in the Universal Spectator for August 17, 1734.

10. Genest records (III, 424) how Theophilus Cibber
earned the name Pistol for his acting in Henry IV, pt. II.
An anonymous play The Stage Mutineers (1733) blamed a quar-

rel with the actors at Covent Garden on "Pistol's work" and
Nichols, "Fielding and the Cibbers," p. 279, believes this
anonymous play may have suggested the Pistol scene in The
Historical Register.

11. For later attacks on Cibber in Joseph Andrews and
The Covent Garden Journal see H. W. Taylor, "Fielding upon
Cibber," MP, 24 (1931-1932), 73-90. D. C. Croissant, "Studies
in the Works of Colley Cibber," University of Kansas Human-
istic Studies (1915), pp. 1-69, says The Egoist or Colley
upon Cibber was written by Cibber as a reply to Fielding
who continued to ridicule Cibber in the very last thing he
wrote, his Journal of a Voyage to Lisbon.

12. Macklin after being excluded from both Drury Lane
and Covent Garden turned to writing satiric afterpieces
such as The New Play Criticiz'd already mentioned. Appleton,
Charles Macklin: An Actor's Life, pp. 65, 79, details their
quarrels.

13. The quarrel of T. Cibber's wife and Mrs. Clive over
who should be assigned to the role of Polly in The Beggar's
Opera was the subject of a dramatic satire The Beggar's Pantomime or the Contending Columbines (1736) which exists in a
copy in the Clarke Library in Los Angeles. Genest, III, 507,
attributes this to Henry Woodward but the title page gives
only Lun junior as author. Despite the disclaimer in the
Dedication to Mrs. Cibber and Mrs. Clive that the pantomime
is "meant only to promote the Theatre to which I belong,"
Lincoln's Inn Fields, it capitalizes on the well-known
squabble with both women scolding as long as they have
breath left until the ghost of Gay comes to judge the quarrel (sc. iv). Fielding referred to the same quarrel in The
Historical Register by having Pistol beg the son of Apollo
to allow his wife to act Polly (II, i).

14. See Chapter II, pp. 80-81.

15. See the Facsimile from the first issue of the original edition of 1729, The Dunciad Variorum with the Proloeg-
omena of Scriberlus (Princeton: Princeton University Press,
1929), p. 33.

16. Great confusion exists about the authorship of
these Taste plays. The Huntington copy of Mr. Taste (KD9) is
a 1734 printing by E. Rayner and bears on its title page "by
the author of Vanelia" generally thought to be James Miller,
but the Biog. Dram. lists Miller's play and another Man of
Taste as separate, #102 and #103. The British Museum Cata-

logue also lists them as separate plays: The Man of Taste
(1733) and Miller's The Man of Taste (1735). Yet the Miller
play, The Man of Taste or the Guardian which was performed
at Drury Lane on March 6, 1735 (Pt. 3, LS, I, 466), is a
completely different play with a different cast of characters. Either Miller revised his earlier play on "the Poetical Fop" or the two plays discussed here are different
printings of a work by an unknown author. Nicoll lists only
the 1735 Miller play with the different subtitle, "or the
Guardian" (344).

17. Probably Lady Mary Wortley Montagu whose quarrel
with Pope is the occasion for Henry Fielding defending her
in some recently discovered poetry which asks for help
against "the injur'd Sappho's wrongs." See Grundy, "New
Verse by Henry Fielding," for the text of Fielding's "An
Epistle to Mr. Lyttleton occasion'd by 2 lines in Mr. Pope's
Paraphrase on the first Satire of the 2d Book of Horace."

18. Grundy, "New Verse by Henry Fielding," pp. 213-45.

19. Dramatists such as Colley Cibber had already questioned the necessity of rules, though not in satiric form,
long before 1720. In the Preface to Women's Wit or The Lady
of Fashion (1697), he acknowledged that while a good play
was the better for being regular, the greatest art was that
which made the drama both regular and diverting; "and of the
two, truly I don't see but men of the greatest sense had
rather have their fancy pleased than their judgment; and I
can't help wishing, though too late, that I had given a
looser reign to the former." Again in the prologue to his
She Wou'd and She Wou'd Not (1702), Cibber opted for the
Moderns in the controversy:

Our humble author thinks a Play shou'd be,
Tho' ty'd to rules, like a good sermon, free
From pride, and stoop to each capacity.
For Rules are but the posts that mark the course,
Which way the rider shou'd direct his horse.

20. Van der Voorde, Henry Fielding: Critic and Satirist,
pp. 68-69, finds other portions of Fielding's work where he
claims that tragedy should set the "highest characters" before us.

21. Undoubtedly this objection to Frenchified taste is
an extension of the social satire discussed earlier.

22. Dougald MacMillan, "David Garrick as Critic," _SP_,
31 (1933), 69-84, argues that it is impossible to know exactly what Garrick's critical standards were since he did
not often express what he thought of plays except in rejec-
tion slips.

23. This idea is suggested in _Biog. Dram._, II, 315.
"But, query, might not both play and epilogue be designed
to expose false taste, fustian, and bombast?" See also
Nicoll, p. 268.

24. See his prologue to Lillo's _Fatal Curiosity_ (1736);
also Nicoll, Appendix C, lists many plays of this type performed at the Haymarket theatre under Fielding's management.

25. Genest, III, 223. Cf. John Loftis, ed., _Essays on
the Theatre_, p. 45.

26. This information is from the notes of "J. P. C." in
the interleaved copy of _Biog. Dram._ at the Huntington Library, facing pages 13 and 15. Aston's play was not performed and "J. P. C." claims his notes are from the only
copy he ever saw.

27. Avery, "Dancing and Pantomime," p. 428.

28. _Ibid._, p. 432.

29. _DNB_, 67, 117, describes how Rich achieved such
stage effects.

30. For the similarity in the attack on Pantomime in
Pasquin and that which appeared three days before the first
performance in the _Grub Street Journal_, see Nichols, "Fielding's Satire on Pantomime."

31. Pt. 3, _LS_, II, 894-96, 899-901, 914.

32. See Genest, III, 641. The scene with Shakespeare's
monument anticipates Mrs. Hoper's _Queen Tragedy Restor'd_
(1749) where the ghost of Shakespeare appears to restore
order and common sense.

33. See Avery, "Dancing and Pantomime," (1934). Wells,
"Some Notes on the Early Eighteenth Century Pantomime,"
(1935), discounts the influence of _commedia dell'arte_.

34. Henry Carey, _Poems on Several Occasions_, 3rd ed.
(London: E. Say, 1729), pp. 17-37. His poem "Blundrella"
also criticized Italianate taste, apparently a favorite
theme of Carey's satire.

35. See especially Bertrand H. Bronson, "The Beggar's
Opera," in John Loftis, ed., _Restoration Drama: Modern Essays in Criticism_ (New York: Oxford University Press, 1966),
pp. 298-327.

36. Nichols, "Social Satire in Fielding's Pasquin and The Historical Register" (1924).

37. J. A. Aitkin, ed., The Tatler (London, 1898), p. 347.

38. See Bernbaum, p. 151, and Nicoll, p. 139. John Kelly's The Married Philosopher (1732) toned down the pathos of his French source, Destouches' Le Philosophe Marié, which may also indicate disapproval of sentimental comedy since Kelly's other plays were laughing comedies.

39. All references in the text are to the expanded three act version, The Tragedy of Tragedies.

40. Van der Voorde, pp. 84 ff., quotes several pages of parallel passages from Dryden and Banks particularly, while Hillhouse, ed., The Tragedy of Tragedies . . ., pp. 24 ff., lists forty-two plays that Fielding parodies, twenty-three of which are from the works of Dryden, Lee and Banks.

41. Hillhouse, pp. 27-28.

42. Two musical versions also appeared, one, The Opera of Operas by Mrs. Eliza Haywood and William Hatchett (1733) and one by Kane O'Hara, Tom Thumb a burletta in 1780 after this period ended.

43. As Samuel L. Macey rightly points out in "Carey's Chrononhotonthologos: A Plea," Carey has other objects of satire; besides heroic tragedy, there is considerable burlesque of pantomime staging as well as acting style.

44. The Monthly Review, II (1749), 90.

45. The date of this play is unknown since it was never acted and appears only in Aaron Hill, The Dramatic Works, 2 vols. (London: T. Lownds, 1760), I, xx and II, 86-114; it was obviously written before Hill's death in 1750. All references are to this edition.

46. Pt. 4, LS, I, p. clxii.

Chapter 5

1. Morris was aware of the dramatic satirists of his day, however, and he suggests that severe satire cannot be answered except by an opposite "Stage of Scurrility,"—a suggestion not unlike that of the anonymous writer for the Gentleman's Magazine in 1737 (VII, 409) who urged Walpole to send Companies of players around the country to answer the stage satire against him.

2. Patricia Meyer Spacks is almost unique among modern critics (except for Northrop Frye and Robert C. Elliott) in calling satire a genre. See "Some Reflections on Satire." Most critics define it in terms of tone or mood; see E. A. and Lillian D. Bloom, "The Satiric Mode of Feeling: A Theory of Intention." The Symposia of Satire Newsletter on the necessity of norms, the satiric persona, and grotesque fantasy (II, No. 1, Fall, 1964 and III, No. 2, Spring, 1966) are primarily discussions of technique.

3. I am indebted to Frye's discussion of the resolution of comedy in his Anatomy of Criticism, pp. 163-86. To illustrate comic resolution, I find the Justice in Fielding's Rape upon Rape a satiric character, but as the subtitle indicates (The Justice Caught in his Own Trap), the Justice pays for his hypocrisy and the play is a comedy ending with the reunion of the lovers who are no longer harrassed by the blocking character of the rascally Justice. The Historical Register, by contrast, has no such resolution; various scenes display a variety of satiric targets carefully pointed out to the audience by Mr. Medley lest the audience miss the point of what would otherwise be a collection of jokes—a farce.

4. For a separate discussion of Fielding's satiric plays, see Kern, "Fielding's Dramatic Satire," in From Chaucer to Gibbon: Essays in Memory of Curt A. Zimansky.

B I B L I O G R A P H Y

PLAYS, 1720-1750, BY AUTHOR

Adams, George. The Plays of Sophocles. 2 vols., London,
    1729. The Heathen Martyr; or, the Death of Socrates.
    London, 1746.
Arthur, John. The Lucky Discovery; or, the Tanner of York.
    York, 1737.
Aston, Anthony. The Fool's Opera; or, the Taste of the Age.
    London, 1731. Cleora; or, the Amorous Old Shepherdess.
    n.p. (1736 perf.).
Aston, Walter. The Restauration of King Charles II; or, the
    Life and Death of Oliver Cromwell. London, 1732.
Aubin, Mrs. The Merry Masqueraders; or, the Humorous Cuckold.
    London, 1730.
Ayre, William. Amintas. London, 1737. Merope. London, 1740.
Ayres, James. Sancho at Court; or, the Mock-Governor. Dublin,
    1742. The Kiss Accepted and Returned. n.p. (1744 perf.).
Baillie, John. The Married Coquet. London, 1746.
Baker, Richard. A Rehearsal of a New Ballad Opera, Bur-
    lesqued, called the Mad-House, after the Manner of Pas-
    quin. London, 1737.
Barford, Richard. The Virgin Queen. London, 1728.
Bellamy, Daniel, Senior and Junior. Love Triumphant; or, the
    Rival Goddesses. London, 1722. The Young Ladies Miscel-
    lany; or, Youth's Innocent and Rational Amusement. Lon-
    don, 1723. Dramatic Pieces. 2 vols., London, 1739-1740.
Bellers, Fettiplace. Injur'd Innocence. London, 1732.
Bennet, Philip. The Beau's Adventures. London, 1733.
Betterton, Thomas. The Sequel of Henry the Fourth; With the
    Humours of Sir John Falstaff, and Justice Shallow. Lon-
    don, 1720.
Blanch, John. Swords into Anchors. Gloucester, 1725. Hoops
    into Spinning Wheels. Gloucester, 1725.
Boadens, Captain Charles. The Modish Couple. London, 1732.
Bond, William. The Tuscan Treaty; or, Tarquin's Overthrow.
    London, 1733.

167

Boyd, Mrs. Elizabeth. Don Sancho; or, The Student's Whim.
    London, 1739.
Breval, Captain John D. The Strolers. London, 1723 (altered
    from The Play is the Plot). The Rape of Helen. London,
    1737.
Brooke, Henry. Gustavus Vasa, The Deliverer of his Country.
    London, 1739. Jack the Giant Queller. London, 1749.
Brown, Anthony. The Fatal Retirement. London, 1739.
Browne, Moses. Polidus; or, Distress'd Love, a Tragedy with
    a Farce call'd All Bedevil'd; or, The House in a Hurry.
    London, 1723.
Carey, Henry. Hanging and Marriage; or, the Dead Man's Wed-
    ding. London, 1722. Amelia. London, 1732. Teraminta.
    London, 1732. Betty; or, the Country Bumpkins. n.p.
    The Songs as they are Sung in Betty. London, 1739.
    Chrononhotonthologos. London, 1734. The Honest York-
    shire Man. London, 1736. The Dragon of Wantley. London,
    1737. Margery; or, A Worse Plague than the Dragon. Lon-
    don, 1738. Nancy; or, the Parting Lovers. London, 1739.
Centlivre, Mrs. Susannah. The Artifice. London, 1723.
Charke, Mrs. Charlotte. The Carnival; or, Harlequin Wanderer.
    London, 1735. The Act of Management; or, Tragedy Ex-
    pell'd. London, 1735. Tit for Tat; or, the Comedy and
    Tragedy of War. London, 1743.
Chetwood, William R. The Stock Jobbers; or, the Humours of
    Exchange Alley. London, 1720. South Sea; or, the Biters
    Bit. London, 1720. The Lover's Opera. London, 1729. The
    Generous Free-Mason; or, the Constant Lady. London,
    1731. The Emperor of China. n.p. (1731 perf.).
Cibber, Colley. The Refusal; or, the Ladies Philosophy.
    London, 1721. Caesar in Aegypt. London, 1725. The
    Provok'd Husband; or, A Journey to London. London,
    1728. Love in a Riddle. London, 1729. Damon and
    Phillida. London, 1729. Papal Tyranny in the Reign of
    King John. London, 1745. The Ladies Lecture. London,
    1748.
Cibber, Theophilus. An Historical Tragedy of the Civil Wars
    in the Reign of King Henry VI. London, 1723. Patie and
    Peggie; or, the Fair Foundling. London, 1730. The
    Lover. London, 1730. The Harlot's Progress; or, the
    Ridotto al'Fresco. London, 1733. Romeo and Juliet.
    London, 1745.

Clancy, Dr. Michael. Tamar, Prince of Nubia. Dublin, 1739.
    Hermon, Prince of Choroea; or, the Extravagant Zealot.
    London, 1746. The Sharper. London, 1750.
Coffey, Charles. The Beggar's Wedding. London, 1729. Phebe;
    or, the Beggar's Wedding. London, 1729. The Devil upon
    Two Sticks; or, the Country Beau. London, 1745. (1729
    perf.). Southwark Fair; or, the Sheep-Shearing. London,
    1729. The Female Parson; or, Beau in the Sudds. London,
    1730. The Devil to Pay; or, the Wives Metamorphos'd.
    London, 1731. A Wife and No Wife. London, 1732. The
    Boarding School; or, the Sham Captain. London, 1733.
    The Merry Cobbler; or, the Second Part of The Devil to
    Pay. London, 1735.
Concanen, Matthew. Wexford Wells. Dublin, 1721.
Conolly, _____. The Connoisseur. London, 1736.
Cooke, Thomas. Albion; or, the Court of Neptune. London,
    1724. Penelope (with John Mottley). London, 1728. The
    Battle of the Poets. London, 1731. The Triumph of Love
    and Honour. London, 1731. The Eunuch; or, the Darby
    Captain. London, 1737. The Mournfull Nuptials; or, Love
    the Cure of all Woes. London, 1744.
Cooper, Mrs. Elizabeth. The Rival Widows; or, the Fair Liber-
    tine. London, 1735. The Nobleman; or, the Family
    Quarrel. London, 1736.
Cross, Richard. The Hen-Peck'd Captain; or, the Humours of
    the Militia. London, 1749.
Croxall, Dr. Samuel. The Fair Circassian. London, 1720.
Cunningham, John. Love in a Mist. Dublin, 1747.
Cutts, John. Rebellion Defeated; or, the Fall of Desmond.
    London, 1745.
Dalton, John. Comus. London, 1739.
Dance, James. Pamela. London, 1742.
Darcy, James. Love and Ambition. Dublin, 1732. The Orphan of
    Venice. Dublin, 1749.
Davey, Samuel. The Treacherous Husband. Dublin, 1737. Whit-
    tington and his Cat. Dublin, 1739.
Davys, Mrs. Mary. The Self Rival. London, 1725.
Dodsley, Robert. The Toy Shop. London, 1735. The King and
    the Miller of Mansfield. London, 1737. Sir John Cockle
    at Court. London, 1738. The Blind Beggar of Bethnal
    Green. London, 1741. Rex and Pontifex. London, 1745
    (in Trifles). The Triumph of Peace. London, 1749.

Dorman, Joseph. Sir Roger de Coverly; or, the Merry Christ-
     mas. London, 1740. The Female Rake; or, Modern Fine
     Lady. London, 1736.
Dower, E. The Salopian Esquire; or, the Joyous Miller. Lon-
     don, 1739.
Downes, Captain. All Vows Kept. Dublin, 1733.
Downing, George. The Tricks of Harlequin. Derby, 1739.
Draper, Matthew. The Spendthrift. London, 1731.
Drury, Robert. The Devil of a Duke; or, Trapolin's Vagaries.
     London, 1732. The Mad Captain. London, 1733. The Fancy'd
     Queen. London, 1733. The Rival Milliners; or the
     Humours of Covent-Garden. London, 1737.
Du Bois, P. B. Aminta. London, 1726.
Duncombe, William. Athaliah. London, 1724. Lucius Junius
     Brutus. London, 1735.
D'Urfey, Thomas. The English Stage Italianiz'd. London,
     1727.
Egleton, Mrs. The Maggot. n.p. (1732 perf.).
Este, Thomas. Methodism Display'd. 1743.
Fabian, R. Trick for Trick. London, 1735.
Fenton, Elijah. Mariamne. London, 1723.
Fielding, Henry. Love in Several Masques. London, 1728.
     The Temple Beau. London, 1730. The Author's Farce; And
     the Pleasures of the Town. London, 1730. Tom Thumb.
     London, 1730 (Revised as The Tragedy of Tragedies).
     Rape upon Rape; or, the Justice Caught in his own Trap.
     London, 1730. The Welsh Opera. London, 1731(Revised as
     The Grub Street Opera). The Letter Writers; or, A New
     Way to Keep a Wife at Home. London, 1731. The Lottery.
     London, 1732. The Modern Husband. London, 1732. The Old
     Debauchees; or, the Jesuit Caught. London, 1732. The
     Covent Garden Tragedy. London, 1732. The Mock Doctor.
     London, 1732. The Miser. London, 1733. Deborah; or, A
     Wife for You All. n.p. (1733 perf.). The Intriguing
     Chambermaid. London, 1734. Don Quixote in England.
     London, 1734. An Old Man Taught Wisdom. London, 1735.
     The Universal Gallant. London, 1735.
     Pasquin. London, 1736. Tumble Down Dick; or, Phaeton in
     the Suds. London, 1736. Eurydice; or, the Devil
     Henpeck'd. London, 1743 (1737 perf.). Eurydice Hiss'd,
     printed with The Historical Register, for the Year
     1736. London, 1737. Plutus, the God of Riches. London,
     1743 (with Rev. Young). Miss Lucy in Town. London,
     1742. The Wedding Day. London, 1743. An Interlude be-

tween Jupiter, Juno, and Mercury. London, 1743.

Foote, Samuel. The Diversions of the Morning. (1747 perf.)
    printed after 1750. The Auction of Pictures. (1748
    perf.).

Forrest, Ebenezer. Momus Turn'd Fabulist. (attributed) Lon-
    don, 1729.

Freeman, Mark. The Downfall of Bribery; or, the Honest Men
    of Taunton. London, 1733.

Frowde, Philip. The Fall of Saguntum. London, 1727. Philotas.
    London, 1731.

Gardiner, Matthew. The Sharpers. Dublin, 1740. The Parthian
    Hero. Dublin, 1741.

Garrick, David. Lethe; or, Aesop in the Shades. London,
    1745. The Lying Valet. London, 1742. Miss in her Teens;
    or, the Medley of Lovers. London, 1747.

Gataker, Thomas. The Jealous Clown; or, The Lucky Mistake.
    London, 1730.

Gay, John. The Captives. London, 1724. The Beggar's Opera.
    London, 1728. Polly. London, 1729. Acis and Galatea.
    London, 1732. Achilles. London, 1733. The Distress'd
    Wife. London, 1743.

Giffard, William. Merlin. London, 1736.

Goodall, William. The False Guardians Outwitted. London,
    1740.

Gordon, Alexander. Lupone; or, The Inquisitor. London,
    1731.

Griffin, Benjamin. Whig and Tory. London, 1720.

Gwinnett, Richard. The Glouchestershire Squire. London,
    1734 (pub. also as The Country Squire. London, 1732).

Hammond, William. The Preceptor. London, 1740.

Harper, Samuel. The Mock Philosopher. London, 1737.

Harrison, Thomas. Beltheshazzar; or, The Heroick Jew. London,
    1729.

Hatchett, William. The Rival Father; or, The Death of
    Achilles. London, 1730. The Chinese Orphan. London,
    1741.

Havard, William. Scanderbeg. London, 1733. King Charles the
    First. London, 1737. Regulus. London, 1744.

Hawker, Essex. The Wedding. London, 1729.

Hawkins, William. Henry and Rosamond. London, 1749.

Hawling, Francis. It Should have Come Sooner; or, the His-
    toric Satiric Tragi-Comic Humours of Exchange Alley.
    n.p. (1723 perf.). The Impertinent Lovers; or, A
    Coquet at her Wit's End. London, 1723.

Haywood, Mrs. Eliza. The Fair Captive. London, 1721. A Wife
    to be Lett. London, 1724. Frederick, Duke of Brunswick-
    Lunenburgh. London, 1729. The Opera of Operas; or, Tom
    Thumb the Great. London, 1733.
Hewitt, John. The Fair Rivals. Bath, 1729. The Fatal False-
    hood; or, Innocence Distress'd. London, 1734. A Tutor
    for the Beaus; or, Love in a Labyrinth. London, 1737.
Hill, Aaron. The Fatal Extravagance. London, 1720. King
    Henry the Fifth; or, The Conquest of France. London,
    1723. Athelwold. London, 1732 (rev. from Elfrid). The
    Tragedy of Zara. London, 1736. Alzira. London, 1736.
    Merope. London, 1749. The Snake in the Grass. The
    Dramatic Works, 2 vols. London, T. Lownds, 1760 (1731
    perf.).
Hill, Sir John. Orpheus. London, 1740.
Hippisley, John. Flora. Southwark, 1729. A Journey to
    Bristol; or, The Honest Welchman. London, 1731. A
    Sequel to the Opera of Flora. London, 1732.
Hoadly, Dr. Benjamin. The Suspicious Husband. London, 1747.
Hoadly, Dr. John. The Contrast. n.p. (1731 perf.) Written
    with Dr. Benjamin Hoadly. Love's Revenge. London,
    1734. Phoebe. London, 1748.
Hoper, Mrs. The Battle of Poictiers; or, The English
    Prince. n.p. (1747 perf.); also perf. as Edward the
    Black Prince; or, The Battle of Poictiers. The Cyclo-
    paedia. n.p. (1748 perf.). Queen Tragedy Restor'd.
    London, 1748.
Hurst, Captain Robert. The Roman Maid. London, 1725.
Jacob, Sir Hildebrand. The Fatal Constancy. London, 1723.
    The Nest of Plays: Consisting of three Comedies: The
    Prodigal Reform'd, The Happy Constancy, and The Tryal
    of Conjugal Love. London, 1738.
Jeffrys, George. Edwin. London, 1724. Merope. London, 1731.
Johnson, Charles. Love in a Forest. London, 1723. The Fe-
    male Fortune-Teller. London, 1726. The Village Opera.
    London, 1729. The Tragedy of Medaea. London, 1731. The
    Ephesian Matron. n.p. (1737 perf.). Caelia; or, The
    Perjur'd Lover. London, 1733.
Johnson, Henry. Regulus. London, 1724.
Johnson, Samuel. Hurlothrumbo. London, 1729. The Cheshire
    Comics; or, The Amours of Lord Flame. n.p. (1730
    perf.). The Blazing Comet. London, 1732. All Alive and
    Merry. n.p. (1737 perf.). The Fool Made Wise. n.p.

(1741 perf.). Sir John Falstaff in Masquerade. n.p.
(1741 perf.).

Johnson, Dr. Samuel. Irene. London, 1749.

Kelly, John. The Married Philosopher. London, 1732. Timon in
Love; or, The Innocent Theft. London, 1733. The Plot.
London, 1735. The Fall of Bob; or, The Oracle of Gin.
London, 1736. The Levee. London, 1741.

Langford, Abraham. The Judgment of Paris. London, 1730. The
Lover his own Rival. London, 1736.

Leigh, John. Hob's Wedding. London, 1720. Kensington Gardens; or The Pretenders. London, 1720.

Lewis, David. Philip of Macedon. London, 1727.

Lillo, George. Sylvia; or, The Country Burial. Dublin, 1730.
The London Merchant; or, The History of George Barnwell.
London, 1731. The Christian Hero. London, 1735. Fatal
Curiosity. London, 1737. Marina. London, 1738. Elmer-
ick; or, Justice Triumphant. London, 1740. Britannia
and Batavia. London, 1740.

Lynch, Francis. The Independent Patriot; or, Musical Folly.
London, 1737.

Lyon, William. The Wrangling Lovers; or, Like Master Like
Man. Edinburgh, 1745.

Macklin, Charles. A Will and No Will. n.p. (1746 perf.).
King Henry VII; or, The Popish Imposter. London, 1746.
The Suspicious Husband Criticized; or, The Plague of
Envy. n.p. (1747 perf.). Also known as The New Play
Criticiz'd. The Fortune-Hunters. London, 1750.

Madden, Dr. Samuel. Themistocles, the Lover of his Country.
London, 1729.

Mallet, David. Eurydice. London, 1731. Mustapha. London,
1739. Alfred. London, 1740 (with James Thomson).

Marsh, Charles. Amasis King of Egypt. London, 1738.

Martyn, Benjamin. Timoleon. London, 1730.

Maxwell, John. The Trepan; or, Virtue Rewarded. York, 1739.
The Shepherd's Opera. York, 1739. The Faithful Pair;
or, Virtue in Distress. York, 1746. The Royal Captives.
York, 1745.

Mendez, Moses. The Double Disappointment; or, The Fortune
Hunters. n.p. until 1760 (1746 perf.). The Chaplet.
London, 1749. Robin Hood. London, 1750.

Miller, James. The Humours of Oxford. London, 1730. The
Mother-in-Law; or, The Doctor the Disease. London,
1734. The Man of Taste. London, 1735. Also known as

Mr. Taste. The Universal Passion. London, 1737. The
    Coffee House. London, 1737. Art and Nature. London,
    1738. An Hospital for Fools. London, 1739. Mahomet the
    Imposter. London, 1744 (with Dr. John Hoadly). Vanelia.
    London, 1732. The Camp Visitants. London, 1740.
Mitchell, Joseph. The Highland Fair; or, Union of the Clans.
    London, 1731.
Moore, Edward. The Foundling. London, 1748.
Morell, Dr. Thomas. Hecuba. London, 1739.
Morris, Robert. The Fatal Necessity; or, Liberty Regain'd.
    London, 1742.
Moss, Theophilus. The General Lover. London, 1748.
Mottley, John. The Imperial Captives. London, 1720.
    Antiochus. London, 1721. Penelope. London, 1728 (with
    Thomas Cooke). The Craftsman, or Weekly Journalist.
    London, 1729. The Widow Bewitch'd. London, 1730.
Nesbit, G. Caledon's Tears; or, Wallace. Edinburgh, 1733.
Newton, James. Alexis's Paradise; or, a Trip to the Garden
    of Love at Vaux-Hall. London, 1722.
Norris, Henry. The Deceit. London, 1723.
Odell, Thomas. The Chimaera. London, 1721. The Patron; or,
    The Statemen's Opera. London, 1729. The Smugglers. Lon-
    don, 1729. The Prodigal; or, Recruits for the Queen of
    Hungary. London, 1744.
Odingsells, Gabriel. The Bath Unmask'd. London, 1725. The
    Capricious Lovers. London, 1726. Bayes's Opera. London,
    1730.
Ozell, John. L'Avare. London, 1732.
Paterson, Joseph. The Raree Show, or the Fox trap't. York,
    1740.
Paterson, William. Arminius. London, 1740.
Peck, Francis. Herod the Great. London, 1740.
Pennecuik, Alexander. Corydon and Cochrania. n.p. (perf.
    1732).
Philips, Ambrose. The Briton. London, 1722. Humphrey, Duke
    of Gloucester. London, 1723.
Phillips, Edward. The Chambermaid. London, 1730. The Mock
    Lawyer. London, 1733. The Livery Rake and Country Lass.
    London, 1733. The Royal Chace; or, Merlin's Cave. Lon-
    don, 1736. Briton's Strike Home; or, The Sailor's Re-
    hearsal. London, 1739.
Phillips, Thomas. Love and Glory. London, 1734. The Rival
    Captives. n.p. (1736 perf.).

Phillips, Captain William. Hibernia Freed. London, 1722.
    Belisarius. London, 1724.
Pilkington, Letitia. The Turkish Court. London, 1748.
Popple, William. The Lady's Revenge; or, The Rover Reclaim'd.
    London, 1734. The Double Deceit; or, A Cure for Jeal-
    ousy. London, 1736.
Potter, Henry. The Decoy. London, 1733.
Pritchard, William. The Fall of Phaeton. London, 1736.
Ralph, James. The Fashionable Lady; or Harlequin's Opera.
    London, 1730. The Fall of the Earl of Essex. London,
    1731. The Lawyer's Feast. London, 1744. The Cornish
    Squire. London, 1734. The Astrologer. London, 1744.
Ramsay, Allan. The Nuptials. London, 1723. The Gentle Shep-
    herd. Edinburgh, 1725.
Randal, John. The Disappointment. London, 1732.
Reed, Joseph. The Superannuated Gallant. Newcastle, 1745.
Rich, John. Jupiter and Europa; or, The Intrigues of
    Harlequin. n.p. (1723 perf.). The Necromancer. n.p.
    (1723 perf.). The Sorcerer. n.p. (1724 perf.).
Robe, Mrs. Jane. The Fatal Legacy. London, 1723.
Robinson, William. The Intriguing Milliners and Attornies
    Clerks. London, 1738.
Ryan, Lacy. The Cobler's Opera. London, 1729.
Sandford, _____. The Female Fop; or, The False One Fitted.
    London, 1724.
Savage, Richard. The Tragedy of Sir Thomas Overbury. London,
    1724.
Sewell, Dr. George. The Tragedy of Richard the I, King of
    England. London, 1728.
Sheridan, Thomas. The Brave Irishman. n.p. until 1754 (1746
    perf.).
Sheridan, Dr. Thomas. Philoctetes. London, 1725.
Shirley, William. The Parricide; or, Innocence in Distress.
    London, 1739. King Pepin's Campaign. n.p. until 1755
    (1745 perf.). Edward the Black Prince. London, 1750.
Shuckburgh, Charles. Antiochus. London, 1740.
Smart, Christopher. The Grateful Fair; or, A Trip to Cam-
    bridge. n.p. (1747 perf.).
Smollett, Tobias. The Regicide; or, James the First, of
    Scotland. London, 1749.
Smythe, James Moore-. The Rival Modes. London, 1727.
Sommer, Henry. Orpheus and Eurydice. London, 1740.
Southerne, Thomas. Money the Mistress. London, 1726.

Spateman, Thomas. _The School-Boy's Mask_. London, 1742.

Steele, Sir Richard. _The Conscious Lovers_. London, 1723.

Sterling, James. _The Rival Generals_. Dublin, 1722. _The Parricide_. London, 1736.

Stevens, John. _The Modern Wife; or, The Virgin her own Rival_. London, 1744.

Sturmy, John. _Love and Duty; or, The Distress'd Bride_. London, 1722. _The Compromise; or Faults on both Sides_. London, 1722. _Sesostris; or, Royalty in Disguise_. London, 1728.

Theobald, Dr. John. _Merope_. London, 1744.

Theobald, Lewis. _Harlequin, A Sorcerer_. London, 1725. _Apollo and Daphne; or, The Burgo-Master trick'd_. London, 1726. _The Rape of Proserpine_. London, 1727. _Double Falsehood; or, The Distrest Lovers_. London, 1728. _Perseus and Andromeda_. London, 1730. _Orestes_. London, 1731. _Merlin; or, the Devil of Stonehenge_. London, 1734. _The Fatal Secret_. London, 1735. _Orpheus and Eurydice_. London, 1740. _The Happy Captive_. London, 1741.

Thomson, Adam. _The Disappointed Gallant; or, Buckram in Armour_. Edinburgh, 1738.

Thomson, James. _The Tragedy of Sophonisba_. London, 1730. _Agamemnon_. London, 1738. _Coriolanus_. London, 1739. _Edward and Eleanora_. London, 1739. _Tancred and Sigismunda_. London, 1745.

Thurmond, John. _The Duke and No Duke_. n.p. (1720 perf.). _The Escapes of Harlequin by Land and Sea; or Columbine Made Happy at Last_. n.p. (1722 perf.). _Harlequin Dr. Faustus_. London, 1724. _Harlequin Sheppard_. London, 1724. _Apollo and Daphne; or, Harlequin Mercury_. London, 1725. _The Miser_. London, 1727.

Tracy, John. _Periander_. London, 1731.

Walker, Thomas. _The Quaker's Opera_. London, 1728. _The Fate of Villany_. London, 1730.

Wandesford, Osborne S. _Fatal Love; or, The Degenerate Brother_. London, 1730.

Ward, Henry. _The Works_ . . . London, 1746 (contains _The Happy Lovers_, _The Petticoat-Plotter_, and _The Widow's Wish_). _The Vintner Trick'd_. London, 1746.

Weddell, Mrs. _The City Farce_. London, 1737. _Inkle and Yarico_. London, 1742.

Weekes, James. _Orpheus and Eurydice_. Cork, 1743.

Welsted, Leonard. _The Dissembled Wanton; or, My Son Get Money_. London, 1727.

West, Richard. Hecuba. London, 1726.

Wetherby, James. Paul the Spanish Sharper. London, 1730.

Whincop, Thomas. Scanderbeg; or, Love and Liberty. London, 1747.

Whitehead, William. The Edinburgh Ball. n.p. (1745 perf.).

Williams, John. Richmond Wells. Richmond, 1722.

Woodward, H. The Beggar's Pantomime. London, 1736. Tit for Tat; or, A Dish for the Auctioneer's own Chocolate. Dublin, 1744.

Worsdale, James. A Cure for a Scold. London, 1735. The Queen of Spain. Dublin, 1741.

Yarrow, Joseph. Love at First Sight. York, 1742. Trick upon Trick. York, 1742. Nancy. York, 1742.

Yonge, Sir William. The Jovial Crew. London, 1731. (with Edward Roome and Matthew Concanen).

Young, Edward. The Revenge. London, 1721. Plutus. London, 1742 (with Fielding).

PLAYS, 1720-1750, ANONYMOUS

The Assembly. London, 1722.

The Author's Triumph; or, The Managers Managed. London, 1737.

Bickerstaff's Unburied Dead. London, 1743.

The British Stage; or, The Exploits of Harlequin. London, 1724.

The Broken Stockjobbers. London, 1720.

Callista. London, 1731.

Colonel Split-Tail. London, 1730.

The Committee; or, King Pepin's Campaign. London, 1745.

The Commodity Excis'd; or, The Women in an Uproar. London, 1733.

The Congress of Beasts. London, 1748.

The Conspirators. London, 1749.

The Contre Temps; or, The Rival Queens. London, 1727.

C—— and Country. London, 1735. (Rev. 1743).

The Court Medley; or, Marriage by Proxy. London, 1733.

The Deposing and Death of Queen Gin. London, 1736.

Diabouloumenon. London, 1723.

The Double Traitor Roasted. London, 1748.

The Downfall of Bribery; or The Honest Men of Taunton. London, 1733. (See Freeman, Mark.)

The Election. London, 1749.

Exchange Alley; or, The Stock-Jobber turn'd Gentleman. Lon-
    don, 1720.
Excise. London, 1733.
The Footman, an Opera. London, 1732.
Fortune's Tricks in Forty Six. London, 1747.
The Happy Marriage; or, The Turn of Fortune. London, 1727.
Harlequin Incendiary; or, Columbine Cameron. London, 1746.
Harlequin Student; or, The Fall of Pantomime: With the Res-
    toration of the Drama. London, 1741.
The Honest Electors; or, The Courtiers Sent back with their
    Bribes. London, 1733.
Hudibrasso. London, 1741.
The Humours of the Court; or Modern Gallantry. London, 1732.
The Humours of the Road. London, 1738.
The Humours of Whist. London, 1743.
The Intriguing Courtiers; or, The Modish Gallants. London,
    1732.
The Intriguing Milliners and Attornies Clerks. London,
    1738.
Jack the Giant Killer. London, 1730.
The Jew Decoy'd; or, The Progress of a Harlot. London,
    1735.
Lethe Rehearsed. London, 1749.
Love and Revenge; or, The Vintners Outwitted. London, 1729.
Majesty Misled; or, The Overthrow of Evil/Ministers.
    London, 1734.
The Mock Preacher. London, 1739.
The Modern Poetasters; or, Directors no Conjurors. London,
    1725.
The Northern Election; or The Nest of Beasts. London, 1749.
The Oxford Act. London, 1733.
The Patriot. London, 1736.
Polite Conversation. Larpent ms. 21.
Politics in Miniature; or, The Humours of Punch's Resigna-
    tion. London, 1742.
The Projectors. London, 1737.
Robin Goodfellow. London, 1738.
St. James Park. London, 1733.
The Stage Mutineers; or, A Play-House to be Lett. London,
    1733.
The Stage Pretenders; or, The Actor turn'd Poet. London,
    1720.
The State Juggler; or, Sir Politick Ribband. London, 1733.

The Stock Jobbers; or, The Humours of Exchange Alley.
    London, 1720.
The Sturdy Beggars. London, 1733.
Tittle Tattle; or, Taste A-la-Mode. London, 1749.
Tyranny Triumphant and Liberty Lost; the Muses Run Mad;
    Apollo Struck Dumb and All Covent Garden Confounded.
    London, 1743.
The Usurpers; or, The Coffee House Politicians. 1741.
The Vintner's Escape; or, Good Luck at Last. n.p. (1733).
The Wanton Countess; or, £10,000 for a Pregnancy. London,
    1733.
The Wanton Jesuit; or, Innocence Seduced. London, 1731.
A Whim. Larpent ms. 28.
The Woman of Taste; or, The Yorkshire Lady. London, 1738.

SELECTED REFERENCES

Alden, R.M. "The Rise of Formal Satire in England under
    Classical Influence," Publications of the University of
    Pennsylvania, Series in Philology, Literature, and
    Archeology, VII, No. 2 (1899).
Appel, Elsa. Henry Fielding als Kritiker der englischen Lit-
    erature. Breslau, 1922.
Appleton, William W. Charles Macklin: An Actor's Life. Cam-
    bridge: Harvard University Press, 1960.
Armens, Sven. John Gay, Social Critic. New York: King's
    Crown Press, Columbia University, 1954.
Avery, Emmett, "Dancing and Pantomime," SP, 31 (1934), 417-
    53.
————. "Fielding's Last Season with the Haymarket Thea-
    tre," MP, 36 (1939), 283-92.
Baker, Sheridan. "Fielding and the Irony of Form," ECS, 2
    (1968), 138-54.
Baskerville, C. R. "Play-Lists and After-Pieces of the Mid-
    Eighteenth Century," MP, 28 (1925-1926), 445-64.
Bateson, F. W. English Comic Drama 1700-1750. Oxford:
    Clarendon Press, 1929.
————. "The Stage in 1713," MLN, 45 (1930), 27-29.
Belden, Mary. "Samuel Foote," Yale Studies in English, 80
    (1929), 1-218.
Bernbaum, Ernest. The Drama of Sensibility. Boston and Lon-
    don: Ginn and Co., 1915.

Biographia Dramatica; Or, A Companion to the Playhouse....
    3 Vols. Ed. D. E. Baker (to 1764), Isaac Reed (to
    1782), Stephen Jones (to 1811). London: T. Longman,
    1812.
Bloom, E. A. and L. D. "The Satiric Mode of Feeling: A
    Theory of Intention," Criticism, 11, No. 2 (1969),
    115-39.
Booth, Wayne C. A Rhetoric of Irony. Chicago: University of
    Chicago Press, 1974.
Bronson, Bertrand H. "The Beggar's Opera," in Restoration
    Drama: Modern Essays in Criticism. Ed. John Loftis.
    New York: Oxford University Press, 1966.
Calverton, J. F. "Social Change and the Sentimental Comedy,"
    MLQ, 3 (1926), 169-88.
Chetwood, William R. The British Theatre; A General History
    of the Stage.... London: W. Owen, 1749.
Clark, Charles C. "Burlesque Writers of England," Gentle-
    man's Magazine, VII (1871), 557-81.
Cornford, Francis M. The Origin of Attic Comedy. London: E.
    Arnold, 1914.
Crean, P. J. "The Stage Licensing Act of 1737," MP, 35
    (1938), 239-55.
Croissant, D. C. "Studies in the Works of Colley Cibber,"
    UKPHS (1915), 1-69.
Cross, Wilbur L. A History of Henry Fielding. 3 Vols. New
    Haven: Yale University Press, 1918.
Elliott, Robert C. The Power of Satire. Princeton: Prince-
    ton University Press, 1960.
Ellis-Fermor, Una M. "Studies in the Eighteenth Century
    Stage," PQ, 11 (1923), 289-302.
Frye, Northrop. The Anatomy of Criticism. Princeton:
    Princeton University Press, 1957.
Genest, John. Some Account of the English Stage, from...
    1660 to 1832. 10 Vols. Bath: H. E. Carrington, 1832.
Grundy, Isobel M. "New Verse by Henry Fielding," PMLA,
    87 (1972), 213-45.
Hodgart, Matthew. Satire. New York and Toronto: McGraw-
    Hill, 1969.
Hume, Robert D. Dryden's Criticism. Ithaca and London:
    Cornell University Press, 1970.
————————. "Diversity and Development in Restoration Comedy,
    1660-1679," ECS, 5 (1972), 365-97.
Jensen, G. E. "Fashionable Society of Fielding's Time,"
    PMLA, 31 (1916), 79-90.

Kern, Jean B. "Modern Satire: A Mini-Symposium," SNL, 6
    (1969), 14-15.

—————. "The Fate of Thomson's Edward and Eleanora," MLN,
    52 (1937), 100-102.

—————. "A Note on The Beggar's Opera," PQ, 17 (1938),
    411-13.

—————, ed. Charles Macklin, The Covent Garden Theatre or
    Pasquin Turn'd Drawcansir (1752). ARS, No. 116 (1965).

—————, ed. Charles Macklin, A Will and No Will or a Bone
    for the Lawyers (1746) and The New Play Criticiz'd or
    The Plague of Envy (1747). ARS, No. 127, 128 (1967).

—————. "Fielding's Dramatic Satire," in From Chaucer to
    Gibbon: Essays in Memory of Curt A. Zimansky. PQ, 54
    (1975), 239-57.

Kernan, Alvin. The Cankered Muse. New Haven: Yale University
    Press, 1959.

—————. The Plot of Satire. New Haven and London: Yale
    University Press, 1965

Kidson, Frank. The Beggar's Opera, Its Predecessors and Suc-
    cessors. Cambridge: Cambridge University Press, 1922.

Krutch, Joseph W. Comedy and Conscience after the Restora-
    tion. New York: Columbia University Press, 1924.

—————. "Governmental Attempts to Regulate the Stage after
    the Jeremy Collier Controversy," PMLA, 38 (1923),
    153-75.

Lecky, W. E. H. A History of England in the Eighteenth Cen-
    tury. 8 Vols. London: Longmans, 1878-1890.

Loftis, John. Comedy and Society from Congreve to Fielding.
    Palo Alto: Stanford University Press, 1959.

—————. The Politics of Drama in Augustan England. Oxford:
    Clarendon Press, 1963.

—————, ed., Essays on the Theatre from Eighteenth Century
    Periodicals. ARS, No. 85, 86 (1960).

Loisseau, Jean. "John Gay et le Beggar's Opera," Revue
    Anglo-Americaine, 12 (1934), 3-19.

The London Stage, 1660-1800. Ed. E. L. Avery et al. 5 pts.
    in 11 Vols. Carbondale: Southern Illinois University
    Press, 1960-1968.

Macey, Samuel. "Carey's Chrononhotonthologos: A Plea," LHR,
    No. 11 (1969), 17-23.

Morris, Corbyn. Essay Toward Fixing the True Standards of
    Wit, Humour, Raillery, Satire and Ridicule.... (1744).
    Reprinted by ARS, No. 10 (1947).

Namier, Lewis B. England in the Age of the American Revolution. London: Macmillan, 1930.

—————. The Structure of Politics at the Accession of
George III. 2 Vols. London: Macmillan, 1929.

Nichols, C. W. "Fielding and the Cibbers," PQ, 1 (1922),
278-98.

—————. "Fielding's Satire on Pantomime," PMLA, 46 (1931),
1107-12.

—————. "Social Satire in Fielding's Pasquin and The Historical Register," PQ, 3 (1924), 309-17.

Nicoll, Allardyce. A History of English Drama, 1660-1900,
Vol. 2: Early Eighteenth Century Drama. Cambridge: Cambridge University Press, 3rd ed. 1952.

Plumb, J. H. Sir Robert Walpole, The King's Minister. London:
Cresset Press, 1960.

Robertson, C. Grant. England under the Hanoverians. New
York and London: Methuen, 1927.

Robertson, J. M. Bolingbroke and Walpole. London: T. F.
Unwin, 1919.

Rosenheim, Edward. Swift and the Satirist's Art. Chicago:
University of Chicago Press, 1963.

Schultz, William E. Gay's Beggar's Opera. New Haven: Yale
University Press, 1923.

Sherbo, Arthur. English Sentimental Drama. East Lansing:
Michigan State University Press, 1957.

Spacks, Patricia M. "Some Reflections on Satire," Genre, 1
(1968), 13-31.

Thorpe, Peter. "Great Satire and the Fragmented Norm," SNL,
4 (1967), 89-95.

Van der Voorde, Frans P. Henry Fielding: Critic and Satirist. Hague: P. Westerbaan, 1931.

Victor, Benjamin. The History of the Theatres of London and
Dublin From the Year 1730 to the Present Time.... London: T. Davies, 1761. 3 Vols. in 2.

Wells, Mitchell P. "Some Notes on the Early Eighteenth Century Pantomime," SP, 32 (1935), 598-608.

Wimsatt, W. K. The Idea of Comedy: Essays in Prose and
Verse, Ben Jonson to George Meredith. Englewood
Cliffs: Prentice-Hall, 1969.

Wood, Frederick T. "Sentimental Comedy in the Eighteenth
Century," Neophil., 18 (1933), 281-89.

—————. "Henry Carey and an Eighteenth Century Satire on
Matrimony," N&Q, 165 (1933), 363-68.

Woods, Charles B. "Captain B——'s Play," Harvard Studies
     and Notes in Philology and Literature, 15 (1933),
     243-55.

Wright, Thomas, ed. Caricature History of the Georges. . . .
     London: Hotten, 1868.

I N D E X

[A complete list of plays used in this study appears in the Bibliography (pp. 167-82). Only those authors and anonymous plays discussed in the text are indexed. From the Selected References (pp. 179-82), the Index includes those works that have helped shape my ideas about satire in general and dramatic satire in particular.]